BUDDHAVACANA

A Pali Reader

Glenn Wallis

Pariyatti Press

Pariyatti Press
an imprint of

Pariyatti Publishing
www.pariyatti.org

© 2010 Glenn Wallis

All rights reserved. No part of this book may be used or reproduced in any manner whatsoever without the written permission of the publisher, except in the case of brief quotations embodied in critical articles and reviews.

ISBN: 978-1-681723-29-7 (print)
ISBN: 978-1-681722-77-1 (ePub)
ISBN: 978-1-681722-78-8 (Mobi)
ISBN: 978-1-928706-86-1 (PDF)
Library of Congress Control Number: 2010904699

CONTENTS

Preface 5

Introduction 9

How to Read a Pali Text 9

Grammar 9

Translation, Vocabulary, and Meaning 14

Pronunciation 18

Notes on the Glossary 21

Sources 24

Sutta 1 *Sakuṇagghisuttaṃ* 26

Sutta 1 Glossary 30

Sutta 2 *Cūḷamālukyasuttaṃ* 34

Sutta 2 Glossary 46

Sutta 3 *Tevijjasuttaṃ* 52

Sutta 3 Glossary 89

Sutta 4 *Kesamuttisuttaṃ* 106

Sutta 4 Glossary 121

Sutta 5 *Sabbasuttaṃ* 128

Sutta 5 Glossary 130

Sutta 6 *Pheṇapiṇḍūpamasuttaṃ* 132

Sutta 6 Glossary 140

Sutta 7 *Anattalakkhaṇasuttaṃ* 146

Sutta 7 Glossary 152

Sutta 8 *Bhārasuttaṃ* 156

Sutta 8 Glossary 160

Sutta 9 *Dhammacakkappavattanasuttaṃ* 164

Sutta 9 Glossary 172

Sutta 10 *Gotamasuttaṃ* 180
Sutta 10 Glossary 190

Sutta 11 *Parāyanasuttaṃ* 194
Sutta 11 Glossary 196

Sutta 12 *Nibbutasuttaṃ* 198
Sutta 12 Glossary 201

Sutta 13 *Saṅkhatalakkhaṇasuttaṃ* 204
Sutta 13 Glossary 205

Sutta 14 *Asaṅkhatalakkhaṇasuttaṃ* 206
Sutta 14 Glossary 207

Sutta 15 *Ānāpānasatisuttaṃ* 208
Sutta 15 Glossary 226

Sutta 16 *Satipaṭṭhānasuttaṃ* 236
Sutta 16 Glossary 262

Sutta Translations 273
Sutta 1 The Hawk 275
Sutta 2 A Brief Talk to Mālukya 277
Sutta 3 Three-fold Knowledge 281
Sutta 4 Discourse in Kesamutta 293
Sutta 5 The All 299
Sutta 6 Like a Ball of Foam 301
Sutta 7 Evidence of Selflessness 305
Sutta 8 The Burden 307
Sutta 9 Turning the Wheel of the Teaching 309
Sutta 10 Gotama's Discourse 313
Sutta 11 Destination 319
Sutta 12 Quenched 321
Sutta 13 Signs of the Fabricated 323
Sutta 14 Signs of the Unfabricated 323
Sutta 15 Present-moment Awareness with Breathing 325
Sutta 16 The Application of Present-moment Awareness 333

PREFACE

This Reader has three related goals. First, it aims to encourage the study of Buddhist canonical literature in Pali (*pāḷi*). While there are, of course, several canonical languages – Tibetan, Chinese, Japanese, Korean, Mongolian, and Sanskrit – the Pali canon is exceptional. It is the repository of what I would like to call Classical Buddhism: the basic teachings, as far as we can determine, of Siddhattha Gotama (c. 480–400 BCE), the man we call the Buddha. As such, the Pali canon constitutes the shared heritage of Buddhists everywhere and at all times.

Buddhism, like everything else, has changed throughout history, is changing now, and will continue to change in the future. It is therefore all the more important that we, as students of Buddhism, not lose sight of the basic teachings of Siddhattha Gotama as recorded in the Pali canon. For, if the term *Buddhism* is to mean anything at all, surely it must, at a minimum, be consonant with the teachings of Gotama. That Buddhism changes is inevitable. It would be irresponsible of us not to adapt, update, clarify, and modify ancient and ascetic teachings to fit the needs of our time and place. But it would be equally irresponsible for us to do so without a genuine understanding of what it is we are changing. I hope this Reader will contribute to such an understanding.

Second, the sixteen texts that comprise the Reader were chosen to provide the student with a reliable overview of Siddhattha Gotama's teachings. I make an argument for why *these* texts are particularly suited to that task in my *Basic Teachings of the Buddha* (New York: Random House, 2007). That book may be seen as a companion to the present one in that it contains in-depth commentaries on the texts given here in Pali. As I mentioned there, the texts that I have selected are just one of numerous possible combinations of "basic teachings of the Buddha." Just to be clear about what I am claiming for these texts, I will repeat what I wrote in the *Basic Teachings*:

> Given the countless idiosyncratic possibilities behind any particular selection of texts, it is unlikely that any two authors would select the exact same sixteen *suttas* as necessarily basic. But I think it is also

> unlikely that many Buddhists or Buddhist scholars would have serious qualms with the present selection of *suttas.* In any case, knowing the contents of the *suttas* presented here, you will have a good grasp of the most vital Buddhist principles for living a fulfilled life. And perhaps that grasp is, after all, the decisive test of what constitutes a reliable selection of "basic teachings."
>
> ... [T]he Buddhist canon contains well over 5000 *suttas.* What, then, is my rationale for selecting the sixteen that I have? My selection is based on two criteria: rate of recurrence and relevance. The first criterion takes into account the frequency with which a theme occurs in the dialogues. There are certain issues that the Buddha raises repeatedly in his discourses. On this principle, I have selected several *suttas* dealing with the Buddha's *ideas* concerning the world, the person, the mind, and perception; and with his *prescriptions* for cultivating meditative concentration, mental and emotional calm, present-moment awareness, and the unbinding from tendencies detrimental to human happiness.
>
> There are other *suttas,* however, that contain material on issues in which the Buddha and his interlocutors placed little importance (again, using rate of recurrence as a yardstick). I have, nonetheless, selected some of these texts because they address issues that the contemporary reader *does* (I assume) consider important. I am not making this assumption on the basis of any complex sociological data analysis, but rather on my own discussions with others throughout my life. These issues include the problematic nature of the idea of a creator deity, or "God"; the manner of conducting a meaningful conversation; methods for countering depression, anxiety, and despair; cultivation of meaningful relationships; healthy reflection on illness and death; and the very nature of a question.
>
> Using these two criteria for the selection of texts, this book should at the very least prove to be a vibrant guide for studying Buddhism and, if the reader so wishes, for applying its principles to life (pp. xli–xlii).

Finally, in including the texts that it does, the Reader aims to help create critics of Buddhism as it begins to take root in the West. Our word "critic" comes from the Greek term for someone who discerns and judges *with care.* So, it is hoped that modern-day Buddhist practitioners would carefully dissect, probe, and question tradition, and not simply accept the views of believers and teachers past and present. Being such a practitioner—a critical one—takes effort. It requires us to know the facts about our shared tradition—i.e., the principles of the

Buddha's basic teachings—and to distinguish these teachings from the countless changes—additions, subtractions, compressions, expansions, innovations, and, yes, manipulations, mutations, distortions, and reversals – that history has brought to these teachings.

Only then are we fit to judge.

INTRODUCTION

How to Read a Pali Text

anujānāmi bhikkhave sakāya niruttiyā buddhavacanam pariyāpuṇituṃ
(*Vinaya, Cūḷavagga* 5.285)

This, according to tradition, was the Buddha's response to a request by two disciples to be permitted to communicate his teachings using Sanskrit, the *lingua franca* of the educated classes in ancient India. Somewhat testily ("fools, how dare you"), he emphatically denies their request, and makes the statement above. What does it mean? Well, a review of the copious literature – from pious to commentarial to scholarly – reveals that no one really knows for sure. Given that the statement obviously has something to do with language (*nirutti*), there is great irony here: the language in an ostensibly decisive canonical statement concerning language contains ambiguous language. Exploring this statement and the irony it contains will allow me to explain the purpose and scope of this Reader. Specifically, this introduction will discuss some basic features of grammar using the statement as an example. I will also make a few remarks about translation strategy and provide some notes on the glossary.

Grammar

Morphology

The first thing that we notice about our statement is that it is composed of letters: *anujānāmi bhikkhave sakāya niruttiyā buddhavacanam pariyāpuṇituṃ.* So, understanding the meaning of the statement as a whole requires that we, in the first instance, comprehend how the letters stand in relation to one another. The system of rules governing these relations is called grammar, from the Greek word for letter: *gramma.*

The subject of grammar, being the colossal, sprawling affair that it is, is beyond the scope of this Reader. It is thus assumed that the student is working with a reliable textbook of Pali grammar, together, perhaps, with a teacher or a group of fellow learners. In any case, this section is composed with the assumption that the student has a grasp of the basics of Pali grammar. If that is not the case, I recommend the following works: A. K. Warder, *Introduction to Pali* (London: Pali Text Society, 1963; revised 1991); Lily de Silva, *Pali Primer* (Igatpuri: Vipassana Research Institute, 1994); Steven Collins, *A Pali Grammar for Students* (Chiang Mai: Silkworm Books, 2005); and, for readers of German, Achim Fahs, *Grammatik des Pali* (Leipzig: VEB Verlag, 1989). There are also many online resources for learning Pali grammar. I would start here:

www.accesstoinsight.org/outsources/pali.html.

For the purpose of reading and translating from Pali, we will be concerned, in the first instance, with morphology, the knowledge of morphemes. The word "morpheme" is derived from the Greek word for "form," *morphē*. In grammar, it refers to the meaning-bearing units of speech that serve to shape or form a word. For instance, *unhelpful* contains three morphemes: *un* (meaning: a lack of, a reversal of, not, a negation); *help* (meaning: rendering assistance, providing what is needed); and *ful* (meaning: full of, characterized by, possessing). The letters used to inflect a word are also morphemes, such as, for instance, the *s* in dogs or *āmi* in *anujānāmi*. Morphemes are distinguished from graphemes (written units, *un* =*u, n*) and phonemes (spoken units, *un* = *ən*) in that the latter two bear neither conceptual (such as *help* or *ful*) nor grammatical meaning (such as *āmi* or *s*).

In the glossary accompanying each text of this Reader, words are given in what is known as stem form, or, in the case of verbs, root form. That means that if you look for *anujānāmi* you will get no further than *anu* + √*jān*. Two important facts emerge here. First, you learn that you are dealing with a verb (√ means verb root); and, second, you know to look for important grammatical information in the additional phonemes, *anu*° and °*āmi* ("°" means that letters precede or follow). Similarly, if you look for *bhikkhave*, you will likely stumble upon *bhikkhu* (m.). Now you can refer to your grammar textbook, under the masculine *u* declension, and uncover crucial grammatical information. So, referring to your grammar textbook, along with the glossary, yields the following possibilities:

anujānāmi is the first-person singular indicative verb composed of *anu* + √*jān* + *āmi*. Possible meanings are: I give permission, I grant, I allow, I advise, I prescribe.

bhikkhave is the masculine vocative plural of the noun *bhikkhu*, mendicant, practitioner, alms-beggar, monk; hence: O, mendicants, O, practitioners, etc.

sakāya is from the adjective *saka,* own, one's own. It is a singular masculine or feminine in one of several possible cases: instrumental (f.), genitive (m.), dative (m.f.), ablative (f.), or locative (f.). As an adjective, it modifies a noun, with which it agrees in number, case, and gender. It may mean: with, by, of, to, from, in, on, one's own *X*.

niruttiyā is derived from the feminine singular noun *nirutti,* which means explanation of words, grammatical analysis, etymological interpretation; pronunciation, dialect, accent, expression. It can be construed as being in any one of the oblique cases (i.e., any case but nominative, accusative, or vocative); namely: instrumental, genitive, dative, ablative, or locative. It may mean: with, by, of, to, from, in, on, interpretation, accent.

buddha° is the past passive participle of √*budh,* awakened, realized. It may also be used adjectively, as an epithet, or as a noun. Here, it is the first member of a determinative compound. As such, it may be construed as being in one of several cases; hence: the *X* of/by/with/from/to *buddha.*

°vacanam is the nominative, accusative, or vocative of the neuter singular noun *vacana,* speech, utterance, word, the speaking, the saying. Final *ṃ* has become *m* because of the *p* that follows. Here, it is the second member of a determinative compound. It may be construed as: the speech, etc., of, by, with, from, to *X*.

pariyāpuṇituṃ is the infinitive form of *pari* + *euphonic y* + √*āp,* meaning: to learn, to master, to know, to be able to. Note: an *m* at the end of a sentence changes to *ṃ*.

So, how do we put all of this together in a meaningful way? To do so requires that we now consider the words not only morphologically, but as comprising a whole. The whole is a sentence. This step involves having an eye on syntax.

Syntax

The word "syntax" derives from the Greek for "arrangement" (*taxis*) and "together" (*syn*). What concerns us here, of course, is the arrangement of words in a sentence. Comprehending the meaning of a sentence requires that we understand how each word in a sentence stands in relation to the other words. Syntax, like grammar, is a large, complicated subject. Unfortunately for the student of Pali, other than a few highly specialized works, there has not been much work done on Pali syntax. As Thomas Oberlies says in his monumental *Pāli: A Grammar of the Language of the Theravāda Tipiṭaka* (Berlin: Walter de Gruyter, 2001), "an up-to-date description of Pali syntax has yet to be written" (p. ix). Here I can only broach the topic by showing how it impacts the understanding of our statement. Students who want to explore the subject further are encouraged to see Lesson 27 of A. K. Warder's *Introduction to Pali.* Specialized works include Oliver Hector de Alwis Wijesekera, *Syntax of the Cases in the Pali Nikayas* (Colombo: University of Kelaniya, 1936 [reprinted 1993]), Hans Hendriksen, *Syntax of the Infinite Verb-forms of Pāli* (Copenhagen: Einar Munksgaard, 1944), and, for readers of German, Oskar von Hinüber, *Studien zur Kasussyntax des Pāli* (Munich: Kitzinger, 1968).

Theoretically, a highly inflected language such as Pali is less bound to any rules and principles governing syntax. The reason for this is that the function of a word in a sentence is revealed in its morphemes. In practice, however, there are serious constraints and conventions governing word order. The combination of the morphemes *anu-jān-ā-mi*, for instance, yields a first-person singular indicative verb meaning "I permit, I prescribe, I allow," and so on. Unlike in English, this meaning remains regardless of where *anujānāmi* appears in the sentence. Compare that with English. *Pass the salt* means one thing; *salt the pass*, quite another, or nothing at all. In contrast, the placement of the word *anujānāmi* does not significantly alter its relationship to the other words, and, hence, its meaning.

Placement may, however, have an impact on the nuance of the sentence. That is why I say "theoretically." After you've read through a number of texts, you will discover that there are indeed certain conventions of syntax. You will, for instance, be curious about the placement of *anujānāmi* at the beginning of the sentence rather than at the end, which is much more common for finite verbs. Of course, you'll immediately notice that there is an infinitive (*pariyāpuṇituṃ*) at the end, which is to be expected. Still, why is the main verb at the beginning? Seeing *anujānāmi* at the beginning of the sentence, I immediately interpreted the term as being particularly forceful, more than usual: I PRESCRIBE. With experience, you will understand the ways in which nuance is created by word placement.

Let's turn again to our statement.

anujānāmi bhikkhave sakāya niruttiyā buddhavacanam pariyāpuṇituṃ

My own approach to analyzing Pali sentences is very simple. Basically, I initially apply the step-by-step method for analyzing English sentences taught to me by my sixth-grade teacher. Sometimes her method proves good enough. More complex sentences, of course, require additional moves. But I always begin with this simple approach.

1. First, I locate the **verb**. That's √*jān* + the prefix *anu,* to allow/permit/prescribe, etc. As I mentioned, the finite verb is typically at the end of the sentence. Somewhat counterintuitively perhaps, the infinitive *pariyāpuṇituṃ*, to learn, is not a verb. Here, it functions as an adverb modifying the finite verb or as a noun modifying the direct object: the learning of *X*.

2. Next, I look for the **subject** by asking who or what *does* the verb. In active verbs, as is the case here, and as opposed to passive verbs, the subject is in the nominative case. In Pali, of course, the subject might also be implicit in the verb. So, we have *anujānāmi,* I allow/permit/prescribe, etc. Typically, the subject, when explicit, is at or near the beginning of the sentence.
3. Because the verb is active in this instance, I look for the **direct object** by asking who or what *receives* the action of the verb. That is, what is being prescribed here? A good first guess for the direct object in Pali is whatever is in the accusative case. Here, that is *buddhavacanam,* "the word/teaching of the Buddha." The direct object often comes just before the verb – so, close to the end of the sentence. For this reason, it often helps to locate the subject, then jump to the end of the sentence and read backwards.
4. Next, I locate the **indirect object** by asking to/for whom/what the action of the verb is done. In other words, who/what is it that is receiving the force of the direct object? The fact that *bhikkhave* is in the vocative case, "O, monks/mendicants," tells us that the speech is being directed *to* these followers. This does not, however, necessarily mean that the monks are the ones receiving the force of the direct object, namely, the learning of the teachings of the Buddha. Precisely who/what is meant here is left implicit. If some specific person or group of persons were meant, this would have to be made explicit. For this reason, I assume an implicit direct object, plural *you* or *one.* This gives us, "O monks, I allow you/one to learn the teachings of the Buddha." In Pali, the indirect object typically comes closer to the subject of the sentence and thus before the direct object.
5. Finally, I account for any other words beyond the basic sentence. I discussed the first of these, *bhikkhave* (O monks/mendicants) above. That leaves *sakāya,* own/one's own, and *niruttiyā,* language. As an adjective, *saka* agrees in case, number, and gender with the term it modifies, which here is the feminine noun *nirutti.* Now, checking the paradigm chart in your grammar textbook (or memory!), you see that the form *niruttiyā* can be either instrumental, genitive, dative, or ablative of the feminine *i* noun stem. I would try each of them to determine which makes the most sense:

- INSTRUMENTAL: Monks, I permit one to learn the teachings of the Buddha *with/through/using/by means of one's own language;*

- GENITIVE: Monks, I permit one to learn the teachings of the Buddha *of one's own language/one's own language;*
- DATIVE: Monks, I permit one to learn the teachings of the Buddha *to one's own language/for the sake of one's own language;*
- ABLATIVE: Monks, I permit one to learn the teachings of the Buddha *because of/from one's own language.*
- LOCATIVE: Monks, I permit one to learn the teachings of the Buddha *in one's own language.*

Given the immediate context of the statement – namely, the disciples' request to be permitted to communicate the teachings in Sanskrit – the instrumental and locative versions make the most sense: *Monks, I permit one to learn the teachings of the Buddha using/in one's own language.* As reader-translators, we have to choose one. I choose the instrumental version. My reason is that the action concerns doing something in a particular manner. It does not concern the placing of something. The former is the most basic function of an instrumental; the latter, of the locative. Hence, my decision to construe *niruttiyā* as an instrumental. Before we end the matter, however, we need to consider some further issues of translation.

Translation, Vocabulary, and Meaning

Sorting out grammar is just the first step toward understanding a word, sentence, passage, and text. Its highly complex nature makes grammar, in one sense, the most difficult part of reading Pali. In another sense, however, it's also the easiest. Grammar constrains your reading of a text. Grammar almost forces you to get it – the grammatical construction – right. For example, if I construe *niruttiyā* to be a dative of direction, say, and translate the statement as "Monks, I permit one to learn the teachings of the Buddha to one's own language," I would have to reconsider my construal: the sentence is nonsensical. There are cases, of course, where a sentence makes sense standing on its own, but, when read from the fuller context of the passage or text, does not. The dative of purpose, for example, might make sense: "Monks, I permit one to learn the teachings of the Buddha for the sake of one's own language." Maybe "the Buddha" was a grammarian of ancient times, and studying his teachings saved his interlocutors from butchering their shared language. Or maybe the text is claiming that the Buddha's *dhamma* could have that effect on their language. Well, it's not difficult to discover that neither of these scenarios is the case. Grammar plus context has constrained, and rejected, those readings; hence, back to the grammar for another try.

As these examples illustrate, translation involves an oscillation between the part and the whole. The part is as limited as a letter, and the whole, as wide as the culture – the social, historical, doctrinal, etc., meaning-making factors – surrounding the text. (I'll say more about this aspect of translation later.) As an example, let's return to our translation: *Monks, I permit one to learn the teachings of the Buddha using one's own language.* This translation is by no means as obvious as I make it seem. First of all, go back and look at all of the other vocabulary possibilities. How would the meaning of the statement be affected if for *anujānāmi* we chose *I prescribe*? Obviously, *prescribing* something is more forceful and decisive than *permitting* it. Consider the nuances suggested in other possibilities: *I give permission, I grant, I allow, I advise.* We could do this exercise in vocabulary choice with each word. Imagine the possibilities if you were to write each possible word meaning on a slip of paper and move them around:

> Monks, I prescribe one to master the sayings of the awakened one using one's own accent.
>
> Beggars, I advise one to know the words of the realized one using one's own etymological interpretation.

And so on.

To get a clear sense of how much can be at stake in determining word meaning, let's look at one of the choices that both Western scholarship and traditional Buddhist exegesis have taken to be controversial. My decision to construe an implicit *one*, and hence, to translate the modifying adjective *saka* as *one's own,* is by no means obvious, it seems. Buddhaghosa, the renowned Theravadin commentator, insisted that *saka* (or as he gives it, *sakā*) is to be construed as *my own,* that is, the Buddha's own. His gloss is as follows: *sakāya niruttiyāti: ettha sakā nirutti nāma sammāsambuddhena vuttappakāro māgadhiko vohāro.* This translates as: "Using his own language: here, the terms *sakā* and *nirutti* refer to the manner spoken by the perfectly awakened one, the Māgadhi language" (*Cūḷavagga-aṭṭhakathā* 5.285). (That Buddhaghosa intends "using *his* own," is, of course, obvious from the remainder of the gloss.)

So, which is it? Have all Buddhists throughout history gone astray by not learning the teachings in the ancient eastern Indian Prakrit (a local dialect or vernacular spoken by the common people at the time of the Buddha) known as Māgadhi? Or are we on the right track in endeavoring to reconstitute the teachings in 21st-century idiomatic English? How can we know, within reasonable boundaries (for we can never know for certain), what the Buddha meant to say here?

Broadening our scope will help resolve some of the uncertainty. For instance, we know from the text within which our statement is embedded that the two monks who were making the request to the Buddha were Brahmin-born, well-spoken brothers. They were, specifically, requesting that the Buddha's teachings be taught and learned in *chandas.* The basic meaning of this term is "verse, metrical form." So, we might conclude that the brothers wanted to transpose the Buddha's words into verse. But the Buddha's harsh response (*moghapurisā,* you morons/fools/twits/imbeciles/dullards – take your choice) would cause me to reconsider that word-choice decision – the response is simply not proportionate to the request. From the study of ancient India, we know, furthermore, that the Vedas were the preëminent metrical compositions of the Brahmins of the time. Perhaps *chandas* refers to the language used by this class of Indian, namely Sanskrit. The grammarian Pāṇini (ca. 4th century BCE), on the other hand, used *chandas* to indicate Vedic Sanskrit as distinct from the form spoken in his day (see B.C. Law, *A History of Pali Literature,* Varanasi: Indica Books, 2000 [1933], p. xii). In any case, it seems safe to say that the brothers were asking for a change from the common and, to their ears, uncouth regional language (or does *nirutti* merely signify *accent* or *dialect*? yet another issue to investigate!) of Māgadhi to some form of melodious high-class Sanskrit.

How will you understand the Buddha's response? Will you side with Buddhaghosa, and construe *sakāya niruttiyā* as referring to the Buddha's language? If so, what will you make of the fact that his teachings proliferated throughout language- and dialect-rich India, and attracted followers from all classes of society, even the most uneducated – and did so right under his nose? Would you have to conclude that the Buddha's decrees – and remember that our statement shows up in the *Vinaya,* the storehouse of ostensibly binding decrees – were toothless, inconsequential? Where would that conclusion lead you? On the other hand, perhaps you, like B.C. Law, find it "incomprehensible" (*ibid.*) that the Buddha could make the declaration suggested by Buddhaghosa in the first place. After all, he's the perfectly enlightened one, right? Law said that it is impossible that the Buddha make such an "irrational, erroneous, and dogmatic" choice (*ibid.*). Maybe he bases his assessment on assumptions he holds about the Buddha's character; or maybe he just finds it too incompatible with other evidence in the texts. Finally, one scholar, John Brough, holds that the controversy concerning the phrase *sakāya niruttiyā* is linguistically baseless, a mere *fata morgana* perpetuated by Buddhaghosa's "sectarian comment" (see John Brough, "Sakāya Niruttiyā: Cauld kale het," in Heinz Bechert, *Die Sprache der Ältesten Buddhistischen Überlieferung* [Göttingen: Vandenhoeck und Ruprecht, 1980], pp. 35–42; citation p. 36).

What do *you* think?

This is just one small example of the many decisions that you, the reader and translator of Pali Buddhist texts, will have to make. When you come across such familiar terms as *nibbāna* or even *buddha,* what will you do? Will you reflexively follow our established Pali-to-English tradition and think *extinguishing* and *enlightened one,* respectively? Well, I hope you will pause, look carefully at the root/stem basis of the term, consider other contexts in which you've seen the term, and, most importantly of all, use your common sense.

One of the greatest benefits of reading in a language as foreign and difficult as Pali is that it forces us to slow down. We have no choice but to give careful, clear thought to the simplest of matters, such as pronouns and word order. Before you begin, please pause to consider the words of one man who mastered the unhurried imbibing of the text, Friedrich Nietzsche (1844–1900).

> A book like this, a problem like this, is in no hurry; we both, I just as much as my book, are friends of lento. It is not for nothing that I have been a philologist, perhaps I am a philologist still, that is to say, A TEACHER OF SLOW READING – in the end I also write slowly. Nowadays it is not only my habit, it is also to my taste – a malicious taste, perhaps? – no longer to write anything which does not reduce to despair every sort of man who is 'in a hurry.' For philology is that venerable art which demands of its votaries one thing above all: to go aside, to take time, to become still, to become slow – it is a goldsmith's art and connoisseurship of the WORD which has nothing but delicate, cautious work to do and achieves nothing if it does not achieve it lento. But precisely for this reason it is more necessary than ever today, by precisely this means does it entice and enchant us the most, in the midst of an age of 'work,' that is to say, of hurry, of indecent and perspiring haste, which wants to 'get everything done' at once, including every old or new book – this art does not so easily get anything done, it teaches to read WELL, that is to say, to read slowly, deeply, looking cautiously before and after, with reservations, with doors left open, with delicate eyes and fingers.... My patient friends, this book desires for itself only perfect readers and philologists: LEARN to read me well! (Friedrich Nietszche, *Morgenröthe,* 1881. Translation: R. J. Hollingdale, *Daybreak* [Cambridge: Cambridge University Press, 1982], p. 5.)

As a student of the Pali *suttas,* you must be a passionate and obsessive reader. I believe that, over time, you, too, will come to this conclusion. Like a connoisseur, you must long to savor each and every word. A text, as Umberto Eco says, is a lazy machine – it requires work from a significant collaborator. That collaborator is you, the reader. When these two – text and reader – come together, horizons are fused and worlds are born.

Pronunciation

Here is a rough guide to pronouncing Pali. I have included some Sanskrit pronunciation as well, since some terms in that language are included in the glossary. The consonants are arranged according to the place of articulation.

Vowels

a, as in **a**nother
ā, as in f**a**ther,
i, as in **it**
ī, as in qu**ee**n
u, as in f**oo**t
ū, as in b**oo**t
e, as in pl**ay**
o, as in g**o**

Nasal

ṃ, as in go**ng**; it also nasalizes the preceding vowel, as the **o** in **gong** as opposed to that in g**o**t.

Gutturals (articulated in the throat)

k, as in **k**ettle
kh, pronounced as k plus slight aspiration, stea**kh**ouse
g, as in **g**one; note: never as in gin
gh, as in bi**g h**ouse
ṅ, as in cra**nk**

Palatals (articulated with tongue pressed against the palate, just above the teeth)

c, as in **ch**urch; note: never as in cat
ch, pronounced as c plus slight aspiration, wit**ch h**azel
j, as in **j**am
jh, pronounced as j plus slight aspiration, sled**geh**ammer
ñ, as in pi**ñ**ata, o**n**ion, ca**ny**on
y, as in **y**es (palatal in name only)
ś, as in **sh**iver (palatal in name only; Sanskrit only)

Cerebrals (articulated with tongue pointing upward, placed toward the middle of the palate)

ṭ, somewhat like **t**ruck
ṭh, pronounced as ṭ plus slight aspiration, ra**t h**ole;
note: never as in thorn
ḍ, somewhat like **d**ry
ḍh, pronounced as ḍ plus slight aspiration, re**d h**ouse
ṇ, somewhat like k**n**owledge
ṛ, as in p**ret**ty (Sanskrit only)
r, as in **r**ain
l, as in **l**ake
ḷ, as in **l**atitude, fe**lt**
ṣ as in **s**ure (Sanskrit only)

Dentals (articulated with tongue pressed against the upper front teeth)

t, as in **t**ake
th, pronounced as t plus slight aspiration, ca**t h**ouse;
note: never as in think
d, as in **d**ay
dh, as in ma**d h**atter
n, as in **n**o
s, as in **s**ane

Labials (articulated with the lips pressed together)

p as in **p**ie
ph, pronounced as p plus slight aspiration, ta**p h**ose;
note: never as in filly, phone
b, as in **b**all
bh, as in clu**b h**ouse
m, as in **m**erry
v, as in **v**ain (labial in name only)

Aspirate (slight release of breath through the mouth)

h, as in **h**ail

Another important aspect of pronunciation is stress. "Stress" is synonymous with "accent." Both terms refer to the placing of emphasis on a given syllable. Unfortunately, we do not know for certain where stress was placed in the Prakrit vernaculars, of which the language of the Pali texts represents an instance. (In written Vedic Sanskrit, by contrast, stress is meticulously indicated by accent notations.)

There seems, furthermore, to be no agreement among contemporary South and Southeast Asian Buddhists and scholars, in both East and West, concerning the spoken pronunciation of Pali. I have heard a wide range of Pali pronunciation among Indian, Sri Lankan, Thai, and Burmese speakers. My impression is that, as with English speakers reading Pali aloud, pronunciation depends as much on the rules and habits governing one's own language as those of Pali. I suppose that the contemporary situation is not much different than that of the ancient and medieval periods. Students who want to investigate this complex matter further can consult A. K. Warder, *Pali Metre* (London: Luzac and Co., 1967). (Good luck.)

We can nonetheless make some commonsensical assumptions about where to place the stress in our spoken Pali. We know, for instance, how to distinguish a short, light syllable from a long, heavy one:

- Short: in *kusala*, all three syllables, *ku sa la*, are short. The rule is that a syllable is short if it is composed of a short vowel and is followed by only one consonant or by nothing.
- Long: the first syllable of *buddha* and *bhūta* are both long. The rule is that a syllable is long if it contains a short vowel followed by two consonants (sometimes called "long by position") or a long vowel.
- Note: nasalization via *ṃ* serves to lengthen a short vowel. For example, the second syllable is prolonged in speaking *bhūtaṃ*, but not in *bhūta*. Remember, however, that *ṃ* is not a consonant.

There are, of course, many exceptions to these basic rules. For example, *e* and *o*, though considered long vowels, do become short on occasion when followed by a double consonant. Particularly in verse, old rules are broken, new rules created, and, at times it seems, anarchy reigns. What we know about syllable length, however, combined with a commonsense assumption about syllable stress, should allow us to begin speaking Pali sentences aloud with some degree of historical integrity. A further assumption is that stress in Pali must share a good deal with classical Sanskrit. And we do have a clear sense of the rules that dictated that pronunciation. Those are basically as follows.

The final (ultimate) syllable never receives the stress, regardless of length. So, to determine where stress lies, begin with the next to last (penultimate) syllable, move backward toward the front of the word, and proceed until you encounter one of the following occurrences: (i) a long vowel, *ā, ī, ū, e, o*, receives the stress; (ii) or *a, i, u* followed by a double consonant does; (iii) or a short vowel + *ṃ* does; (iv) or, if you make it all the way back to the first syllable and none of these possibilities has occurred, that first one gets the accent. For example (stressed syllable is indicated by bold letter), (i) *bh**ā**ra, **ā**sana, rajan**ī**ya, j**ī**va, r**ū**pa, Vās**e**ṭṭha,* *ass**o**suṃ*, *G**o**tama*; (ii) *an**a**ttā*, *l**a**kkhaṇa*, *bh**i**kkhu*, *p**u**cchati*; (iii) *ahi**ṃ**sā*, *va**ṃ**sa*; (iv) *y**a**didaṃ*, *k**a**tama*.

I have encountered various interpretations – usually implicit – of the pronunciation of compound Sanskrit words (including those with affixes). Some speakers and scholars seem to hold that each term in the compound retains its accent; for example, *an**a**ttal**a**kkhaṇa*, *b**u**ddhav**a**cana*, ***a**nujān**ā**mi*. Others, that only the final term receives stress. It may, in this case, be proper to speak of secondary accent or pitch. That is, the second term receives the primary accent, or stress, while the first term receives pitch. Pitch occurs where stress would if the term stood alone. It is shorter than stress. For instance, (pitch = ′): *anáttal**a**kkhaṇa*, *búddhav**a**cana*, *ánujān**ā**mi*.

Be careful not to confuse stress with length and pitch. Vowels retain their value even if they don't receive the stress. For instance, *licchavī* = *l**i**cchavee*. The *ī*, pronounced like the *e* in *easy*, does not receive the stress because it is the final syllable, yet is still long. Pitch is a shorter accentuation than stress. Together, stress, length, and pitch give spoken language its musicality.

Taking all of the above into account, this is how our statement might read:

*ánujān**ā**mi bh**i**kkhave sák**ā**ya nír**u**ttiyā búddhav**a**canam páriy**ā**puṇituṃ*

Notes on the Glossary

A glossary is provided at the end of each *sutta*. The basic organizing principle of the glossary is to offer just enough information about a word to enable the student of Pali to begin the work of translation; namely, determining grammar, syntax, sense, and meaning. Therefore, when consulting the glossary, the following points should be kept in mind.

- With the exception of pronouns, words are given in their stem or root form.
- Verbs are given either under prefix or root form, depending on how they appear in the text. For instance, *saṃvatteyya* is located under *saṃ* + √*vatt*, and *gacchati*, under √*gam*. Common verbal prefixes include: *ati*, *adhi*, *anu*, *apa*, *api*, *abhi*, *ā*, *ud*, *upa*, *du(r)*, *ni(r)*, *pa*, *paṭi*, *pati*, *parā*, *pari*, *vi*, *saṃ*. Note that *a* and *an* are not verbal prefixes per se. However, *a* (i) is augmented to the stem in certain conjugations; (ii) represents the verbal prefix *ā* before a double consonant; and, (iii) along with *an*, denotes negation. Also, remember that *sandhi* and contraction alter many forms. Common examples are:

  ati > acc before vowels
  adhi + ā > ajjhā

adhi + pra	>	adhipa
anu	>	anv before vowels
apa	>	o occasionally
abhi	>	abbh before vowels other than i
ava	>	o before consonants
paṭi, pati	>	pacc before vowels
pari	>	pariy or pall before vowels, payir before u
pari + ā	>	pariyā
pari + ava	>	pariyo
vi	>	by, v, viy, vy before vowels
vi + ati	>	vīti
vi + apa	>	vyapa, vapa
vi + ava	>	vo
vi + ā	>	byā, viyā, vyā
vi + ud	>	vud
vi + upa	>	vupa, vūpa

(Based on: Achim Fahs, *Grammatik des Pali* [Leipzig: VEB Verlag, 1989], p. 42.)

In order to show the elements comprising the verb, compound verbs are given in their pre-sandhi form. For instance: *paccakkhāya* appears in the glossary as *paṭi + ā + khā*.)

- Particularly difficult-to-recognize terms are included under their stem or root form. Example: *avocumhā* is mentioned under √*vac.*
- In the majority of cases, past passive participles (ppp.) are given as such even when used as adjectives or nouns, though gender is given in the latter case.
- Nonfinite verbs are generally omitted when the root form has already been given. For example, when *vi + ni +* √*bhuj* is given, *vinibbhujant* (present active participle [prap.]) is not.
- "Line 2," "Line 208," etc., refer to the superscripted number in the *sutta* Only the first instance of a word is given.
- When only the gender designation is given (m., f. or n.), it indicates that the word is a noun.
- A given word meaning does not necessarily cover the lexical range of the term, but rather corresponds roughly to the specific text passage in which it occurs.
- Compounds are generally broken up. For example, *buddhavacana* comprises two entries: *buddha* and *vacana.*

- Words are given in Pali alphabetical order, which is as follows:

  a, ā, i, ī, u, ū, e, o, ṃ
  k, kh, g, gh, ṅ
  c, ch, j, jh, ñ
  ṭ, ṭh, ḍ, ḍh, ṇ
  t, th, d, dh, n
  p, ph, b, bh, m
  y, r, l, ḷ, v, s, h

- The following abbreviations are used:

abs.	absolutive
act.	active
adj.	adjective
adv.	adverb
ag.n.	agent noun
aor.	aorist
caus.	causitive
cf.	compare
cond.	conditional
dat.	dative
dem.	demonstrative
den.	denominative
desid.	desiderative
E.	English
encl.	enclitic
f.	feminine
fpp.	future passive participle
fut.	future
gen.	genitive
imper.	imperative
ind.	indeclinable
indef.	indefinite
indic.	indicative
inf.	infinitive
inj.	injunctive
inst.	instrumental
int.	intensive
interg.	interrogative
lit.	literally
loc.	locative
m.	masculine
n.	neuter
neg.	negative
nom.	nominative
num.	numeral
opt.	optative
ord.	ordinal
P.	Pali
part.	particle (always indeclinable; frequently an adverb)
partic.	participle
pass.	passive
per.	personal
pers.	person
pl.	plural
ppp.	past passive participle
pr. adj.	pronominal adjective
prap.	present active participle
prep.	preposition
prmp.	present middle participle
prpp.	present passive participle
pres.	present
pron.	pronoun
S.	Sanskrit
sg.	singular
tech.	technically
voc.	vocative
√	verb root
°	elision
+	affixed to; in addition to
[]	amended to text

Sources

The following sources were referred to in compiling the glossaries.

Collins, Steven, *A Pali Grammar for Students* (Chiang Mai: Silkworm Books, 2005).

Cone, Margaret, *A Dictionary of Pāli; Part 1, a-kh* (Oxford: The Pali Text Society, 2001).

Fahs, Achim, *Grammatik des Pali* (Leipzig: VEB Verlag, 1989).

Oberlies, Thomas, *Pāli: A Grammar of the Language of the Theravāda Tipiṭaka.* (Berlin: Walter de Gruyter: 2001).

Rhys Davids, T. W., Stede, William (editors), *The Pali Text Society's Pali–English Dictionary* (London: The Pali Text Society, 1986) [original: Chipstead: The Pali Text Society, 1921–5].

Trenckner, V., Andersen, D., Smith, H., et. al., *A Critical Pāli Dictionary, vols. 1-3*; online version: http://pali.hum.ku.dk/cpd/intro

Warder, A. K., *Introduction to Pali* (Oxford: The Pali Text Society, 1991).

NOTE: The texts in the present volume are constituted on the basis of the *Chaṭṭha Saṅgāyana Pāli Tipiṭaka* (Dhamma Giri, Igatpuri, India: Vipassana Research Institute, 1990). All references are to the CD-ROM/online edition unless otherwise noted. That edition is available here: http://www.tipitaka.org.

The references are as follows.

- *Dīghanikāya* = division, text number, paragraph number; e.g., *Dīghanikāya* 1.13.518
- *Majjhimanikāya* = division, section, text number, and paragraph number; e.g., *Majjhimanikāya* 1.1.10.105.
- *Saṃyuttanikāya* = division, *saṃyutta*, subsection, text number, and paragraph number; e.g., *Saṃyuttanikāya* 5.3.1.6.372.
- *Aṅguttaranikāya* = numerical division, subdivision, section, text number, paragraph number; e.g., *Aṅguttaranikāya* 3.2.2.5.66.

The Suttas

Sutta 1

Sakuṇagghisuttaṃ

(*Saṃyuttanikāya* 5.3.1.6.372)

"Bhūtapubbaṃ, bhikkhave, sakuṇagghi lāpaṃ sakuṇa ṃ sahasā ajjhappattā aggahesi. Atha kho, bhikkhave, lāpo sakuṇo sakuṇagghiyā hariyamāno evaṃ paridevasi – 'mayamevamha alakkhikā, mayaṃ appapuññā, ye mayaṃ agocare carimha paravisaye. Sacejja mayaṃ gocare careyyāma sake pettike visaye, na myāyaṃ, sakuṇagghi, alaṃ abhavissa, yadidaṃ – yuddhāyā'ti. 'Ko pana te, lāpa, gocaro sako pettiko visayo'ti? 'Yadidaṃ – naṅgalakaṭṭhakaraṇaṃ leḍḍuṭṭhāna'"nti. "Atha kho, bhikkhave, sakuṇagghi sake bale apatthaddhā sake bale asaṃvadamānā lāpaṃ sakuṇaṃ pamuñci – 'gaccha kho tvaṃ, lāpa, tatrapi me gantvā na mokkhasī'"ti.

"Atha kho, bhikkhave, lāpo sakuṇo naṅgalakaṭṭhakaraṇaṃ leḍḍuṭṭhānaṃ gantvā mahantaṃ leḍḍuṃ abhiruhitvā sakuṇagghiṃ vadamāno aṭṭhāsi – 'ehi kho dāni me, sakuṇagghi, ehi kho dāni me, sakuṇagghī'ti. Atha kho sā, bhikkhave, sakuṇagghi sake bale apatthaddhā sake bale asaṃvadamānā ubho pakkhe sannayha lāpaṃ sakuṇaṃ sahasā ajjhappattā. Yadā kho, bhikkhave, aññāsi lāpo sakuṇo 'bahuāgato kho myāyaṃ sakuṇagghī'ti, atha tasseva leḍḍussa antaraṃ paccupādi. Atha kho, bhikkhave, sakuṇagghi tattheva uraṃ paccatāḷesi. Evañhi taṃ, bhikkhave, hoti yo agocare carati paravisaye.

"Tasmātiha, bhikkhave, mā agocare carittha paravisaye. Agocare, bhikkhave, caratam paravisaye lacchati māro otāram, lacchati māro ārammaṇaṃ. Ko ca, bhikkhave, bhikkhuno agocaro paravisayo? Yadidaṃ – pañca kāmaguṇā. Katame pañca? Cakkhuviññeyyā rūpā iṭṭhā kantā manāpā piyarūpā kāmūpasaṃhitā rajanīyā, sotaviññeyyā saddā...pe... ghānaviññeyyā gandhā... jivhāviññeyyā rasā... kāyaviññeyyā phoṭṭhabbā iṭṭhā kantā manāpā piyarūpā kāmūpasaṃhitā rajanīyā – ayaṃ, bhikkhave, bhikkhuno agocaro paravisayo.

"Gocare, bhikkhave, caratha sake pettike visaye. Gocare, bhikkhave, carataṃ sake pettike visaye na lacchati māro otāraṃ, na lacchati māro ārammaṇaṃ. Ko ca, bhikkhave, bhikkhuno gocaro sako pettiko visayo? Yadidaṃ – cattāro satipaṭṭhānā. Katame cattāro? Idha, bhikkhave, bhikkhu kāye kāyānupassī viharati ātāpī sampajāno satimā, vineyya loke abhijjhādomanassaṃ; vedanāsu...pe... citte...pe... dhammesu dhammānupassī viharati ātāpī sampajāno satimā, vineyya loke abhijjhādomanassaṃ – ayaṃ, bhikkhave, bhikkhuno gocaro sako pettiko visayo"ti.

Sutta 1 ♦ Glossary

a

agocara (m.), improper pasture, foreign domain.

ajja (adv.), today.

atha (part.), then.

atha kho (part.), then, moreover.

adhi + *ā* + √*pat*, to swoop down on, to descend on, to attack. (Line 1, *ajjhappatta* = ppp.)

anatara (adj.), inside, within, internal.

anupassin (adj.), observing, viewing, considering.

apatthaddha (ppp. √*thambh* + *apa*), relied on, trusted in.

api (part.), *adds emphasis to preceding term*; even, even though, also; but.

appapuñña (adj.), having little merit.

abhijjhā (f.), longing, yearning.

abhi + √*ruh*, to ascend, to climb.

ayaṃ (m.f. dem. pron.), this, *etc.*

alaṃ (part.), certainly, alas, enough.

alakkhika (adj.), unfortunate.

ā

ā + √*gam*, to come, to arrive.

ātāpin (adj.), ardent, strenuous, energetic, applying oneself.

ārammaṇa (n.), basis, foundation.

i

√*i*, to come. (Line 12, *ehi* = 2nd pers. sg. imper.)

iṭṭha (ppp. √*is*), pleasing, wished for.

idaṃ (n. dem. pron), this, *etc.*

idāni (adv.), now. (Line 13, *dāni* = abbreviation.)

idha (part.), here, in this connection, now.

√*is*, to desire, to want, to wish.

iha (part.), here, in this case, in this instance.

u

upasaṃhita (adj.), possessing, accompanied by, connected with.

ubho (adj.), both.

ura (m.n.), chest.

e

eva (part.), *adds emphasis to preceding term*; so, just, even.

evaṃ (part.), thus, so, such, in this way; yes.

o

otāra (m.), opening, access, weak point.

k

kaṭṭha (ppp. √*kas*), ploughed.

katama (m.f.n. interg. pron.), which (of several)?, *etc.*

kanta (ppp. √*kam*), desirable.

√*kam*, to desire.

karaṇa (n.), instrument; in the condition of.

√*kas*, to plough.

kāma (m.n.), desire, sensory pleasure, passion.

kāya (m.), body.

ko (m. interg. pron.), who, which, what?, *etc.*

kh

kho pana (interrog. part.), what then?

g

gandha (m.), scent.

√*gam*, to go.

√*gah*, to grasp, to hold, to seize.

guṇa (m.), quality; strand, aspect, element.

gocara (m.), proper pasture, native domain.

gh

ghāna (n.), nose.

c

ca (encl. part.), and.

cakkhu (n.), eye.

catu(r) (num.), four. (Line 28, *cattāro* = four.)

√*car*, to wander. (Line 18, *mā ... carittha* = 2nd pers. pl. inj.)

citta (n.), mind, discursive thought, discursive mind.

j

jivhā (f.), tongue.

ñ

√*ñā*, to know, to realize.

ṭh

√*ṭhā*, to stand.

ṭhāna (n.), place, location.

t

taṃ (m.f.n. dem. pron.), him, her, it, that, this, the, *etc.*

taṃ (part.), then, now, so.

tattha (part.), there, that place. (Line 16, *tattheva*, right there.)

tatra (part.), there.

tasmā (part.), therefore.

ti (part.), marks end of direct speech, a thought, or quoted term. (Note: A short vowel preceding *ti* is lengthened, and *ṃ* is converted to *n*.)

te (2nd pers. per. pron; m. dem. pron.), by you, yours, to you (sg); those, them, *etc.*

tvaṃ (2nd pers. per. pron.), you, *etc.*

th

√*thambh*, to support, to be firm, to make firm.

d

dāni, see idāni.

domanassa (n.), heavy heartedness, depression, abjection.

dh

dhamma (m.), phenomenon, thing; quality, mental quality, thought; nature; teaching; standard.

n

na (part.), no, not.

naṅgala (m.), plough.

p

pakkha (m.), wing, side.

pañca (num.), five.

paṭṭhāna (n.), foundation, establishment; *tech.*, setting forth.

paṭi + *upa* + *ā* + √*dā*, to take up again, to return to. (Line 16, *paccupādi* = aor.)

paṭi + √*tud*, to strike, to strike a blow. (Line 17, *paccatāḷesi* = aor.)

√*pat*, to fall.

pana (encl. part.), *see kho pana.*

pa + √*muc*, to free, to release.

para (prep.), beyond, outside of.

pari +√*div*, to lament.

piya (adj.), dear, agreeable, likable, beloved.

pe (part.), abridgement of *peyyāla*: repetition, etcetera.

pettika (adj.), ancestral.

ph

phoṭṭhabba (n.), tactile feeling, touch.

b

bala (n.), strength, power.

bahu (adj.), much, many, great.

bh

bhikkhu (m.), mendicant; *lit.* beggar.

√*bhū*, to be, to become; to cultivate, to nurture, to develop. (Line 5, *abhavissa* = cond.)

bhūtapubbaṃ (adv.), formerly, distant past.

m

manāpa (adj.), charming, pleasing, pleasant.

mayaṃ (1st pers. per. pron.), we, *etc*; (can be used to indicate singular "I").

mahant (adj.), large, great, extensive.

mā (part.), not, do not.

māra (m.), death; Mara, *the personification of mortality.*

√*muc*, to release, to free, to liberate; to escape. (Line 9, *mokkhasi* = 2nd pers. sing. fut.)

me (1st pers. per. pron.), to me, *etc*. (Line 5, *myāyaṃ* = *me* + *ayaṃ*.)

y

yad (n. rel. pron), which, that, *etc.*

yadā (part.), when.

yadidaṃ (part.), namely, as follows, that is to say; *literally*, which is this.

yuddha (n.), battle.

ye (m. rel. pron.), those who, those which, that, *etc.*

yo (m. rel. pron.), he who, that which, *etc.*

r

rajanīya (adj.), enticing

rūpa (n.), form, appearance, body, object.

l

lacch° = √*labh*.

√*labh*, to gain, to aquire. (Line 26, *lacchati* = fut.)

lāpa (m.), quail.

leḍḍu (m.), clod of earth.

loka (m.), world.

v

√*vad*, to say, to speak.

vi + √*ñā*, to perceive, to discern, to know. (Line 21, *viññeyya* = fpp.)

vi + √*nī*, to give up, to put down, to remove. (Line 31, *vineyya* = abs.)

visaya (m.), habitat, area, domain.

vi + √*har*, to live, to stay, to dwell, to abide.

vedanā (f.), feeling, sensation.

s

saṃ + √*nah*, to bind together, to arrange. (Line 14, *sannayha* = aor.)

saṃ + √*vad*, to boast.

saka (adj.), own, one's own.

sakuṇa (m.), bird.

sakuṇagghi (f.), hawk; *lit.* bird-(*sakuṇa*) killer (from °*ghin*, that which destroys).

sace (part.), if.

sati (f.), present-moment awareness, presence of mind, reflective clarity, non-interfering consciousness, lucidity; *lit.*, memory; *tech.*, memory-in-the-present.

satimant (adj.), aware, attentive, watchful.

sadda (m.), sound, report.

sampajāna (adj.), attentive, conscientious, thoughtful, fully comprehending.

sahasā (adv.), suddenly, forcibly.

sā (f. pers. pron.), she, that, *etc.*

sutta (n.), discourse, dialogue, text; *lit.*, thread, stitching, textile.

sota (n.), ear.

h

ha, see iha

hariyamāna (prpp. √*har*), being taken, being carried away.

Sutta 2

Cūḷamālukyasuttaṃ

(Majjhimanikāya 2. 2.3.122)

Evaṃ me sutaṃ – ekaṃ samayaṃ bhagavā sāvatthiyaṃ viharati jetavane anāthapiṇḍikassa ārāme. Atha kho āyasmato mālukyaputtassa rahogatassa paṭisallīnassa evaṃ cetaso parivitakko udapādi – "yānimāni diṭṭhigatāni bhagavatā abyākatāni ṭhapitāni paṭikkhittāni – 'sassato loko'tipi, 'asassato loko'tipi, 'antavā loko'tipi, 'anantavā loko'tipi, 'taṃ jīvaṃ taṃ sarīra'ntipi, 'aññaṃ jīvaṃ aññaṃ sarīra'ntipi, 'hoti tathāgato paraṃ maraṇā'tipi, 'na hoti tathāgato paraṃ maraṇā'tipi, 'hoti ca na ca hoti tathāgato paraṃ maraṇā'tipi, 'neva hoti na na hoti tathāgato paraṃ maraṇā'tipi – tāni me bhagavā na byākaroti. Yāni me bhagavā na byākaroti taṃ me na ruccati, taṃ me nakkhamati. Sohaṃ bhagavantaṃ upasaṅkamitvā etamatthaṃ pucchissāmi. Sace me bhagavā byākarissati – 'sassato loko'ti vā 'asassato loko'ti vā...pe... 'neva hoti na na hoti tathāgato paraṃ maraṇā'ti vā – evāhaṃ bhagavati brahmacariyaṃ carissāmi; no ce me bhagavā byākarissati – 'sassato loko'ti vā 'asassato loko'ti vā...pe... 'neva hoti na na hoti tathāgato paraṃ maraṇā'ti vā – evāhaṃ sikkhaṃ paccakkhāya hīnāyāvattissāmī"ti. Atha kho āyasmā mālukyaputto sāyanhasamayaṃ paṭisallānā vuṭṭhito yena bhagavā tenupasaṅkami; upasaṅkamitvā bhagavantaṃ abhivādetvā ekamantaṃ nisīdi. Ekamantaṃ nisinno kho āyasmā mālukyaputto bhagavantaṃ etadavoca –

"Idha mayhaṃ, bhante, rahogatassa paṭisallīnassa evaṃ cetaso parivitakko udapādi – yānimāni diṭṭhigatāni bhagavatā abyākatāni ṭhapitāni paṭikkhittāni –

'sassato loko'tipi, 'asassato loko'tipi...pe... 'neva hoti na na hoti tathāgato paraṃ maraṇā'tipi – tāni me bhagavā na byākaroti. Yāni me bhagavā na byākaroti taṃ me na ruccati, taṃ me nakkhamati. Sohaṃ bhagavantaṃ upasaṅkamitvā etamatthaṃ pucchissāmi. Sace me bhagavā byākarissati – 'sassato loko'ti vā, 'asassato loko'ti vā...pe... 'neva hoti na na hoti tathāgato paraṃ maraṇā'ti vā – evāhaṃ bhagavati, brahmacariyaṃ carissāmi. No ce me bhagavā byākarissati – 'sassato loko'ti vā, 'asassato loko'ti vā...pe... 'neva hoti na na hoti tathāgato paraṃ maraṇā'ti vā – evāhaṃ sikkhaṃ paccakkhāya hīnāyāvattissāmīti. Sace bhagavā jānāti – 'sassato loko'ti, 'sassato loko'ti me bhagavā byākarotu; sace bhagavā jānāti – 'asassato loko'ti, 'asassato loko'ti me bhagavā byākarotu. No ce bhagavā jānāti – 'sassato loko'ti vā, 'asassato loko'ti vā, ajānato kho pana apassato etadeva ujukaṃ hoti yadidaṃ – 'na jānāmi, na passāmī'ti. Sace bhagavā jānāti – 'antavā loko'ti, 'anantavā loko'ti me bhagavā byākarotu; sace bhagavā jānāti – 'anantavā loko'ti, 'anantavā loko'ti me bhagavā byākarotu. No ce bhagavā jānāti – 'antavā loko'ti vā, 'anantavā loko'ti vā, ajānato kho pana apassato etadeva ujukaṃ hoti yadidaṃ – 'na jānāmi, na passāmī'ti. Sace bhagavā jānāti – 'taṃ jīvaṃ taṃ sarīra'nti, 'taṃ jīvaṃ taṃ sarīra'nti me bhagavā byākarotu; sace bhagavā jānāti – 'aññaṃ jīvaṃ aññaṃ sarīra'nti, 'aññaṃ jīvaṃ aññaṃ sarīra'nti me bhagavā byākarotu. No ce bhagavā jānāti – 'taṃ jīvaṃ taṃ sarīra'nti vā, 'aññaṃ jīvaṃ aññaṃ sarīra'nti vā, ajānato kho pana apassato etadeva ujukaṃ hoti yadidaṃ – 'na jānāmi, na passāmī'ti. Sace bhagavā jānāti – 'hoti tathāgato paraṃ maraṇā'ti, 'hoti tathāgato paraṃ maraṇā'ti me bhagavā byākarotu; sace bhagavā jānāti – 'na hoti tathāgato paraṃ maraṇā'ti, 'na hoti tathāgato paraṃ maraṇā'ti me bhagavā byākarotu. No ce bhagavā jānāti – 'hoti tathāgato paraṃ maraṇā'ti vā, 'na hoti tathāgato paraṃ maraṇā'ti vā, ajānato kho pana apassato etadeva ujukaṃ hoti yadidaṃ – 'na jānāmi na passāmī'ti. Sace bhagavā jānāti – 'hoti ca na ca hoti tathāgato paraṃ maraṇā'ti, 'hoti ca na ca hoti tathāgato paraṃ maraṇā'ti me bhagavā byākarotu; sace bhagavā jānāti – 'neva hoti na na hoti tathāgato paraṃ maraṇā'ti, 'neva hoti na na hoti tathāgato paraṃ maraṇā'ti

me bhagavā byākarotu. No ce bhagavā jānāti – 'hoti ca na ca hoti tathāgato paraṃ maraṇā'ti vā, 'neva hoti na na hoti tathāgato paraṃ maraṇā'ti vā, ajānato kho pana apassato etadeva ujukaṃ hoti yadidaṃ – 'na jānāmi, na passāmī'"ti.

"Kiṃ nu tāhaṃ, mālukyaputta, evaṃ avacaṃ – 'ehi tvaṃ, mālukyaputta, mayi brahmacariyaṃ cara, ahaṃ te byākarissāmi – 'sassato loko'ti vā, 'asassato loko'ti vā, 'antavā loko'ti vā, 'anantavā loko'ti vā, 'taṃ jīvaṃ taṃ sarīra'nti vā, 'aññaṃ jīvaṃ aññaṃ sarīra'nti vā, 'hoti tathāgato paraṃ maraṇā'ti vā, 'na hoti tathāgato paraṃ 'maraṇā'ti vā, 'hoti ca na ca hoti tathāgato paraṃ maraṇā'ti vā, 'neva hoti na na hoti tathāgato paraṃ maraṇā'ti vā"ti? "No hetaṃ, bhante". "Tvaṃ vā pana maṃ evaṃ avaca – ahaṃ, bhante, bhagavati brahmacariyaṃ carissāmi, bhagavā me byākarissati – 'sassato loko'ti vā, 'asassato loko'ti vā, 'antavā loko'ti vā, 'anantavā loko'ti vā, 'taṃ jīvaṃ taṃ sarīra'nti vā, 'aññaṃ jīvaṃ aññaṃ sarīra'nti vā, 'hoti tathāgato paraṃ maraṇā'ti vā, 'na hoti tathāgato paraṃ maraṇā'ti vā, 'hoti ca na ca hoti tathāgato paraṃ maraṇā'ti vā, 'neva hoti na na hoti tathāgato paraṃ maraṇā'ti vā"ti? "No hetaṃ, bhante". "Iti kira, mālukyaputta, nevāhaṃ taṃ vadāmi – ehi tvaṃ, mālukyaputta, mayi brahmacariyaṃ cara, ahaṃ te byākarissāmi – 'sassato loko'ti vā, 'asassato loko'ti vā...pe... 'neva hoti na na hoti tathāgato paraṃ maraṇāti vā'ti; napi kira maṃ tvaṃ vadesi – ahaṃ, bhante, bhagavati brahmacariyaṃ carissāmi, bhagavā me byākarissati – 'sassato loko'ti vā 'asassato loko'ti vā...pe... 'neva hoti na na hoti tathāgato paraṃ maraṇā'ti vā"ti. Evaṃ sante, moghapurisa, ko santo kaṃ paccācikkhasi?

"Yo kho, mālukyaputta, evaṃ vadeyya – 'na tāvāhaṃ bhagavati brahmacariyaṃ carissāmi yāva me bhagavā na byākarissati – "sassato loko"ti vā, "asassato loko"ti vā...pe... "neva hoti na na hoti tathāgato paraṃ maraṇā"ti vāti, abyākatameva taṃ, mālukyaputta, tathāgatena assa, atha so puggalo kālaṃ kareyya. Seyyathāpi, mālukyaputta, puriso sallena viddho assa savisena gāḷhapalepanena. Tassa mittāmaccā ñātisālohitā bhisakkaṃ sallakattaṃ upaṭṭhapeyyuṃ. So evaṃ vadeyya – 'na tāvāhaṃ

imaṃ sallaṃ āharissāmi yāva na taṃ purisaṃ jānāmi yenamhi viddho, khattiyo vā brāhmaṇo vā vesso vā suddo vā'ti; so evaṃ vadeyya – 'na tāvāhaṃ imaṃ sallaṃ āharissāmi yāva na taṃ purisaṃ jānāmi yenamhi viddho, evaṃnāmo evaṃgotto iti vā'ti; so evaṃ vadeyya – 'na tāvāhaṃ imaṃ sallaṃ āharissāmi yāva na taṃ purisaṃ jānāmi yenamhi viddho, dīgho vā rasso vā majjhimo vā'ti; so evaṃ vadeyya – 'na tāvāhaṃ imaṃ sallaṃ āharissāmi yāva na taṃ purisaṃ jānāmi yenamhi viddho, kāḷo vā sāmo vā maṅguracchavī vā'ti; so evaṃ vadeyya – 'na tāvāhaṃ imaṃ sallaṃ āharissāmi yāva na taṃ purisaṃ jānāmi yenamhi viddho, amukasmiṃ gāme vā nigame vā nagare vā'ti; so evaṃ vadeyya – 'na tāvāhaṃ imaṃ sallaṃ āharissāmi yāva na taṃ dhanuṃ jānāmi yenamhi viddho, yadi vā cāpo yadi vā kodaṇḍo'ti; so evaṃ vadeyya – 'na tāvāhaṃ imaṃ sallaṃ āharissāmi yāva na taṃ jiyaṃ jānāmi yāyamhi viddho, yadi vā akkassa yadi vā saṇhassa yadi vā nhārussa yadi vā maruvāya yadi vā khīrapaṇṇino'ti; so evaṃ vadeyya – 'na tāvāhaṃ imaṃ sallaṃ āharissāmi yāva na taṃ kaṇḍaṃ jānāmi yenamhi viddho, yadi vā gacchaṃ yadi vā ropima'nti; so evaṃ vadeyya – 'na tāvāhaṃ imaṃ sallaṃ āharissāmi yāva na taṃ kaṇḍaṃ jānāmi yenamhi viddho, yassa pattehi vājitaṃ. yadi vā gijjhassa yadi vā kaṅkassa yadi vā kulalassa yadi vā morassa yadi vā sithilahanuno'ti; so evaṃ vadeyya – 'na tāvāhaṃ imaṃ sallaṃ āharissāmi yāva na taṃ kaṇḍaṃ jānāmi yenamhi viddho, yassa nhārunā parikkhittaṃ yadi vā gavassa yadi vā mahiṃsassa yadi vā bheravassa yadi vā semhārassā'ti; so evaṃ vadeyya – 'na tāvāhaṃ imaṃ sallaṃ āharissāmi yāva na taṃ sallaṃ jānāmi yenamhi viddho, yadi vā sallaṃ yadi vā khurappaṃ yadi vā vekaṇḍaṃ yadi vā nārācaṃ yadi vā vacchadantaṃ yadi vā karavīrapatta'nti – aññātameva taṃ, mālukyaputta, tena purisena assa, atha so puriso kālaṃ kareyya. Evameva kho, mālukyaputta, yo evaṃ vadeyya – 'na tāvāhaṃ bhagavati brahmacariyaṃ carissāmi yāva me bhagavā na byākarissati – "sassato loko"ti vā "asassato loko"ti vā…pe…

“neva hoti na na hoti tathāgato paraṃ maraṇā”ti vāti – abyākatameva taṃ, mālukyaputta, tathāgatena assa, atha so puggalo kālaṅkareyya.

“‘Sassato loko’ti, mālukyaputta, diṭṭhiyā sati brahmacariyavāso abhavissāti, evaṃ ‘no asassato loko’ti, mālukyaputta, diṭṭhiyā sati brahmacariyavāso abhavissāti, evampi ‘no sassato loko’ti vā, mālukyaputta, diṭṭhiyā sati, ‘asassato loko’ti vā diṭṭhiyā sati attheva jāti, atthi jarā, atthi maraṇaṃ, santi sokaparidevadukkhadomanassupāyāsā; yesāhaṃ diṭṭheva dhamme nighātaṃ paññapemi. ‘Antavā loko’ti, mālukyaputta, diṭṭhiyā sati brahmacariyavāso abhavissāti, evaṃ ‘no anantavā loko’ti, mālukyaputta, diṭṭhiyā sati brahmacariyavāso abhavissāti, evampi ‘no antavā loko’ti vā, mālukyaputta, diṭṭhiyā sati, ‘anantavā loko’ti vā diṭṭhiyā sati attheva jāti, atthi jarā, atthi maraṇaṃ, santi sokaparidevadukkhadomanassupāyāsā; yesāhaṃ diṭṭheva dhamme nighātaṃ paññapemi. ‘Taṃ jīvaṃ taṃ sarīra’nti, mālukyaputta, diṭṭhiyā sati brahmacariyavāso abhavissāti, evaṃ ‘no aññaṃ jīvaṃ aññaṃ sarīra’nti, mālukyaputta, diṭṭhiyā sati brahmacariyavāso abhavissāti, evampi ‘no taṃ jīvaṃ taṃ sarīra’nti vā, mālukyaputta, diṭṭhiyā sati, ‘aññaṃ jīvaṃ aññaṃ sarīra’nti vā diṭṭhiyā sati attheva jāti...pe... nighātaṃ paññapemi. ‘Hoti tathāgato paraṃ maraṇā’ti, mālukyaputta, diṭṭhiyā sati brahmacariyavāso abhavissāti, evaṃ ‘no na hoti tathāgato paraṃ maraṇā’ti, mālukyaputta, diṭṭhiyā sati brahmacariyavāso abhavissāti, evampi ‘no hoti tathāgato paraṃ maraṇā’ti vā, mālukyaputta, diṭṭhiyā sati, ‘na hoti tathāgato paraṃ maraṇā’ti vā diṭṭhiyā sati attheva jāti...pe... yesāhaṃ diṭṭheva dhamme nighātaṃ paññapemi. ‘Hoti ca na ca hoti tathāgato paraṃ maraṇā’ti, mālukyaputta, diṭṭhiyā sati brahmacariyavāso abhavissāti, evaṃ ‘no neva hoti na na hoti tathāgato paraṃ maraṇā’ti, mālukyaputta, diṭṭhiyā sati brahmacariyavāso abhavissāti, evampi ‘no hoti ca na ca hoti tathāgato paraṃ maraṇā’ti, mālukyaputta, diṭṭhiyā sati, ‘neva hoti na na hoti tathāgato paraṃ maraṇā’ti vā diṭṭhiyā sati attheva jāti...pe... yesāhaṃ diṭṭheva dhamme nighātaṃ paññapemi.

“Tasmātiha, mālukyaputta, abyākatañca me abyākatato dhāretha; byākatañca me byākatato dhāretha. Kiñca, mālukyaputta, mayā abyākataṃ? ‘Sassato loko’ti

mālukyaputta, mayā abyākataṃ; 'asassato loko'ti – mayā abyākataṃ; 'antavā loko'ti – mayā abyākataṃ; 'anantavā loko'ti – mayā abyākataṃ; 'taṃ jīvaṃ taṃ sarīra'nti – mayā abyākataṃ; 'aññaṃ jīvaṃ aññaṃ sarīra'nti – mayā abyākataṃ; 'hoti tathāgato paraṃ maraṇā'ti – mayā abyākataṃ; 'na hoti tathāgato paraṃ maraṇā'ti – mayā abyākataṃ; 'hoti ca na ca hoti tathāgato paraṃ maraṇā'ti – mayā abyākataṃ; 'neva hoti na na hoti tathāgato paraṃ maraṇā'ti – mayā abyākataṃ. Kasmā cetaṃ, mālukyaputta, mayā abyākataṃ? Na hetaṃ, mālukyaputta, atthasaṃhitaṃ na ādibrahmacariyakaṃ na nibbidāya na virāgāya na nirodhāya na upasamāya na abhiññāya na sambodhāya na nibbānāya saṃvattati. Tasmā taṃ mayā abyākataṃ. Kiñca, mālukyaputta, mayā byākataṃ? 'Idaṃ dukkha'nti, mālukyaputta, mayā byākataṃ; 'ayaṃ dukkhasamudayo'ti – mayā byākataṃ; 'ayaṃ dukkhanirodho'ti – mayā byākataṃ; 'ayaṃ dukkhanirodhagāminī paṭipadā'ti – mayā byākataṃ. Kasmā cetaṃ, mālukyaputta, mayā byākataṃ? Eta hi, mālukyaputta, atthasaṃhitaṃ etaṃ ādibrahmacariyakaṃ nibbidāya virāgāya nirodhāya upasamāya abhiññāya sambodhāya nibbānāya saṃvattati. Tasmā taṃ mayā byākataṃ. Tasmātiha, mālukyaputta, abyākatañca me abyākatato dhāretha; byākatañca me byākatato dhārethā"ti.

Idamavoca bhagavā. Attamano āyasmā mālukyaputto bhagavato bhāsitaṃ abhinandīti.

Sutta 2 ♦ Glossary

a

akka (m.), swallowwort plant.

añña (pr. adj.), other, another.

aññāta (ppp. √*ñā* + *an*), unknown.

attamana (adj.), mentally uplifted, exalted, pleased, assured, satisfied.

attha (m.), meaning, sense, reason, import.

atthasaṃhita (adj.), beneficial, profitable, meaningful.

atthi, see √*as.*

atha (part.), then.

atha kho (part.), then, moreover.

anantavant (adj.), infinite, not having an end.

anāthapiṇḍika (m.), personal name.

antavant (adj.), finite, having an end.

api (part.), adds emphasis to preceding term; even, even though, also; but.

abyākata (ppp. √*kar* + *vi* + *ā*), undetermined, indeterminate.

abhiññā (f.), direct knowledge, wisdom.

abhi + √*nand,* to rejoice, to take delight, to be glad.

abhi + √*vad,* to greet, to address.

amacca (m.), friend, companion.

amu (m.f.n. dem. pron.), this, *etc.* (Line 87, *amu* + suffix *ka* = such and such, this or that.)

amhi, see √as.

ayaṃ (m.f. dem. pron.), this, *etc.*

√*as,* to be. (Line 80, *amhi* = 1st pers. sing. indic. Line 112, *attheva* = 3. pers. sing. indic. *atthi* + *eva.*)

asassata (adj.), not eternal, not perpetual.

assa (m.n. dem. pron.), to him, his, to that one, *etc.*

ahaṃ (1st pers. per. pron.), I.

ā

ādi (m.), beginning, starting.

āyasmant (adj.), venerable.

ārāma (m.), park, garden.

ā + √*vatt,* to turn toward.

ā + √*har,* to take out, to remove.

i

√*i,* to go, to come. (Line 53, *ehi* = 2nd pers. imper.)

iti (part.), here, in this/that case; marks quotation of speech or thought.

idaṃ (n. dem. pron.), this, *etc.*

idha (part.), here.

imaṃ (m.f.n. dem. pron.), this, *etc.*

imāni (n. dem. pron.), those, *etc.*

iha (part.), here, in this case, in this instance.

u

ujuka (adj.), upright, straight.

ud + √*pad,* to arise, to originate, to come into existence, to occur. (Line 3, *udapādi* = aor.)

ud + √*ṭhā, see vuṭṭhita.*

upa + √*ṭha,* to serve; caus. to hire.

upa + *saṃ* + √*kam,* to approach, to come near.

upasama (m.), quietness, calmness, peace.

upāyāsā (m.), anxiety, trouble, disturbance.

e

eka (num.; adj.), one; a certain, some.

ekamantaṃ (adv.), on one side, beside.

etaṃ (m.f.n. dem. pron.), this, *etc.* (Line 18, n. *etad* before vowel.)

eva (part.), adds emphasis to preceding term; so, just, even.

evaṃ, (part.), thus, so, such, in this way; yes.

ehi, see √*i.*

k

kaṃ (m.f. interog. pron.), what, whom?, *etc.*

kaṅka (m.), heron.

kaccha (adj.), naturally grown.

kaṇḍa (m.n), arrow shaft.

kattar (ag.n. √*kar*), one who works on.

√*kar,* to do, to make. (Line 75, *kālaṃ kareyya* = lit., would make time; fig., would make and end, would die.)

karavīrapatta (m.), oleander (shaped?) arrow.

kasmā (part.), why?

kāla (m.), time. (Line 75, *kālaṃ kareyya* = lit., would make time; fig., would make and end, would die.)

kāḷa (adj.), dark, black.

kiṃ (n. interrog. pron.), what?, *etc.*

kiṃ nu (part.) = question marker.

kira (part.), adds emphasis to preceding term or phrase; then.

kulala (m.), crow.

ko (m. interg. pron.), who, which, what?, *etc.*

kodaṇḍa (n.), crossbow.

kh

khattiya (m.), class designation: the administrative and warrior class.

√*kham,* to approve, to please, to seem fit. (Line 10, *nakkhamati* = *na* + *khamati.*)

khīrapaṇṇin (m.), a kind of plant; *tech.*, milky-leafed.

khurappa (m.), razor-tipped arrow.

kho pana (part.), marks continuation of narrative; emphasizes preceeding term or phrase.

g

gaccha = *kaccha.*

gava (m.), cattle.

gāma (m.), village.

gāmin (adj.), leading to, going toward.

gāḷha (adj.), thick.

gijjha (m.), vulture.

gotta (n.), family lineage, clan.

c

ca (encl. part.), and. (Line 7, *ca* ... *ca* = both … and.)

√*car,* to go, to wander, to walk, to go on rounds.

cāpa (m.n.), longbow.

cetas (n.), mind. (Line 3, *cetaso* = gen. dat. sg., of the mind, to mind, *etc.*)

j

jarā (f.), aging.

jāti (f.), birth, generation.

√*jān*, to know, to realize.

jiyā (f.), bow string.

jīva (n.), life, life force, animating function.

jeta (m.), personal name.

ñ

√*ñā*, to know.

ñāti (m.), a family relation, a relative.

ṭh

ṭhapita (ppp. √ṭhā), set aside, put down, suspended.

t

taṃ (dem. pron.), him, her, it, that, this, the, *etc.*

tathāgata (adj.; m.), come to [know] reality, come to suchness; epithet of Gotama.

tasmā (part.), therefore. (Note: *t* inserted before following vowel: *tasmāt.*)

tassa (m.n. dem. pron.), his, to him, for him, *etc.*

tāni (n. dem. pron.), these, *etc.*

tāva (part.), until, as long as, so long. (Lines 71-72, tāva … *yāva* = until, as long as.)

ti (part.), marks end of direct speech, a thought, or quoted term. (Note: A short vowel preceding *ti* is lengthened, and *ṃ* is converted to *n.*)

te (2nd pers. per. pron.; m. dem. pron.), by you, yours, to you (sg); those, them, *etc.* (Line 53, *tāhaṃ* = *te ahaṃ.*)

tvaṃ (2nd pers. per. pron.), you, *etc.*

d

diṭṭha (ppp. √das), seen, visible. (Line 113, *diṭṭhe dhamme* = in this world, here and now, in the present.)

diṭṭhi (f.), theory, speculative view, dogma.

diṭṭhigata (n.), speculative view, groundless opinion.

dīgha (adj.), long, tall.

dukkha (n.; adj.), unease, distress, trouble, unhappiness, pain; distressful, painful, troublesome.

domanassa (n.), depression, dejection, mental disturbance.

dh

dhanu (n.), bow.

dhamma (m.), phenomenon, thing; quality, mental quality, thought; nature; teaching; standard. (Line 113, *diṭṭhe dhamme* = in this world.)

√*dhar,* to bear in mind, to memorize; to hold, to sustain, to bear.

n

na (part.), no, not.

nagara (n.), city.

nāma (n.), name; *tech.* mental functions, e.g. feeling, perception, conceptualization, intention, attentiveness.

nārāca (m.), tubular arrow.

nigama (m.), town.

nighāta (m.), destruction.

nibbāna (n.), extinguishing, unbinding, letting go, releasing.

nibbidā (f.), disenchantment, world-weariness, disillusionment.

nirodha (m.), cessation, ending, stopping.

ni + √*sad,* to sit down. (Line 17, *nisīdi* = aor.; *nissino* = ppp.)

nisinna (ppp. √*sad* + *ni*), seated.

neva = *na eva* (part.), certainly not, indeed not. (Line 8, *neva* ... *na na* = neither … nor.)

no (part.), no, not.

no ce (part.), if not.

nhāru (m.), sinew.

p

pa + √*ñā,* to know, to realize. caus.to declare, to proclaim.

paṭi + *ā* + √*khā,* to reject, to repudiate, to disavow, to speak against. (Line 70, *paccācikkhasi* = int.)

paṭikkhitta (ppp. √*khip* +*paṭi*), rejected, refused.

paṭipadā (f.), path, course, practice, way.

paṭisallāna (m.), solitude, seclusion, separation; *tech.*, isolation for the purpose of meditation..

paṭisallīna (ppp. √*lī* + *paṭi* + *saṃ*), solitary, secluded, separated; *tech.*, isolated for the purpose of meditation.

patta (n.), feather.

paraṃ (part.), beyond, over.

parikkhitta (ppp. √*khip* + *pari*), wrapped, enclosed.

parideva (m.), regret, weeping, crying.

parivitakko (m.), reflection, thought, consideration.

palepana (adj.), smeared with.

√*pas,* to see.

pi (encl. part.), even, also, just so, too; but; adds emphasis to preceding term.

puggala (m.), person.

√*pucch,* to ask.

purisa (m.), man, person, people.

b

byākar° = *vi* + *ā* + √*kar.*

brahmacariya (n.), life of training, the expansive life. (Line 143, *°ka* = suffix, not effecting meaning.)

brāhmaṇa (m.), class designation: Brahmin.

bh

bhagavant (adj.), fortunate, illustrious, honorable; fortunate one: epithet of Gotama.

bhante (ind.), form of respectful address, like E. sir.

bhāsita (n.), speech, words.

bhisakka (m.), physician.

√*bhū,* to be, to become; to cultivate, to nurture, to develop. (Line 109, *abhavissā* = cond.)

bherava (m.), deer; *tech.*, stricken with terror; timid.

m

maṅguracchavi (adj.), golden.

majjhima (adj.), medium, middle.

mayā (1st pers. per. pron.), by me, *etc.*

mayi (1st pers. per. pron.), around (with) me, *etc.*

mayhaṃ (1st pers. per. pron.), to me, *etc.*

maraṇa (n.), death.

maruvā (f.), hemp.

mahiṃsa (m.), water buffalo.

mālukyaputta (m.), personal name.

mitta (m.n.), friend.

me (1st pers. per. pron.), me, by me, *etc.*

mogha (adj.), dull, stupid, foolish.

mora (m.), peacock.

y

yadi (part.), if.

yadidaṃ (part.), namely, as follows, that is to say; literally, which is this.

yā (f. rel. pron.), which, that which, *etc.*

yāni (n. rel. pron.), which, that, *etc.*

yāva, see tāva.

yena (part.), where, to where, at which place; with *tena* = where (*yena*) X was, there (*tena*) he went.

yena (m.n. rel. pron.), by whom, *etc.*

yesaṃ (m.n. rel. pron.), of which, *etc.*

yo (m. rel. pron.), he who, that which, someone, anyone, *etc.*

r

rassa (adj.), short.

rahogata (adj.), living in a solitary place, being alone, gone into seclusion.

√*ruc,* to please, to find pleasure in.

ropima (adj.), cultivated, planted.

l

loka (m.), world.

v

√*vac,* to speak. (Line 18, *avoca* = *aor.*)

vacchadanta (m.), calf-toothed arrow.

√*vad,* to speak, to say.

vana (n.), grove, wood.

vā (encl. part.), or.

vāsa (m.), life, living; state, condition.

vājita (adj.), feathered.

vi + *ā* + √*kar,* to determine, to explain, to answer.

viddha (ppp. √*vyadh*), pierced, shot.

virāga (m.), dispassion, detatchment.

visa (n.), poison.

vi + √*har,* to live, to stay, to dwell, to abide.

vuṭṭhita (ppp. √*ṭhā* +*ud*), emerged, returned, risen. (Following a vowel, as in line 16, *u* > *vu.*)

vekaṇḍa (m.), curved or barbed arrow.

vessa (m.), class designation: the merchant class.

s

sa prefix denoting with, possessed of, having.

saṃ + √*vatt,* to lead to.

sace (part.), if, if so.

saṇha (adj.), smooth; delicate.

sat (prap. √*as*), being. (Line 109, *sati* = f. loc. sing.)

samaya (m.), time, occasion.

samudaya (m.), origin, arising, source.

sambodha (m.), awakening.

sarīra (n.), body.

salla (n.), arrow, dart.

sassata (adj.), eternal, perpetual.

sāma (adj.), brown.

sāyanhasamayaṃ (adv.), in the evening.

sālohita (m), blood relative.

sāvatthi (f.), place name.

sikkhā (f.), training, study, discipline.

sithilahanu (m.), stork.

suta (ppp. √*su*), heard.

sutta (n.), discourse, dialogue, text; lit., thread, stitching, textile.

sudda (m.), class designation: the lower, underpriviledged, class.

semhāra (m.), monkey.

seyyathā (part.), as if, just as.

so (m. dem. pron.), he, that, the, *etc.*

soka (m), sadness, sorrow, grief.

h

hi (part.), surely, indeed. (Line 58, *hetaṃ* = *hi etaṃ.*)

hīna (adj.; ppp. √*hā*), lowly, inferior. (Line 14, *hīnāya* + *ā* + √*vatt* = *tech.*, return to the world, renounce training vows.)

hoti = √*bhū.*

Sutta 3
Tevijjasuttaṃ

(Dighanikāya 1.13.518)

Evaṃ me sutaṃ – ekaṃ samayaṃ bhagavā kosalesu cārikaṃ caramāno mahatā bhikkhusaṅghena saddhiṃ pañcamattehi bhikkhusatehi yena manasākaṭaṃ nāma kosalānaṃ brāhmaṇagāmo tadavasari. Tatra sudaṃ bhagavā manasākaṭe viharati uttarena manasākaṭassa aciravatiyā nadiyā tīre ambavane.

Tena kho pana samayena sambahulā abhiññātā abhiññātā brāhmaṇamahāsālā manasākaṭe paṭivasanti, seyyathidaṃ – caṅkī brāhmaṇo tārukkho brāhmaṇo pokkharasāti brāhmaṇo jāṇusoṇi brāhmaṇo todeyyo brāhmaṇo aññe ca abhiññātā abhiññātā brāhmaṇamahāsālā.

Atha kho vāseṭṭhabhāradvājānaṃ māṇavānaṃ jaṅghavihāraṃ anucaṅkamantānaṃ anuvicarantānaṃ maggāmagge kathā udapādi. Atha kho vāseṭṭho māṇavo evamāha –

"Ayameva ujumaggo, ayamañjasāyano niyyāniko niyyāti takkarassa brahmasahabyatāya, yvāyaṃ akkhāto brāhmaṇena pokkharasātinā"ti. Bhāradvājopi māṇavo evamāha – "ayameva ujumaggo, ayamañjasāyano niyyāniko, niyyāti takkarassa brahmasahabyatāya, yvāyaṃ akkhāto brāhmaṇena tārukkhenā"ti. Neva kho asakkhi vāseṭṭho māṇavo bhāradvājaṃ māṇavaṃ saññāpetuṃ, na pana asakkhi bhāradvājo māṇavopi vāseṭṭhaṃ māṇavaṃ saññāpetuṃ.

Atha kho vāseṭṭho māṇavo bhāradvājaṃ māṇavaṃ āmantesi – "ayaṃ kho, bhāradvāja, samaṇo gotamo sakyaputto sakyakulā pabbajito manasākaṭe viharati uttarena manasākaṭassa aciravatiyā nadiyā tīre ambavane. Taṃ kho pana bhavantaṃ gotamaṃ evaṃ kalyāṇo kittisaddo abbhuggato – "itipi so bhagavā arahaṃ sammāsambuddho vijjācaraṇasampanno sugato lokavidū anuttaro purisadammasārathi satthā devamanussānaṃ buddho bhagavā"ti. Āyāma, bho bhāradvāja, yena samaṇo gotamo tenupasaṅkamissāma; upasaṅkamitvā etamatthaṃ samaṇaṃ gotamaṃ pucchissāma. Yathā no samaṇo gotamo byākarissati, tathā naṃ dhāressāmā"ti. "Evaṃ, bho"ti kho bhāradvājo māṇavo vāseṭṭhassa māṇavassa paccassosi.

Maggāmaggakathā

Atha kho vāseṭṭhabhāradvājā māṇavā yena bhagavā tenupasaṅkamiṃsu; upasaṅkamitvā bhagavatā saddhiṃ sammodiṃsu. Sammodanīyaṃ kathaṃ sāraṇīyaṃ vītisāretvā ekamantaṃ nisīdiṃsu. Ekamantaṃ nisinno kho vāseṭṭho māṇavo bhagavantaṃ etadavoca – "idha, bho gotama, amhākaṃ jaṅghavihāraṃ anucaṅkamantānaṃ anuvicarantānaṃ maggāmagge kathā udapādi. Ahaṃ evaṃ vadāmi – 'ayameva ujumaggo, ayamañjasāyano niyyāniko niyyāti takkarassa brahmasahabyatāya, yvāyaṃ akkhāto brāhmaṇena pokkharasātinā'ti. Bhāradvājo māṇavo evamāha – 'ayameva ujumaggo ayamañjasāyano niyyāniko niyyāti takkarassa brahmasahabyatāya, yvāyaṃ akkhāto brāhmaṇena tārukkhenā'ti. Ettha, bho gotama, attheva viggaho, atthi vivādo, atthi nānāvādo"ti.

"Iti kira, vāseṭṭha, tvaṃ evaṃ vadesi – "ayameva ujumaggo, ayamañjasāyano niyyāniko niyyāti takkarassa brahmasahabyatāya, yvāyaṃ akkhāto brāhmaṇena pokkharasātinā"ti. Bhāradvājo māṇavo evamāha – "ayameva ujumaggo ayamañjasāyano niyyāniko niyyāti takkarassa brahmasahabyatāya, yvāyaṃ akkhāto brāhmaṇena tārukkhenā"ti. Atha kismiṃ pana vo, vāseṭṭha, viggaho, kismiṃ vivādo, kismiṃ nānāvādo"ti?

"Maggāmagge, bho gotama. Kiñcāpi, bho gotama, brāhmaṇā nānāmagge paññapenti, addhariyā brāhmaṇā tittiriyā brāhmaṇā chandokā brāhmaṇā bavhārijjhā brāhmaṇā, atha kho sabbāni tāni niyyānikā niyyanti takkarassa brahmasahabyatāya.

"Seyyathāpi, bho gotama, gāmassa vā nigamassa vā avidūre bahūni cepi nānāmaggāni bhavanti, atha kho sabbāni tāni gāmasamosaraṇāni bhavanti; evameva kho, bho gotama, kiñcāpi brāhmaṇā nānāmagge paññapenti, addhariyā brāhmaṇā tittiriyā brāhmaṇā chandokā brāhmaṇā bavhārijjhā brāhmaṇā, atha kho sabbāni tāni niyyānikā niyyanti takkarassa brahmasahabyatāyā"ti.

Vāseṭṭhamāṇavānuyogo

"Niyyantīti vāseṭṭha vadesi"? "Niyyantīti, bho gotama, vadāmi". "Niyyantīti, vāseṭṭha, vadesi"? "Niyyantīti, bho gotama, vadāmi". "Niyyantīti, vāseṭṭha, vadesi"? "Niyyantī"ti, bho gotama, vadāmi".

"Kiṃ pana, vāseṭṭha, atthi koci tevijjānaṃ brāhmaṇānaṃ ekabrāhmaṇopi, yena brahmā sakkhidiṭṭho"ti? "No hidaṃ, bho gotama".

"Kiṃ pana, vāseṭṭha, atthi koci tevijjānaṃ brāhmaṇānaṃ ekācariyopi, yena brahmā sakkhidiṭṭho"ti? "No hidaṃ, bho gotama".

"Kiṃ pana, vāseṭṭha, atthi koci tevijjānaṃ brāhmaṇānaṃ ekācariyapācariyopi, yena brahmā sakkhidiṭṭho"ti? "No hidaṃ, bho gotama".

"Kiṃ pana, vāseṭṭha, atthi koci tevijjānaṃ brāhmaṇānaṃ yāva sattamā ācariyāmahayugā yena brahmā sakkhidiṭṭho"ti? "No hidaṃ, bho gotama".

"Kiṃ pana, vāseṭṭha, yepi tevijjānaṃ brāhmaṇānaṃ pubbakā isayo mantānaṃ kattāro mantānaṃ pavattāro, yesamidaṃ etarahi tevijjā brāhmaṇā porāṇaṃ mantapadaṃ gītaṃ pavuttaṃ samihitaṃ, tadanugāyanti, tadanubhāsanti, bhāsitamanubhāsanti, vācitamanuvācenti, seyyathidaṃ – aṭṭhako vāmako

vāmadevo vessāmitto yamataggi aṅgīraso bhāradvājo vāseṭṭho kassapo bhagu. Tepi evamāhaṃsu – 'mayametaṃ jānāma, mayametaṃ passāma, yattha vā brahmā, yena vā brahmā, yahiṃ vā brahmā'"ti? "No hidaṃ, bho gotama".

"Iti kira, vāseṭṭha, natthi koci tevijjānaṃ brāhmaṇānaṃ ekabrāhmaṇopi, yena brahmā sakkhidiṭṭho. Natthi koci tevijjānaṃ brāhmaṇānaṃ ekācariyopi, yena brahmā sakkhidiṭṭho. Natthi koci tevijjānaṃ brāhmaṇānaṃ ekācariyapācariyopi, yena brahmā sakkhidiṭṭho. Natthi koci tevijjānaṃ brāhmaṇānaṃ yāva sattamā ācariyāmahayugā yena brahmā sakkhidiṭṭho. Yepi kira tevijjānaṃ brāhmaṇānaṃ pubbakā isayo mantānaṃ kattāro mantānaṃ pavattāro, yesamidaṃ etarahi tevijjā brāhmaṇā porāṇaṃ mantapadaṃ gītaṃ pavuttaṃ samihitaṃ, tadanugāyanti, tadanubhāsanti, bhāsitamanubhāsanti, vācitamanuvācenti, seyyathidaṃ – aṭṭhako vāmako vāmadevo vessāmitto yamataggi aṅgīraso bhāradvājo vāseṭṭho kassapo bhagu, tepi na evamāhaṃsu – 'mayametaṃ jānāma, mayametaṃ passāma, yattha vā brahmā, yena vā brahmā, yahiṃ vā brahmā'ti. Teva tevijjā brāhmaṇā evamāhaṃsu – 'yaṃ na jānāma, yaṃ na passāma, tassa sahabyatāya maggaṃ desema. Ayameva ujumaggo ayamañjasāyano niyyāniko, niyyāti takkarassa brahmasahabyatāyā'"ti.

"Taṃ kiṃ maññasi, vāseṭṭha, nanu evaṃ sante tevijjānaṃ brāhmaṇānaṃ appāṭihīrakataṃ bhāsitaṃ sampajjatī"ti? "Addhā kho, bho gotama, evaṃ sante tevijjānaṃ brāhmaṇānaṃ appāṭihīrakataṃ bhāsitaṃ sampajjatī"ti.

"Sādhu, vāseṭṭha, te vata, vāseṭṭha, tevijjā brāhmaṇā yaṃ na jānanti, yaṃ na passanti, tassa sahabyatāya maggaṃ desessanti. 'Ayameva ujumaggo, ayamañjasāyano niyyāniko, niyyāti takkarassa brahmasahabyatāyā'ti, netaṃ ṭhānaṃ vijjati.

"Seyyathāpi, vāseṭṭha, andhaveṇi paramparasaṃsattā purimopi na passati, majjhimopi na passati, pacchimopi na passati. Evameva kho, vāseṭṭha, andhaveṇūpamaṃ maññe tevijjānaṃ brāhmaṇānaṃ bhāsitaṃ, purimopi na

passati, majjhimopi na passati, pacchimopi na passati. Tesamidaṃ tevijjānaṃ brāhmaṇānaṃ bhāsitaṃ hassakaññeva sampajjati, nāmakaññeva sampajjati, rittakaññeva sampajjati, tucchakaññeva sampajjati.

"Taṃ kiṃ maññasi, vāseṭṭha, passanti tevijjā brāhmaṇā candimasūriye, aññe cāpi bahujanā, yato ca candimasūriyā uggacchanti, yattha ca ogacchanti, āyācanti thomayanti pañjalikā namassamānā anuparivattantī"ti?

"Evaṃ, bho gotama, passanti tevijjā brāhmaṇā candimasūriye, aññe cāpi bahujanā, yato ca candimasūriyā uggacchanti, yattha ca ogacchanti, āyācanti thomayanti pañjalikā namassamānā anuparivattantī"ti.

"Taṃ kiṃ maññasi, vāseṭṭha, yaṃ passanti tevijjā brāhmaṇā candimasūriye, aññe cāpi bahujanā, yato ca candimasūriyā uggacchanti, yattha ca ogacchanti, āyācanti thomayanti pañjalikā namassamānā anuparivattanti, pahonti tevijjā brāhmaṇā candimasūriyānaṃ sahabyatāya maggaṃ desetuṃ – "ayameva ujumaggo, ayamañjasāyano niyyāniko, niyyāti takkarassa candimasūriyānaṃ sahabyatāyā"ti? "No hidaṃ, bho gotama".

"Iti kira, vāseṭṭha, yaṃ passanti tevijjā brāhmaṇā candimasūriye, aññe cāpi bahujanā, yato ca candimasūriyā uggacchanti, yattha ca ogacchanti, āyācanti thomayanti pañjalikā namassamānā anuparivattanti, tesampi nappahonti candimasūriyānaṃ sahabyatāya maggaṃ desetuṃ – "ayameva ujumaggo, ayamañjasāyano niyyāniko, niyyāti takkarassa candimasūriyānaṃ sahabyatāyā"ti.

"Iti pana na kira tevijjehi brāhmaṇehi brahmā sakkhidiṭṭho. Napi kira tevijjānaṃ brāhmaṇānaṃ ācariyehi brahmā sakkhidiṭṭho. Napi kira tevijjānaṃ brāhmaṇānaṃ ācariyapācariyehi brahmā sakkhidiṭṭho. Napi kira tevijjānaṃ brāhmaṇānaṃ yāva sattamā ācariyāmahayugehi brahmā sakkhidiṭṭho. Yepi kira tevijjānaṃ brāhmaṇānaṃ pubbakā isayo mantānaṃ kattāro mantānaṃ

pavattāro, yesamidaṃ etarahi tevijjā brāhmaṇā porāṇaṃ mantapadaṃ gītaṃ pavuttaṃ samihitaṃ, tadanugāyanti, tadanubhāsanti, bhāsitamanubhāsanti, vācitamanuvācenti, seyyathidaṃ – aṭṭhako vāmako vāmadevo vessāmitto yamataggi aṅgīraso bhāradvājo vāseṭṭho kassapo bhagu, tepi na evamāhaṃsu – "mayametaṃ jānāma, mayametaṃ passāma, yattha vā brahmā, yena vā brahmā, yahiṃ vā brahmā"ti. Teva tevijjā brāhmaṇā evamāhaṃsu – "yaṃ na jānāma, yaṃ na passāma, tassa sahabyatāya maggaṃ desema – ayameva ujumaggo ayamañjasāyano niyyāniko niyyāti takkarassa brahmasahabyatāyā"ti.

"Taṃ kiṃ maññasi, vāseṭṭha, nanu evaṃ sante tevijjānaṃ brāhmaṇānaṃ appāṭihīrakataṃ bhāsitaṃ sampajjatī"ti? "Addhā kho, bho gotama, evaṃ sante tevijjānaṃ brāhmaṇānaṃ appāṭihīrakataṃ bhāsitaṃ sampajjatī"ti.

"Sādhu, vāseṭṭha, te vata, vāseṭṭha, tevijjā brāhmaṇā yaṃ na jānanti, yaṃ na passanti, tassa sahabyatāya maggaṃ desessanti – "ayameva ujumaggo, ayamañjasāyano niyyāniko, niyyāti takkarassa brahmasahabyatāyā"ti, netaṃ ṭhānaṃ vijjati.

Janapadakalyāṇīupamā

"Seyyathāpi, vāseṭṭha, puriso evaṃ vadeyya – "ahaṃ yā imasmiṃ janapade janapadakalyāṇī, taṃ icchāmi, taṃ kāmemī"ti. Tamenaṃ evaṃ vadeyyuṃ – "ambho purisa, yaṃ tvaṃ janapadakalyāṇiṃ icchasi kāmesi, jānāsi taṃ janapadakalyāṇiṃ – khattiyī vā brāhmaṇī vā vessī vā suddī vā"ti? Iti puṭṭho "no"ti vadeyya.

"Tamenaṃ evaṃ vadeyyuṃ – "ambho purisa, yaṃ tvaṃ janapadakalyāṇiṃ icchasi kāmesi, jānāsi taṃ janapadakalyāṇiṃ – evaṃnāmā evaṃgottāti vā, dīghā vā rassā vā majjhimā vā kāḷī vā sāmā vā maṅguracchavī vāti, amukasmiṃ gāme vā nigame vā nagare vā"ti? Iti puṭṭho 'no'ti vadeyya. Tamenaṃ evaṃ

vadeyyuṃ – “ambho purisa, yaṃ tvaṃ na jānāsi na passasi, taṃ tvaṃ icchasi kāmesī”ti? Iti puṭṭho “āmā”ti vadeyya.

“Taṃ kiṃ maññasi, vāseṭṭha, nanu evaṃ sante tassa purisassa appāṭihīrakataṃ bhāsitaṃ sampajjatī”ti? “Addhā kho, bho gotama, evaṃ sante tassa purisassa appāṭihīrakataṃ bhāsitaṃ sampajjatī”ti.

“Evameva kho, vāseṭṭha, na kira tevijjehi brāhmaṇehi brahmā sakkhidiṭṭho, napi kira tevijjānaṃ brāhmaṇānaṃ ācariyehi brahmā sakkhidiṭṭho, napi kira tevijjānaṃ brāhmaṇānaṃ ācariyapācariyehi brahmā sakkhidiṭṭho. Napi kira tevijjānaṃ brāhmaṇānaṃ yāva sattamā ācariyāmahayugehi brahmā sakkhidiṭṭho. Yepi kira tevijjānaṃ brāhmaṇānaṃ pubbakā isayo mantānaṃ kattāro mantānaṃ pavattāro, yesamidaṃ etarahi tevijjā brāhmaṇā porāṇaṃ mantapadaṃ gītaṃ pavuttaṃ samihitaṃ, tadanugāyanti, tadanubhāsanti, bhāsitamanubhāsanti, vācitamanuvācenti, seyyathidaṃ – aṭṭhako vāmako vāmadevo vessāmitto yamataggi aṅgīraso bhāradvājo vāseṭṭho kassapo bhagu, tepi na evamāhaṃsu – “mayametaṃ jānāma, mayametaṃ passāma, yattha vā brahmā, yena vā brahmā, yahiṃ vā brahmā”ti. Teva tevijjā brāhmaṇā evamāhaṃsu – “yaṃ na jānāma, yaṃ na passāma, tassa sahabyatāya maggaṃ desema – ayameva ujumaggo ayamañjasāyano niyyāniko niyyāti takkarassa brahmasahabyatāyā”ti.

“Taṃ kiṃ maññasi, vāseṭṭha, nanu evaṃ sante tevijjānaṃ brāhmaṇānaṃ appāṭihīrakataṃ bhāsitaṃ sampajjatī”ti? “Addhā kho, bho gotama, evaṃ sante tevijjānaṃ brāhmaṇānaṃ appāṭihīrakataṃ bhāsitaṃ sampajjatī”ti.

“Sādhu, vāseṭṭha, te vata, vāseṭṭha, tevijjā brāhmaṇā yaṃ na jānanti, yaṃ na passanti, tassa sahabyatāya maggaṃ desessanti – ayameva ujumaggo ayamañjasāyano niyyāniko niyyāti takkarassa brahmasahabyatāyāti netaṃ ṭhānaṃ vijjati.

Nisseṇīupamā

“Seyyathāpi, vāseṭṭha, puriso cātumahāpathe nisseṇiṃ kareyya – pāsādassa ārohaṇāya. Tamenaṃ evaṃ vadeyyuṃ – “ambho purisa, yassa tvaṃ pāsādassa ārohaṇāya nisseṇiṃ karosi, jānāsi taṃ pāsādaṃ – puratthimāya vā disāya dakkhiṇāya vā disāya pacchimāya vā disāya uttarāya vā disāya ucco vā nīco vā majjhimo vā”ti? Iti puṭṭho “no”ti vadeyya.

“Tamenaṃ evaṃ vadeyyuṃ – “ambho purisa, yaṃ tvaṃ na jānāsi, na passasi, tassa tvaṃ pāsādassa ārohaṇāya nisseṇiṃ karosī”ti? Iti puṭṭho “āmā”ti vadeyya.

“Taṃ kiṃ maññasi, vāseṭṭha, nanu evaṃ sante tassa purisassa appāṭihīrakataṃ bhāsitaṃ sampajjatī”ti? “Addhā kho, bho gotama, evaṃ sante tassa purisassa appāṭihīrakataṃ bhāsitaṃ sampajjatī”ti.

“Evameva kho, vāseṭṭha, na kira tevijjehi brāhmaṇehi brahmā sakkhidiṭṭho, napi kira tevijjānaṃ brāhmaṇānaṃ ācariyehi brahmā sakkhidiṭṭho, napi kira tevijjānaṃ brāhmaṇānaṃ ācariyapācariyehi brahmā sakkhidiṭṭho, napi kira tevijjānaṃ brāhmaṇānaṃ yāva sattamā ācariyāmahayugehi brahmā sakkhidiṭṭho. Yepi kira tevijjānaṃ brāhmaṇānaṃ pubbakā isayo mantānaṃ kattāro mantānaṃ pavattāro, yesamidaṃ etarahi tevijjā brāhmaṇā porāṇaṃ mantapadaṃ gītaṃ pavuttaṃ samihitaṃ, tadanugāyanti, tadanubhāsanti, bhāsitamanubhāsanti, vācitamanuvācenti, seyyathidaṃ – aṭṭhako vāmako vāmadevo vessāmitto yamataggi aṅgīraso bhāradvājo vāseṭṭho kassapo bhagu, tepi na evamāhaṃsu – mayametaṃ jānāma, mayametaṃ passāma, yattha vā brahmā, yena vā brahmā, yahiṃ vā brahmāti. Teva tevijjā brāhmaṇā evamāhaṃsu – “yaṃ na jānāma, yaṃ na passāma, tassa sahabyatāya maggaṃ desema, ayameva ujumaggo ayamañjasāyano niyyāniko niyyāti takkarassa brahmasahabyatāyā”ti.

“Taṃ kiṃ maññasi, vāseṭṭha, nanu evaṃ sante tevijjānaṃ brāhmaṇānaṃ

appāṭihīrakataṃ bhāsitaṃ sampajjatī"ti? "Addhā kho, bho gotama, evaṃ sante tevijjānaṃ brāhmaṇānaṃ appāṭihīrakataṃ bhāsitaṃ sampajjatī"ti.

"Sādhu, vāseṭṭha. Te vata, vāseṭṭha, tevijjā brāhmaṇā yaṃ na jānanti, yaṃ na passanti, tassa sahabyatāya maggaṃ desessanti. Ayameva ujumaggo ayamañjasāyano niyyāniko niyyāti takkarassa brahmasabyatāyāti, netaṃ ṭhānaṃ vijjati.

Aciravatīnadīupamā

"Seyyathāpi, vāseṭṭha, ayaṃ aciravatī nadī pūrā udakassa samatittikā kākapeyyā. Atha puriso āgaccheyya pāratthiko pāragavesī pāragāmī pāraṃ taritukāmo. So orime tīre ṭhito pārimaṃ tīraṃ avheyya – "ehi pārāpāraṃ, ehi pārāpāra"nti.

"Taṃ kiṃ maññasi, vāseṭṭha, api nu tassa purisassa avhāyanahetu vā āyācanahetu vā patthanahetu vā abhinandanahetu vā aciravatiyā nadiyā pārimaṃ tīraṃ orimaṃ tīraṃ āgaccheyyā"ti? "No hidaṃ, bho gotama".

"Evameva kho, vāseṭṭha, tevijjā brāhmaṇā ye dhammā brāhmaṇakārakā te dhamme pahāya vattamānā, ye dhammā abrāhmaṇakārakā te dhamme samādāya vattamānā evamāhaṃsu – "indamavhayāma, somamavhayāma, varuṇamavhayāma, īsānamavhayāma, pajāpatimavhayāma, brahmamavhayāma, mahiddhimavhayāma, yamamavhayāmā"ti.

"Te vata, vāseṭṭha, tevijjā brāhmaṇā ye dhammā brāhmaṇakārakā te dhamme pahāya vattamānā, ye dhammā abrāhmaṇakārakā te dhamme samādāya vattamānā avhāyanahetu vā āyācanahetu vā patthanahetu vā abhinandanahetu vā kāyassa bhedā paraṃ maraṇā brahmānaṃ sahabyūpagā bhavissantī"ti, netaṃ ṭhānaṃ vijjati.

"Seyyathāpi, vāseṭṭha, ayaṃ aciravatī nadī pūrā udakassa samatittikā kākapeyyā. Atha puriso āgaccheyya pāratthiko pāragavesī pāragāmī pāraṃ taritukāmo. So orime tīre daḷhāya anduyā pacchābāhaṃ gāḷhabandhanaṃ baddho.

"Taṃ kiṃ maññasi, vāseṭṭha, api nu so puriso aciravatiyā nadiyā orimā tīrā pārimaṃ tīraṃ gaccheyyā"ti? "No hidaṃ, bho gotama".

"Evameva kho, vāseṭṭha, pañcime kāmaguṇā ariyassa vinaye andūtipi vuccanti, bandhanantipi vuccanti. Katame pañca? Cakkhuviññeyyā rūpā iṭṭhā kantā manāpā piyarūpā kāmūpasaṃhitā rajanīyā. Sotaviññeyyā saddā...pe... ghānaviññeyyā gandhā... jivhāviññeyyā rasā... kāyaviññeyyā phoṭṭhabbā iṭṭhā kantā manāpā piyarūpā kāmūpasaṃhitā rajanīyā.

"Ime kho, vāseṭṭha, pañca kāmaguṇā ariyassa vinaye andūtipi vuccanti, bandhanantipi vuccanti. Ime kho vāseṭṭha pañca kāmaguṇe tevijjā brāhmaṇā gadhitā mucchitā ajjhopannā anādīnavadassāvino anissaraṇapaññā paribhuñjanti. Te vata, vāseṭṭha, tevijjā brāhmaṇā ye dhammā brāhmaṇakārakā, te dhamme pahāya vattamānā, ye dhammā abrāhmaṇakārakā, te dhamme samādāya vattamānā pañca kāmaguṇe gadhitā mucchitā ajjhopannā anādīnavadassāvino anissaraṇapaññā paribhuñjantā kāmandubandhanabaddhā kāyassa bhedā paraṃ maraṇā brahmānaṃ sahabyūpagā bhavissantī"ti, netaṃ ṭhānaṃ vijjati.

"Seyyathāpi, vāseṭṭha, ayaṃ aciravatī nadī pūrā udakassa samatittikā kākapeyyā. Atha puriso āgaccheyya pāratthiko pāragavesī pāragāmī pāraṃ taritukāmo. So orime tīre sasīsaṃ pārupitvā nipajjeyya.

"Taṃ kiṃ maññasi, vāseṭṭha, api nu so puriso aciravatiyā nadiyā orimā tīrā pārimaṃ tīraṃ gaccheyyā"ti? "No hidaṃ, bho gotama".

"Evameva kho, vāseṭṭha, pañcime nīvaraṇā ariyassa vinaye āvaraṇātipi vuccanti, nīvaraṇātipi vuccanti, onāhanātipi vuccanti, pariyonāhanātipi vuccanti. Katame pañca? Kāmacchandanīvaraṇaṃ, byāpādanīvaraṇaṃ, thīnamiddhanīvaraṇaṃ, uddhaccakukkuccanīvaraṇaṃ, vicikicchānīvaraṇaṃ. Ime kho, vāseṭṭha, pañca nīvaraṇā ariyassa vinaye āvaraṇātipi vuccanti, nīvaraṇātipi vuccanti,

onāhanātipi vuccanti, pariyonāhanātipi vuccanti.

"Imehi kho, vāseṭṭha, pañcahi nīvaraṇehi tevijjā brāhmaṇā āvuṭā nivuṭā onaddhā pariyonaddhā. Te vata, vāseṭṭha, tevijjā brāhmaṇā ye dhammā brāhmaṇakārakā te dhamme pahāya vattamānā, ye dhammā abrāhmaṇakārakā te dhamme samādāya vattamānā pañcahi nīvaraṇehi āvuṭā nivuṭā onaddhā pariyonaddhā kāyassa bhedā paraṃ maraṇā brahmānaṃ sahabyūpagā bhavissantī"ti, netaṃ ṭhānaṃ vijjati.

Saṃsandanakathā

"Taṃ kiṃ maññasi, vāseṭṭha, kinti te sutaṃ brāhmaṇānaṃ vuddhānaṃ mahallakānaṃ ācariyapācariyānaṃ bhāsamānānaṃ, sapariggaho vā brahmā apariggaho vā"ti? "Apariggaho, bho gotama". "Saveracitto vā averacitto vā"ti? "Averacitto, bho gotama". "Sabyāpajjacitto vā abyāpajjacitto vā"ti? "Abyāpajjacitto, bho gotama". "Saṅkiliṭṭhacitto vā asaṅkiliṭṭhacitto vā"ti? "Asaṅkiliṭṭhacitto, bho gotama". "Vasavattī vā avasavattī vā"ti? "Vasavattī, bho gotama".

"Taṃ kiṃ maññasi, vāseṭṭha, sapariggahā vā tevijjā brāhmaṇā apariggahā vā"ti? "Sapariggahā, bho gotama". "Saveracittā vā averacittā vā"ti? "Saveracittā, bho gotama". "Sabyāpajjacittā vā abyāpajjacittā vā"ti? "Sabyāpajjacittā, bho gotama". "Saṅkiliṭṭhacittā vā asaṅkiliṭṭhacittā vā"ti? "Saṅkiliṭṭhacittā, bho gotama". "Vasavattī vā avasavattī vā"ti? "Avasavattī, bho gotama".

"Iti kira, vāseṭṭha, sapariggahā tevijjā brāhmaṇā apariggaho brahmā. Api nu kho sapariggahānaṃ tevijjānaṃ brāhmaṇānaṃ apariggahena brahmunā saddhiṃ saṃsandati sametī"ti? "No hidaṃ, bho gotama". "Sādhu, vāseṭṭha, te vata, vāseṭṭha, sapariggahā tevijjā brāhmaṇā kāyassa bhedā paraṃ maraṇā apariggahassa brahmuno sahabyūpagā bhavissantī"ti, netaṃ ṭhānaṃ vijjati.

"Iti kira, vāseṭṭha, saveracittā tevijjā brāhmaṇā, averacitto brahmā...pe... sabyāpajjacittā tevijjā brāhmaṇā abyāpajjacitto brahmā... saṅkiliṭṭhacittā tevijjā brāhmaṇā asaṅkiliṭṭhacitto brahmā... avasavattī tevijjā brāhmaṇā vasavattī brahmā, api nu kho avasavattīnaṃ tevijjānaṃ brāhmaṇānaṃ vasavattinā brahmunā saddhiṃ saṃsandati sametī"ti? "No hidaṃ, bho gotama". "Sādhu, vāseṭṭha, te vata, vāseṭṭha, avasavattī tevijjā brāhmaṇā kāyassa bhedā paraṃ maraṇā vasavattissa brahmuno sahabyūpagā bhavissantī"ti, netaṃ ṭhānaṃ vijjati.

"Idha kho pana te, vāseṭṭha, tevijjā brāhmaṇā āsīditvā saṃsīdanti, saṃsīditvā visāraṃ pāpuṇanti, sukkhataraṃ maññe taranti. Tasmā idaṃ tevijjānaṃ brāhmaṇānaṃ tevijjāiriṇantipi vuccati, tevijjāvivanantipi vuccati, tevijjābyasanantipi vuccatī"ti.

Evaṃ vutte, vāseṭṭho māṇavo bhagavantaṃ etadavoca – "sutaṃ metaṃ, bho gotama, samaṇo gotamo brahmānaṃ sahabyatāya maggaṃ jānātī"ti. "Taṃ kiṃ maññasi, vāseṭṭha. Āsanne ito manasākaṭaṃ, na ito dūre manasākaṭa"nti? "Evaṃ, bho gotama, āsanne ito manasākaṭaṃ, na ito dūre manasākaṭa"nti.

"Taṃ kiṃ maññasi, vāseṭṭha, idhassa puriso manasākaṭe jātasaṃvaddho. Tamenaṃ manasākaṭato tāvadeva avasaṭaṃ manasākaṭassa maggaṃ puccheyyuṃ. Siyā nu kho, vāseṭṭha, tassa purisassa manasākaṭe jātasaṃvaddhassa manasākaṭassa maggaṃ puṭṭhassa dandhāyitattaṃ vā vitthāyitattaṃ vā"ti? "No hidaṃ, bho gotama". "Taṃ kissa hetu"? "Amu hi, bho gotama, puriso manasākaṭe jātasaṃvaddho, tassa sabbāneva manasākaṭassa maggāni suviditānī"ti.

"Siyā kho, vāseṭṭha, tassa purisassa manasākaṭe jātasaṃvaddhassa manasākaṭassa maggaṃ puṭṭhassa dandhāyitattaṃ vā vitthāyitattaṃ vā, na tveva tathāgatassa brahmaloke vā brahmalokagāminiyā vā paṭipadāya puṭṭhassa dandhāyitattaṃ vā vitthāyitattaṃ vā. Brahmānaṃ cāhaṃ, vāseṭṭha, pajānāmi brahmaloka ca brahmalokagāminiñca paṭipadaṃ, yathā paṭipanno ca brahmalokaṃ upapanno,

tañca pajānāmī”ti.

Evaṃ vutte, vāseṭṭho māṇavo bhagavantaṃ etadavoca – “sutaṃ metaṃ, bho gotama, samaṇo gotamo brahmānaṃ sahabyatāya maggaṃ desetī”ti. “Sādhu no bhavaṃ gotamo brahmānaṃ sahabyatāya maggaṃ desetu ullumpatu bhavaṃ gotamo brāhmaṇiṃ paja”nti. “Tena hi, vāseṭṭha, suṇāhi; sādhukaṃ manasi karohi; bhāsissāmī”ti. “Evaṃ bho”ti kho vāseṭṭho māṇavo bhagavato paccassosi.

Brahmalokamaggadesanā

Bhagavā etadavoca – “idha, vāseṭṭha, tathāgato loke uppajjati arahaṃ, sammāsambuddho vijjācaraṇasampanno sugato lokavidū anuttaro purisadammasārathi satthā devamanussānaṃ buddho bhagavā. So imaṃ lokaṃ sadevakaṃ samārakaṃ sabrahmakaṃ sassamaṇabrāhmaṇiṃ pajaṃ sadevamanussaṃ sayaṃ abhiññā sacchikatvā pavedeti. So dhammaṃ deseti ādikalyāṇaṃ majjhekalyāṇaṃ pariyosānakalyāṇaṃ sātthaṃ sabyañjanaṃ, kevalaparipuṇṇaṃ parisuddhaṃ brahmacariyaṃ pakāseti.

“Taṃ dhammaṃ suṇāti gahapati vā gahapatiputto vā aññatarasmiṃ vā kule paccājāto. So taṃ dhammaṃ sutvā tathāgate saddhaṃ paṭilabhati. So tena saddhāpaṭilābhena samannāgato iti paṭisañcikkhati – ‘sambādho gharāvāso rajopatho, abbhokāso pabbajjā. Nayidaṃ sukaraṃ agāraṃ ajjhāvasatā ekantaparipuṇṇaṃ ekantaparisuddhaṃ saṅkhalikhitaṃ brahmacariyaṃ carituṃ. Yaṃnūnāhaṃ kesamassuṃ ohāretvā kāsāyāni vatthāni acchādetvā agārasmā anagāriyaṃ pabbajeyya’nti.

“So aparena samayena appaṃ vā bhogakkhandhaṃ pahāya mahantaṃ vā bhogakkhandhaṃ pahāya appaṃ vā ñātiparivaṭṭaṃ pahāya mahantaṃ vā ñātiparivaṭṭaṃ pahāya kesamassuṃ ohāretvā kāsāyāni vatthāni acchādetvā agārasmā anagāriyaṃ pabbajati.

"So evaṃ pabbajito samāno pātimokkhasaṃvarasaṃvuto viharati ācāragocarasampanno, aṇumattesu vajjesu bhayadassāvī, samādāya sikkhati sikkhāpadesu, kāyakammavacīkammena samannāgato kusalena, parisuddhājīvo sīlasampanno, indriyesu guttadvāro, satisampajaññena samannāgato, santuṭṭho.

"Kathañca, vāseṭṭha, bhikkhu sīlasampanno hoti? Idha, vāseṭṭha, bhikkhu pāṇātipātaṃ pahāya pāṇātipātā paṭivirato hoti. Nihitadaṇḍo nihitasattho lajjī dayāpanno sabbapāṇabhūtahitānukampī viharati. Idampissa hoti sīlasmiṃ.

"Adinnādānaṃ pahāya adinnādānā paṭivirato hoti dinnādāyī dinnapāṭikaṅkhī, athenena sucibhūtena attanā viharati. Idampissa hoti sīlasmiṃ.

"Abrahmacariyaṃ pahāya brahmacārī hoti ārācārī virato methunā gāmadhammā. Idampissa hoti sīlasmiṃ.

"Musāvādaṃ pahāya musāvādā paṭivirato hoti saccavādī saccasandho theto paccayiko avisaṃvādako lokassa. Idampissa hoti sīlasmiṃ.

"Pisuṇaṃ vācaṃ pahāya pisuṇāya vācāya paṭivirato hoti; ito sutvā na amutra akkhātā imesaṃ bhedāya; amutra vā sutvā na imesaṃ akkhātā, amūsaṃ bhedāya. Iti bhinnānaṃ vā sandhātā, sahitānaṃ vā anuppadātā, samaggārāmo samaggarato samagganandī samaggakaraṇiṃ vācaṃ bhāsitā hoti. Idampissa hoti sīlasmiṃ.

"Pharusaṃ vācaṃ pahāya pharusāya vācāya paṭivirato hoti; yā sā vācā nelā kaṇṇasukhā pemanīyā hadayaṅgamā porī bahujanakantā bahujanamanāpā tathārūpiṃ vācaṃ bhāsitā hoti. Idampissa hoti sīlasmiṃ.

"Samphappalāpaṃ pahāya samphappalāpā paṭivirato hoti kālavādī bhūtavādī atthavādī dhammavādī vinayavādī, nidhānavatiṃ vācaṃ bhāsitā hoti kālena sāpadesaṃ pariyantavatiṃ atthasaṃhitaṃ. Idampissa hoti sīlasmiṃ.

Indriyasaṃvaro

“Kathañca, vāseṭṭha, bhikkhu indriyesu guttadvāro hoti? Idha, vāseṭṭha, bhikkhu cakkhunā rūpaṃ disvā na nimittaggāhī hoti nānubyañjanaggāhī. Yatvādhikaraṇamenaṃ cakkhundriyaṃ asaṃvutaṃ viharantaṃ abhijjhā domanassā pāpakā akusalā dhammā anvāssaveyyuṃ, tassa saṃvarāya paṭipajjati, rakkhati cakkhundriyaṃ, cakkhundriye saṃvaraṃ āpajjati. Sotena saddaṃ sutvā...pe... ghānena gandhaṃ ghāyitvā...pe... jivhāya rasaṃ sāyitvā...pe... kāyena phoṭṭhabbaṃ phusitvā...pe... manasā dhammaṃ viññāya na nimittaggāhī hoti nānubyañjanaggāhī. Yatvādhikaraṇamenaṃ manindriyaṃ asaṃvutaṃ viharantaṃ abhijjhā domanassā pāpakā akusalā dhammā anvāssaveyyuṃ, tassa saṃvarāya paṭipajjati, rakkhati manindriyaṃ, manindriye saṃvaraṃ āpajjati. So iminā ariyena indriyasaṃvarena samannāgato ajjhattaṃ abyāsekasukhaṃ paṭisaṃvedeti. Evaṃ kho, vāseṭṭha, bhikkhu indriyesu guttadvāro hoti.

Satisampajaññaṃ

“Kathañca, vāseṭṭha, bhikkhu satisampajaññena samannāgato hoti? Idha, vāseṭṭha, bhikkhu abhikkante paṭikkante sampajānakārī hoti, ālokite vilokite sampajānakārī hoti, samiñjite pasārite sampajānakārī hoti, saṅghāṭipattacīvaradhāraṇe sampajānakārī hoti, asite pīte khāyite sāyite sampajānakārī hoti, uccārapassāvakamme sampajānakārī hoti, gate ṭhite nisinne sutte jāgarite bhāsite tuṇhībhāve sampajānakārī hoti. Evaṃ kho, vāseṭṭha, bhikkhu satisampajaññena samannāgato hoti.

Santoso

“Kathañca, vāseṭṭha, bhikkhu santuṭṭho hoti? Idha, vāseṭṭha, bhikkhu santuṭṭho hoti kāyaparihārikena cīvarena, kucchiparihārikena piṇḍapātena. So yena yeneva pakkamati, samādāyeva pakkamati. Seyyathāpi, vāseṭṭha, pakkhī

sakuṇo yena yeneva ḍeti, sapattabhārova ḍeti. Evameva kho, vāseṭṭha, bhikkhu santuṭṭho hoti kāyaparihārikena cīvarena kucchiparihārikena piṇḍapātena. So yena yeneva pakkamati, samādāyeva pakkamati. Evaṃ kho, vāseṭṭha, bhikkhu santuṭṭho hoti.

Nīvaraṇappahānaṃ

"So iminā ca ariyena sīlakkhandhena samannāgato, iminā ca ariyena indriyasaṃvarena samannāgato, iminā ca ariyena satisampajaññena samannāgato, imāya ca ariyāya santuṭṭhiyā samannāgato, vivittaṃ senāsanaṃ bhajati araññaṃ rukkhamūlaṃ pabbataṃ kandaraṃ giriguhaṃ susānaṃ vanapatthaṃ abbhokāsaṃ palālapuñjaṃ. So pacchābhattaṃ piṇḍapātappaṭikkanto nisīdati pallaṅkaṃ ābhujitvā ujuṃ kāyaṃ paṇidhāya parimukhaṃ satiṃ upaṭṭhapetvā.

"So abhijjhaṃ loke pahāya vigatābhijjhena cetasā viharati, abhijjhāya cittaṃ parisodheti. Byāpādapadosaṃ pahāya abyāpannacitto viharati sabbapāṇabhūtahitānukampī, byāpādapadosā cittaṃ parisodheti. Thīnamiddhaṃ pahāya vigatathīnamiddho viharati ālokasaññī, sato sampajāno, thīnamiddhā cittaṃ parisodheti. Uddhaccakukkuccaṃ pahāya anuddhato viharati, ajjhattaṃ vūpasantacitto, uddhaccakukkuccā cittaṃ parisodheti. Vicikicchaṃ pahāya tiṇṇavicikiccho viharati, akathaṃkathī kusalesu dhammesu, vicikicchāya cittaṃ parisodheti.

Tassime pañca nīvaraṇe pahīne attani samanupassato pāmojjaṃ jāyati, pamuditassa pīti jāyati, pītimanassa kāyo passambhati, passaddhakāyo sukhaṃ vedeti, sukhino cittaṃ samādhiyati.

Paṭhamajjhānaṃ

"So vivicceva kāmehi, vivicca akusalehi dhammehi savitakkaṃ savicāraṃ vivekajaṃ pītisukhaṃ paṭhamaṃ jhānaṃ upasampajja viharati. So imameva kāyaṃ vivekajena pītisukhena abhisandeti parisandeti paripūreti parippharati,

nāssa kiñci sabbāvato kāyassa vivekajena pītisukhena apphuṭaṃ hoti.

[Brahmaviharā]

"So mettāsahagatena cetasā ekaṃ disaṃ pharitvā viharati. Tathā dutiyaṃ. Tathā tatiyaṃ. Tathā catutthaṃ. Iti uddhamadho tiriyaṃ sabbadhi sabbattatāya sabbāvantaṃ lokaṃ mettāsahagatena cetasā vipulena mahaggatena appamāṇena averena abyāpajjena pharitvā viharati.

"Seyyathāpi, vāseṭṭha, balavā saṅkhadhamo appakasireneva catuddisā viññāpeyya; evameva kho, vāseṭṭha, evaṃ bhāvitāya mettāya cetovimuttiyā yaṃ pamāṇakataṃ kammaṃ na taṃ tatrāvasissati, na taṃ tatrāvatiṭṭhati. Ayampi kho, vāseṭṭha, brahmānaṃ sahabyatāya maggo.

"Puna caparaṃ, vāseṭṭha, bhikkhu karuṇāsahagatena cetasā...pe... muditāsahagatena cetasā...pe... upekkhāsahagatena cetasā ekaṃ disaṃ pharitvā viharati. Tathā dutiyaṃ. Tathā tatiyaṃ. Tathā catutthaṃ. Iti uddhamadho tiriyaṃ sabbadhi sabbattatāya sabbāvantaṃ lokaṃ upekkhāsahagatena cetasā vipulena mahaggatena appamāṇena averena abyāpajjena pharitvā viharati.

"Seyyathāpi, vāseṭṭha, balavā saṅkhadhamo appakasireneva catuddisā viññāpeyya. Evameva kho, vāseṭṭha, evaṃ bhāvitāya upekkhāya cetovimuttiyā yaṃ pamāṇakataṃ kammaṃ na taṃ tatrāvasissati, na taṃ tatrāvatiṭṭhati. Ayaṃ kho, vāseṭṭha, brahmānaṃ sahabyatāya maggo.

"Taṃ kiṃ maññasi, vāseṭṭha, evaṃvihārī bhikkhu sapariggaho vā apariggaho vā"ti? "Apariggaho, bho gotama". "Saveracitto vā averacitto vā"ti? "Averacitto, bho gotama". "Sabyāpajjacitto vā abyāpajjacitto vā"ti? "Abyāpajjacitto, bho gotama". "Saṅkiliṭṭhacitto vā asaṅkiliṭṭhacitto vā"ti? "Asaṅkiliṭṭhacitto, bho gotama". "Vasavattī vā avasavattī vā"ti? "Vasavattī, bho gotama".

"Iti kira, vāseṭṭha, apariggaho bhikkhu, apariggaho brahmā. Api nu kho

apariggahassa bhikkhuno apariggahena brahmunā saddhiṃ saṃsandati sametī"ti? "Evaṃ, bho gotama". "Sādhu, vāseṭṭha, so vata vāseṭṭha apariggaho bhikkhu kāyassa bhedā paraṃ maraṇā apariggahassa brahmuno sahabyūpago bhavissatī"ti, ṭhānametaṃ vijjati.

"Iti kira, vāseṭṭha, averacitto bhikkhu, averacitto brahmā...pe... abyāpajjacitto bhikkhu, abyāpajjacitto brahmā... asaṅkiliṭṭhacitto bhikkhu, asaṅkiliṭṭhacitto brahmā... vasavattī bhikkhu, vasavattī brahmā, api nu kho vasavattissa bhikkhuno vasavattinā brahmunā saddhiṃ saṃsandati sametī"ti? "Evaṃ, bho gotama". "Sādhu, vāseṭṭha, so vata, vāseṭṭha, vasavattī bhikkhu kāyassa bhedā paraṃ maraṇā vasavattissa brahmuno sahabyūpago bhavissatīti, ṭhānametaṃ vijjatī"ti.

Evaṃ vutte, vāseṭṭhabhāradvājā māṇavā bhagavantaṃ etadavocuṃ – "abhikkantaṃ, bho gotama, abhikkantaṃ, bho gotama! Seyyathāpi, bho gotama, nikkujjitaṃ vā ukkujjeyya, paṭicchannaṃ vā vivareyya, mūḷhassa vā maggaṃ ācikkheyya, andhakāre vā telapajjotaṃ dhāreyya 'cakkhumanto rūpāni dakkhantī'ti. Evamevaṃ bhotā gotamena anekapariyāyena dhammo pakāsito. Ete mayaṃ bhavantaṃ gotamaṃ saraṇaṃ gacchāma, dhammañca bhikkhusaṅghañca. Upāsake no bhavaṃ gotamo dhāretu ajjatagge pāṇupete saraṇaṃ gate"ti.

Sutta 3 ♦ Glossary

a

a = *negative prefix* (*an* before vowel): non°, un°, not, without, lacking, *etc.*

akusala (adj.; n.), detrimental, unskillful, bad; *tech., a quality or an action that is disadvantageous to well being.*

akkhāta (ppp. √*khā* + *ā*), related, proclaimed.

agāra (n.), house, household life.

agāri (f.), living in a home.

aṅgīrasa (m.), *personal name.*

aciravatī (f.), *place and river name.*

ajjatagge (part.), from this day forward.

ajjhattaṃ (part.), in, inner, subjective, within oneself.

ajjhāvasatar (ag. n.), person living indoors.

ajjhopanna (ppp. √*pad* + *adhi* + *o*), enthralled, addicted to.

añjasa (adj.), straight, straightforward.

añña (pr. adj.), other, another.

aññatara (m.n. pr. adj.), a, a certain.

aṭṭhaka (m.), *personal name.*

aṇumatta (adj.), minute, slightest amount; *tech., measuring an atom* (*aṇu*).

atipāta (m.), destruction, killing.

attan (m.; reflexive pron.), self; oneself. (Line 340, *attanā* = inst: on one's on account, spontaneously.)

attha (m.n.), matter, affair, concern; benefit, advantage, profit; meaning, import. (Line 39, *attheva* = *atthi eva*; line 318, *sātthaṃ* = *sa* + *atthaṃ*)

atthi = √*as.*

atthika (adj.), wanting, desiring.

atha (part.), then, so.

atha kho (part.), now, then, moreover; continuation of narrative.

adinna (ppp. √*dā* + *a*), that which is not given.

addhariya (m.), name of a class of Brahmins.

addhā (part.), certainly, truly, indeed.

adho (part.), below, beneath.

an = *negative prefix* (*a* before consonant): non°, un°, not, without, lacking, *etc.*

anu + *ā* + √*su,* to flow on, to flow continually after; to attack, to overcome.

anu + √*kam,* to stroll. (Line 10, *anucaṅkamant* = prap. int.)

anukampin (adj.), compassionate.

anu + √*gā,* to sing.

anuttara (adj.), unsurpassed.

anu + *pari* + √*vatt,* to worship.

anuppadātar (ag. n.), encourager, inspirer.

anu + √*bhās,* to repeat.

anuyoga (m.), question, examination, enquiry; application, devotion to, practice, pursuit.

anu + √*vac,* to be recited again, to be spoken again, to be repeated.

anu + *vi* + √*car,* to wander.

aneka (adj.), various, many; lit., not one.

andu (f.), shackle, cord, fetter.

andū = *andu.*

andha (adj.), blind.

andhakāra (m.n.), darkness.

aparaṃ, see puna.

aparena (part.), afterward, later.

api (part.), but; *adds emphasis to preceding term;* even, even though, also, too; *at beginning of sentence* = *interrog. part.*

appa (adj.), small, insignificant, little, trifling.

appamāṇa (adj.), immeasurable, boundless.

abbhuggata (ppp. √*gam* + *abhi* + *ud*), gone out, spread out, preceded.

abbhokāsa (m.), open space.

abyāpajja (adj.), kind, caring, humane.

abyāseka (adj.), unimpaired, untouched, unimpeded.

abhikkanta (ppp. √*kam* + *abhi*), going forward, advancing; excellent, splendid wonderful.

abhijjhā (f.), longing, desire.

abhiññā (f.), realization; *tech.*, realization concerning the nature of reality.

abhiññāta (ppp. √*ñā*), well-known.

abhi + √*nand,* welcome, delight in, entice, cajole.

abhi √*sand,* caus., to saturate, to pervade, to make full, to fill.

amu (m. dem. pron.), that, *etc.*

amukasmiṃ (m.n. indef. pron.). in whatever, *etc.*

amutra (part.), there.

amba (m.), mango.

ambho (part.), exclamation used to attract someone's attention.

amhākaṃ (1st pers. per. pron.), our, *etc.*

ayaṃ (m.f. dem. pron.), this, *etc.*

ayana (n.), path, road.

arañña (n.), forest, wilderness.

arahant (adj.), worthy.

ariya (adj.), noble, preëminent, superlative; Buddhist.

ava + √*sar,* to go, to leave, to withdraw to. (Line 294, °*saṭa* = ppp.)

ava √*sis,* to be left over, to remain.

ava √*sthā,* to be lasting, to settle.

avidūra (adj.), near, not far.

avera (adj.), peaceful.

avheyya, see ā + √*hvā.*

√*as,* be. (Line 295, *siyā* = opt.)

asita (ppp. √*as*), eaten, eating.

assa (m.n. dem. pron.), his, of his, for him, *etc.* (Line 338, *pissa* = *pi* + *assa.*)

√*ah,* to say, to speak. (Line 11, *āha,* is a rare perfect tense, formed by reduplication, *a* + *ah* + 3rd pers. sing. ending *a.* Line 72, *āhaṃsu* = aor.)

ahaṃ (1st pers. per. pron.), I.

ā

ā √*khā,* to relate, to reveal, to divulge. (Line 445, *ācikkheyya* = int.)

ā + √*gam,* to come, to arrive

ācariya (m.), teacher.

ācāra (m.), good conduct.

ā + √*chad,* caus., to put on, to dress.

ājīva (m.), livelihood.

ādāna (n.), taking.

ādāyin (adj.), taking.

ādi (m.), beginning.

ādīnava (m.), danger, disadvantage, wretchedness.

ā + √*pad,* to come to, to reach; to exhibit, to manifest.

āpanna (ppp. √*pad* + *ā*), possessed of, having.

ā + √*bhuj,* to bend down, to assume a posture.

āma (part.), *expresses consent.*

ā + √*mant,* to address, to advise.

ā + √*yā,* to go.

ā + √*yāc,* to entreat, to pray.

ārācārin (adj), living remote.

ārāma (m.), pleasure, delight.

ārohaṇa (n.), ascending, climbing, mounting.

āloka (adj.), bright, luminous.

ālokita (ppp. √*lok* + *ā*), looking forwards.

āvaraṇa (n.), covering, obstruction.

āvāsa (m.), living, dwelling.

āvuṭā (ppp. √*var* + *ā*), obstructed, covered.

ā + √*sad,* to come near.

āsanna (ppp. √*sad* + *ā*), to be near.

ā + √*hvā,* to call.

i

√*i,* to come. (Line 210, *ehi* = 2nd pers. sg. imper.)

icch° = √*is*

iṭṭha (ppp. √*is*), desired, wish for.

iti (part.), here, in this/that case; marks quotation of speech or thought.

ito (part.), from here.

idaṃ (n. dem. pron), this, *etc.*

idha (part.), here.

inda (m.), *name of a Vedic deity* (S. *indra*).

indriya (n.), sense faculty.

imasmiṃ (m.n. dem. pron.), in the, *etc.*

imāya (f. dem. pron.), by this; from this, because of this, *etc.*

iminā (m.n. dem. pron.), with this, *etc.*

ime (m. dem. pron.), these, *etc.*

imesaṃ (m.n. dem. pron.), among them, *etc.*

iriṇa (n.), desert.

√*is,* to desire, to want, to wish.

isi (m.), visionary, seer.

ī

īsāna (m.), *name of a Vedic deity* (Skt. *īśvara*).

u

ucca (adj.), high, elevated.

uccāra (m.), feces.

uju (adj.), direct, going in a straight direction; straight, upright.

ut + √*kujj,* to set up, to set upright.

uttara (adj.), northern.

udaka (n.), water.

ud + √*gam,* to rise.

uddhaṃ (part.), above, vertically.

uddhacca (n.), agitation, over-excitement, distraction.

ud + √*pad,* to arise, to originate, to come into existence, to occur. (Line 10, *udapādi* = aor.)

ud + √*lup,* to save.

upa + √*ṭha,* to set up, to establish; caus., to bring near, to make present.

upapanna (ppp. √*pad* + *upa*), possessed of, furnished with, attained.

upamā (adj.; f.), like, similar to; simile.

upa + *saṃ* + √*kam,* to approach.

upa + *saṃ* + √*pad,* enter on, attain, reach. (Line 404, *upasampajja* = abs.)

upasaṃhita (adj.), accompanied by, possessing, connected with.

upasanta (ppp. √*sam* + *upa*), calmed, quieted, become tranquil.

upāsaka (m.), lay follower.

upekkhā (f.), equanimity, balance.

upeta (ppp. √*i* + *upa*), endowed with, possessed of.

e

eka (num.; adj.), one; a certain, some.

ekanta (adj.), utmost, extreme.

ekamantaṃ (adv.), on one side, beside.

etaṃ (m.f.n. dem. pron.), this, *etc.* (Line 33, n. *etad* before vowel.)

etarahi (part.), at present, now.

ete (m. dem. pron.), these, *etc.*

ettha (part.), here, in this case.

enaṃ (m.f.n. dem. pron.), him, her, it, that, this, the, *etc.*

enena (m.n. pers. pron), by him, *etc.*

eva (part.), adds emphasis to preceding term; so, just, even.

evaṃ, (part.), thus, so, such, in this way; yes.

o

o + √*gam,* to descend, to set.

onaddhā (ppp. √*nah* + *o*), covered, stretched over.

onāhana (m.), covering.

orima (adj.; n.), nearer, nearest; this side.

o + √*har,* caus., to remove.

k

ka = *suffix added to various parts of speech either: (i) without significant meaning; (ii) forming a diminutive; (iii) expressing contempt; or (iv) creating an adjective from a noun.* (Line 99, °*kaññeva* = *kaṃ* + [*ñ*]*eva.*)

kaṇṇa (m.), ear.

kata (ppp. √*kar*), made, done, created.

katama (m.f.n. interg. pron.), which (of several)?, *etc.*

kattar (ag.n.), maker, creator, doer.

kathaṃ (part), how?

kathaṃkathin (adj.), doubtful, questioning, uncertain; *lit.*, "how-saying."

kathā (f.), discussion, conversation; dispute.

kanta (ppp. √*kam*), desired; pleasing.

kandarā (f.), ravine, valley.

√*kam,* to desire.

kamma (n.), action, behavior.

√*kar,* to make, to create, to build.

karaṇī (f.), doing, making, creating.

karuṇā (f.), compassion, care, concern.

kalyāṇa (adj.), good, fine, excellent, favorable, beautiful.

kalyāṇī (f.), a beautiful woman.

kasira (n.), difficulty, trouble, labor.

kassapa (m.), personal name.

kākapeyya (adj.), brimful; *tech.,* crow-(*kāka*) drinkable (*peyya*).

kāma (m.n.), wish, desire, sensory pleasure.

kāya (m.), body.

kāraka (m.n.), doer of, participant in.

kārin (adj.), doing, making, creating, producing.

kāla (m.), time; the proper time.

kāḷī (f.), dark.

kāsāya (adj.), yellow.

kiṃ (part.) = *question marker.*

kiñci (n. indef. pron.), certain, some; *with negation,* whatsoever.

kitti (f.), renown, fame.

kinti (part.), *emphasizes interrog*: haven't you X, have you indeed X, *etc.*

kira (part.), apparently, so it seems; indeed.

kismiṃ (m.n. interrog. pron.), in what? about what?, *etc.*

kissa (m.n. interrog. pron.), for what?, *etc.*

kukkucca (n.), worry, remorse, anxiety.

kucchi (m.), stomach.

kula (n.), family, clan, peoples.

kusala (adj.; n.), beneficial, skillful, good; *tech., a quality or an action that is conducive to well being.*

kevala (adj.), entire, whole, all.

kesa (m.), hair.

koci (m. indef. pron), any.

kosala (m.), *place and peoples' name.*

kh

khattiya (m.), *class designation: administrative and warrior class.*

khandha (m.), complex, mass, accumulation.

khāyita (ppp. √*khā*), chewing.

kho (encl. part.), indeed, clearly, surely, certainly.

kho pana (part.), *marks continuation of narrative; emphasizes preceeding.*

g

gata (ppp. √*gam*), going, gone.

gathita (ppp. √*ganth*), bound to, enslaved, greedy for.

gadhita = *gathita*

gandha (m.), scent.

√*gam,* to go.

gama (adj.), going.

gavesin (adj.), seeking, striving for.

gahapati (m.), householder.

gāma (m.), village.

gāmin (adj.), going.

gāminiyā (adj.), leading to.

gāḷha (adj.), tight.

gāhin (adj.), grasping.

giri (m.), mountain.

gīta (ppp. √*gā*), sung.

guṇa (m.), cord, string, strand.

gutta (ppp. √*gup*), guarded.

guhā (f.), grotto, cave.

gocara (m.), pasture, field, sphere.

gotama (m.), family name of the Buddha.

gotta (n.), family lineage, clan.

gh

ghara (n.), home, house.

√*ghā, to smell.*

ghāna (n.), nose.

c

ca (encl. part.), and.

cakkhu (n.), eye.

cakkhumant (adj.), having eyes.

caṅkin (m.), personal name.

catu° = *catur in compound.*

catuttha (ord. num.), fourth.

catur (num.), four.

candimā (m.), moon.

√*car,* to go, to wander, to walk, to go on rounds.

caraṇa (n.), conduct, behavior.

cātumahāpatha (m.), crossroad, intersection.

cārikā (f.), travel, walk, journey.

citta (n.), mind, discursive thought, discursive mind.

cīvara (n.), robe.

cetas (n.), mind.

ch

chanda (m.), impulse, will, resolution, intention.

chandoka (m.), *name of a class of Brahmins.*

j

°*ja* (suffix), produced, born, emerged, arisen.

jaṅghā (f.), a walk. (Line 9, *jaṅgavihāra* = short *a* in compounds.)

√*jan,* to create, to produce, to generate.

jana (m.), people.

janapada (m.), country, land.

jāgarita (ppp. √*gar*), awakened.

jāṇusoṇi (m.), personal name.

jāta (ppp. √*jan*), born.

jāy° = √*jan.*

jivhā (f.), tongue.

jh

jhāna (n.), meditation, meditative absorption.

ñ

√*ñā,* to know, to realize.

ñāti (m.), relative.

ṭh

√*ṭhā,* to stand, to be situated.

ṭhāna (n.), possibility, soundness, plausibility.

ṭhita (ppp. √*ṭhā*), stood, standing.

ḍ

√*ḍi,* to fly.

t

taṃ (m.f.n. dem. pron.), him, her, it, that, this, the, *etc.* (Line 3, n. *tad* before vowel; also, used adverbially = there.)

takkara (m.), doer of that [which precedes the term].

tatiya (ord. num.), third.

tatra (part.), there.

tathā (part.), that, thus, in that manner; such, so. (Line 26-27, *yathā* ... *tathā,* whatever X … that Y.)

tathāgata (adj.; m.), come to [know] reality, come to suchness; *epithet of Gotama.*

√*tar,* to cross over.

tara (n.), crossing, bank.

tasmā (part.), therefore.

tassa (m.n. dem. pron.), as the, of that, *etc.*

tāni (n. pers. pron.), they, *etc.*

tārukkha (m.), personal name.

tāvadeva (part.), just now. (Line 294, *tāva-d-eva* = *d* before vowel.)

ti (part.), marks end of direct speech, a thought, or quoted term. (Note: A short vowel preceding *ti* is lengthened, and *ṃ* is converted to *n.*)

tiṇṇa (ppp. √*tar*), to overcome, to surmount, to cross over from.

tittiriya (m.), *name of a class of Brahmins.*

tiriyaṃ (part.), across, horizontally.

tīra (n.), bank, shore.

tuccha (adj.), desolate, deserted, empty, vacuous.

tuṇhībhāva (m.), silence.

te (2nd pers. per. pron.; m. dem. pron.), by you, yours, to you (sg.); those, them, *etc.*

tena (m.n. dem. pron.), at that, *etc.*

tela (n.), sesame oil.

tevijja (adj.), *tech.,* possessing the three-fold knowledge; *fig.,* versed in the three Vedas.

todeyya (m.), personal name.

tvaṃ (2nd pers. per. pron.), you, *etc.*

th

thīna (n.), stagnation, stiffness, unwieldiness, impiability, inflexibility.

theta (adj.), reliable, firm, trustworthy.

thoma, a hymn of praise. (Line 103, *thomayanti* = den., praise, extol.)

d

dakkh° = √*das*

dakkhiṇa (adj.), southern.

daṇḍa (m.), stick, weapon.

dandhāyitatta (n.), mental slowness, stupidity.

damma (adj), to be tamed.

dayā (f.), kindness, compassion.

daḷha (adj.), strong.

√*das,* to see.

dassāvin (adj.), recognizing, seeing, perceiving.

diṭṭha (ppp. √*das*), seen.

dinna (ppp. √*dā*), given.

√*dis,* to show; *caus.* to teach, to declare; to point to, to point out.

disā (f.), direction; region.

dīgha (adj.), tall, long.

dutiya (ord. num.), second.

dūra (adj.), distant.

deva (m.), resplendent being; god.

desanā (f.), teaching, instruction, discourse.

domanassa (n.), discontentment, dejection, depression.

dvāra (n.), door, gate, entrance.

dh

dhamma (m.), phenomenon, thing; quality, mental quality, thought; nature; teaching; standard, custom, way; justice, righteousness, goodness.

√*dhar,* to bear in mind, to memorize; to hold, to sustain, to bear, to provide; *with double acc.* = take, to accept, to admit.

dhāraṇa (n.), wearing, bearing, holding.

n

na (part.), no, not.

naṃ (mfn. dem. pron.), that, *etc.*

nagara (n.), city.

nadī (f.), river.

nanu (part.), *expresses affirmation*: isn't, doesn't; surely, certainly.

nandī (f.), enjoyment, pleasure, delight.

namas (n.), honor, veneration. (Line 103, *namassamānā* = den., honoring.)

nāna (part.), various, all kinds.

nānā (adj.), various, different.

nāma (ind.), by name, called.

nāman (n.), name, concept, notion.

nikkujjita (ppp. √*kujj* + *ni*), turn over, upset, unsettle.

nigama (m.), town.

nidhānavant (adj.), precious, valuable, worth treasuring. (Line 354, *nidhānavatiṃ* = f.)

ni + √*pad,* to lie down. (Line 245, *nipajjeyya* = opt.)

nimitta (n.), characteristic, feature, sign, mark.

niyyānika (adj.), leading out, leading toward; *tech.,* leading to salvation.

nir + √*yā,* to lead.

nihita (ppp. √*dhā* + *ni*), put down.

nīvaraṇa (m.), hindrance, obstacle, envelopment.

nivuṭā (ppp. √*var* + *ni*), enveloped, covered, hemmed in.

ni + √*sad,* to sit down. (Line 32, *nisīdiṃsu* = aor.)

nisinna (ppp. √*sad* + *ni*), seated, sitting.

nisīd° = *ni* + √*sad.*

nissaraṇa (n.), giving up, leaving behind, escape.

nisseṇi (f.), staircase.

nīca (adj), low.

nu (part.), emphasizes preceeding term: now, then, now then, *etc.*

nūna, see yaṃ nūna.

nela (adj.), humane, gentle.

no (1st pers. per. pron.), us, *etc.*

no hi (part.), indeed not.

p

pa + √*āp,* to attain, to arrive at, to reach.

pa + √*kam,* to proceed, to set out, to go forth.

pa + √*kās,* to shine, to be visible; caus., to illuminate.

pakāsita (ppp. √*kās* + *pa*), illuminated, made clear.

pakkhin (adj.), winged.

paccayika (adj.), trustworthy.

paccājāta (ppp. √*jan* + *paṭi* + *ā*), born.

pacchā (adv.), behind.

pacchābhattaṃ (part.), in the afternoon.

pacchima (adj.), last, final; western.

pajā (f.), progeny, humanity.

pajāpati (m.), *name of Vedic deity* (S. *prājapati*).

pañca (num.) five.

pañjalika (adj.), *gesture of folded hands placed at the chest, as in prayer.*

pajjota (m.), lamp.

pa + √*ñā*, to know, to realize; *caus.* to declare, to proclaim.

pañña (adj.), possessed of knowledge, knowing.

paṭikkanta (ppp. √*kam* + *paṭi*), going backwards, returning.

paṭicchanna (ppp. √*chad* + *paṭi*), hidden, concealed.

paṭi + √*pad,* to follow a method, to take a course of action, to practice.

paṭipadā (f.), path, course, practice, way.

paṭi + √*labh,* to acquire, to get.

paṭi + √*vas,* to reside, to live.

paṭivirata (ppp. √*ram* + *paṭi* + *vi*), abstaining from.

paṭi + *saṃ* + √*khā,* to reflect, to consider. (Line 322, *paṭisañcikkhati* = int.)

paṭi + *saṃ* + √*vid,* to experience, to feel, to undergo.

paṭi + √*su,* to respond, to answer; to agree, to assent. (Line 28, *paccassosi* = aor.)

paṭhama (ord. num.), first.

pa + *ṇi* + √*dhā,* to apply, to hold.

patta (m.n.), bowl; bowl used by Buddhist mendicants for begging food.

patta (n.), wing.

√*patth,* to desire, to long for, to request.

pattha (m.), elevated land, plateau.

pada (n.), verse.

padosa (m.), hostility, anger, hatred.

pana (encl. part.), but, however; moreover; now (continuing particle).

pabbajita (ppp. √*vaj* + *pa*), wandered forth; *tech.,* left the householder life for the training life.

pabbajjā (f.), mendicant.

pabbata (m.), hill, mountain.

pa + √*bhū,* to be able.

pamāṇa (n.), measure, amount.

pamudita (ppp. √*mud* + *pa*), pleased, delighted.

paramparā (f.), succession.

pariggaha (m.), possessions, belongings, property.

paripuṇṇa (ppp. √*pūr* + *pari*), complete, fulfilled.

pari √*pūr, caus.,* to make full, to fulfill.

pari √*phar,* to permeate, to pervade.

pari + √*bhuj,* to enjoy.

parimukhaṃ (part.), in front, immediately before; *lit.,* around the mouth.

pariyantavant (adj.), discriminating, precise, well-defined. (Line 355, *pariyantavatiṃ* = f.)

pariyāya (m.), way, manner, method.

pariyonaddhā (ppp. √*nah* + *pari* + *o*), ensnared, covered over, enveloped.

pariyonāhana (m.), enveloping, covering.

pariyosāna (n.), end, conclusion.

parivaṭṭa (m.), circle.

pari + √*sand, caus.,* to saturate, to drench, to soak, to steep.

pari + √*sudh, caus.,* to cleanse, to clarify, to purify.

parisuddha (ppp. √*sudh* + *pari*), clear, purified.

parihārika (adj.), keeping, preserving, caring for.

palāpa (m.), chatter, nonsense, yammering.

palālapuñja (m.), straw pile.

palālapuñjapara (adv.), after, further, beyond.

pallaṅka (adj.), crossed-legged.

pa + √*vaj,* to wander, to go forth.

pavattar (ag.n.), expounder, teacher.

pa + √*vid, caus.,* to make known.

pavutta (ppp. √*vac* + *pa*), declared, announced.

√*pas,* to see.

pa + √*sambh,* to be calm.

pasārita (ppp. √*sār* + *pa*), to stretch.

passaddha (ppp. √*sambh* + *pa*), become calm, quieted, reposed.

passāva (m.), urine.

pa + √*hā,* to reject, to leave, to give up, to abandon.

pahāna (n.), abandonment, rejection, reliquishment.

pa + √*hā,* to forsake, to abandon, to give up. (Line 215, *pahāya* = abs.)

pahīna (ppp. √*hā*), abandoned, eliminated, put down, left alone.

paho° = *pa* + √*bhū.*

pācariya (m.), teacher of teachers.

pāṭikaṅkhin (adj.), desiring.

pāṇa (m.), sentient being; life; breath.

pātimokkha (n.), *tech.*,= collection of rules for Buddhist mendicants.

pāpaka (adj.), detrimental, harmful.

pāmojja (n.), delight, gladness.

pāra (adj.; n.), beyond, over, across; distant bank, other shore.

pārima (adj.), farther.

pārupitvā (abs. √*var* + *pari*), covered, veiled.

pāsāda (m.), lofty platform, terrace, palace.

pi (encl. part.), even, also, just so, too; but; *adds emphasis to preceding term.*

piṇḍapāta (m.), alms.

piya (adj.), agreeable, dear, pleasing.

pisuṇa (adj.), malicious.

pīta (ppp. √*pī*), having drunk, drinking.

pīti (f.), joy, delight, exuberance, bliss.

√*pucch,* to ask.

puṭṭha (ppp. √*pucch*), asked.

putta (m.), son. (Line 20, *sakyaputta, can be personal name.*)

puna (part.), again. (Line 416, *puna caparaṃ,* moreover, and something else, furthermore.)

pubbaka (adj.), ancient, former, previous.

puratthima (adj.), eastern.

purima (adj.), first, preceeding.

purisa (m.), man, person, people.

pūra (adj.), full.

pe (part.), abridgement of *peyyāla*: repetition, etcetera.

pemanīya (adj.), affectionate, loving.

pokkharasāti (m.), *personal name.*

porāṇa (adj.), ancient, former, old.

porin (adj.), humane, polite.

ph

√*phar,* to saturate, to pervade, to permeate.

pharusa (adj.), harsh, rough, mean.

phuṭa (ppp. √*phar*), saturated, pervaded, permeated.

√*phus,* to feel.

phoṭṭhabba (n.), tactile feeling, touch.

b

baddha (ppp. √*bandh*), bound.

bandhana (n.), binding, bond.

balavant (adj.), powerful.

bavhārijjha (m.), *name of a class of Brahmins.*

bahu (adj.), many.

bāhā (f.), arm.

buddha (ppp. √*budh*), awakened, realized.

byañjana (n.), letter, sign, appearance.

byasana (n.), ruin, destruction.

byākar° = *vi* + *ā* + *√kar*

byāpajja (m.), trouble, disturbance.

byāpāda (m.), hostility, anger, ill-will, antagonism.

brahmacariya (n.), life of training, the expansive life; chastity.

brahmacārin (adj.), chaste.

brahmavihara (m.), *tech.*, meditative practice for developing and expanding a particular disposition.

brahman (n.), Brahma, name of Vedic creator deity; God; the ideal; possessing exceptional integrity.

brāhmaṇa (m.), *class designation*: Brahmin; *Vedic religious authority.*

bh

bhagavant (adj.), fortunate, illustrious, honorable; fortunate one: *epithet of Gotama.*

bhagu (m.), *personal name.*

√bhaj, to resort to, to retreat to.

bhaya (n.), fear.

bhavaṃ see bhavant.

bhavant (pron.; m.), (i) *respectable form of* you; (ii) *synonomous with bhagavant,* (iii) *form of address like E.* friend *or* comrade. (Line 25, *bho* = voc. sg.; line 308, *bhavaṃ* = 2nd pers. per. pron., used with 3rd pers. verb; line 446, *bhotā* = inst. sg.; line 22, *bhavantaṃ* = acc. sg.)

bhāra (m.), load, burden.

bhāradvāja (m.), *personal name.*

bhāvita (ppp. caus. *√bhū*), made to become, cultivated, cultured, developed.

√bhās, to speak, to say.

bhāsita (ppp. *√bhās;* n.), spoken, speeking; speech, talk.

bhikkhu (m.), mendicant; *tech.*, beggar.

bhinna (ppp. *√bhid*), divided.

√bhū, to be, to become; to cultivate, to nurture, to develop.

bhūta (m.; adj.), living being, existent, that which is; genuine, natural.

bheda (m.), cutting off, distruction, dissolution; division, dissension, disunion.

bho, see bhavant.

bhoga (m.), possession, wealth.

m

magga (m.), path, road, way.

maggāmagga (m.), right and wrong paths.

maṅguracchavi (adj.), golden.

majjha (adj.), middle.

majjhima (adj.), middle, medium.

maññ° = *√man.*

matta (adj.), measured, by measure, as much as; merely, only, not even.

√man, to think.

manasākaṭa (m.), *place name.*

manas (n.), mind.

manāpa (adj.), charming.

manussa (m.), human being.

manasākaṭa (m.), name of town.
mano (n.), mind.
manta (m.), scripture, sacred verse, incantation.
maraṇa (n.), death.
mayaṃ (1st pers. per. pron.), we, *etc.*
massu (n.), beard.
mahaggata (adj.), extensive, expansive.
mahant (adj.), large, great, extensive, significant.
mahayuga (n.), generation, eon, age.
mahallaka (adj.), venerable, old.
mahāsāla (adj.), wealthy, prosperous.
māṇava (m.), youth; young Brahman.
māra (m.), death; Mara, the personification of mortality.
middha (n.), lethargy, torpor.
mucchita (ppp. √*mucch*), infatuated, dulled, become stupid.
muditā (f.), gladness, joy.
musā (adv.), falsely, uselessly, neglectfully.
mūla (n.), root.
mūḷha (ppp. √*muh*), become confused, get lost, go astray.
me (1st pers. per. pron.), by me, *etc.*
mettā (f.), friendliness, kindness, love, concern.
methuna (n.), sexual intercourse.

y

yaṃ (mfn. rel. pron.), that which, *etc.*
yaṃ nūna (part.), what if? let me.
yato (part.), when; since, because.
yattha (part.), when.
yatvādhikaraṇaṃ (part.), since, because, on account of.
yathā (part.), as. (Line 26-27, *yathā* ... *tathā,* whatever X ... that Y.)
yamataggi (m.), *personal name.*
yassa (m.n. rel. pron.), that, which, *etc.*
yahiṃ (part.), where, wherever.
yā (f. rel. pron.), which, that which, those which, *etc.*
yāva (part.), as far as.
ye (m. rel. pron.), those who, those which, that, *etc.*
yena (part.), where, to where, at which place; *with tena* = where (*yena*) X was, there (*tena*) he went; how, by what means. (Line 381, *yena yena* = everywhere, wherever.)
yena (m.n. rel. pron.), by whom, *etc.*
yesaṃ (m.n. rel. pron.), of which, *etc.*
yo (m. rel. pron.), who, he who, one who, *etc.* (Line 13, *yvāyaṃ* = *yo ayaṃ.*)

r

√*rakkh,* to protect.
rajanīya (adj.), enticing.
rajopatha (n.), dustiness.
rata (ppp. √*ram*), delighting in, enjoying.
rasa (m.), taste.
rassa (adj.), short.
√*ric,* to leave, to abandon.
ritta (ppp. √*ric*), empty, vacuous.
rukkha (m.), tree.

rūpa (n.), form, appearance, body, object.

rūpin (adj.), possessing qualities.

l

lajjin (adj.), modest, conscientious.

loka (m.), world; people.

v

√*vac,* to speak. (Line 33, *avoca* = aor.; line 229, *vuccanti* = pass.)

vacī (m.), speech.

vajja (n.), fault.

vata (encl. part.), exclamation: indeed! of course! surely!

√*vatt,* to turn toward; to do; to occur.

vattha (n.), robe.

√*vad,* to speak, to say.

vana (m.), grove, forest.

varuṇa (m.), *name of a Vedic deity.*

vasavattin (adj.), domineering, autocratic.

vā (encl. part.), or.

vācā (f.), speech.

vācita (ppp. √*vac*), recited, spoken.

vāda (m.), viewpoint, opinion; speech, talk.

vādin (adj.), speaking, talking.

vāmaka (m.), *personal name.*

vāmadeva (m.), *personal name.*

vāseṭṭha (m.), *personal name.*

vi + *ati* + √*sar,* to exchange, to converse.

vi + *ñā* + √*kar,* to determine, to explain, to answer.

vigata (ppp. √*gam* + *vi*), devoid of, ceased; without.

viggaha (m.), dispute, argument.

vicāra (m.), *tech.,* sustained thought, continuous attention.

vicikicchā (f.), doubt, perplexity, uncertainty.

vijjā (f.), knowledge, comprehension, understanding.

vi + √*ñā,* to perceive, to discern, to know; *caus.,* to make known, to proclaim. (Line 230, *viññeyya* = fpp.)

vitakka (m.), *tech.,* applied thought, directed attention.

vitthāyitatta (n.), confusion, hesitation.

√*vid,* to find; to be. (Line 94, *vijjati* = pass.)

√*vid,* to know, to experience.

vidita (ppp. √*vid*), found.

vidū (adj.), knowledgable, skilled.

vinaya (m.), discipline, code of conduct; instructional, educational.

vipula (adj.), extensive, abundant, great.

vimutti (f.), freedom, liberation, release.

virata (ppp. √*ram* + *vi*), abstaining from.

vilokita (ppp. √*lok* + *vi*), looking backwards.

vivana (n.), wilderness.

vi √*var,* to uncover, to open up, to make clear.

vivāda (m.), argument, contention, disagreement.

vivicca (part.), disengaged, isolated, separated.

vivitta (ppp. √*vic* + *vi*), isolated, secluded, separated.

viveka (m.), seclusion, separation, withdrawal; discrimination.

visaṃvādaka (adj.), deceitful.

visāda (m.), despair, dejection, depression.

visāra, see visāda.

vi + √*har,* to live, to stay, to dwell, to abide; to be in the condition or state of.

vutta (ppp. √*vac*), said, spoken.

vuddha (ppp. √*vaḍḍh*), developed, ripened.

veṇi (f.), braid; *fig.,* line.

vera (n.), hostile, ill-tempered.

vessa (m.), class designation: merchant class.

vessāmitta (m.), personal name.

S

sa, prefix denoting with, possessed of, having.

saṃ + *ā* + √*dā,* to undertake, to take up, to take upon oneself.

saṃ + *ā* + √*dhā,* to concentrate, to compose, to bring together, to fully integrate, to thoroughly gather.

saṃ + √*i,* to come togther, to correspond to, to associate with, to agree with.

saṃ + √*ñā, caus.* to convince.

saṃ + √*pad,* to turn out to be, to come to, to become.

saṃ + √*mud,* to be friendly, to be polite; *tech.,* to exchange friendly greetings.

saṃvaddha (ppp. √*vaḍḍh* + *saṃ*), raised.

saṃvara (m.), restraint.

saṃvuta (ppp. √*var* + *saṃ*), restrained, guarded, governed.

saṃsatta (ppp. √*sañj* + *saṃ*), clinging.

saṃ + √*sad,* to sink down, to lose heart.

saṃ √*sand,* to flow together, to fuse, to associate, to unite, to combine.

saṃsandanā (f.), *tech.,* coming together; communion.

saṃhita (ppp. √*dhā* + *saṃ*), connected to, possessed of, endowed with, accompanying; preserved, collected.

√*sak,* can, to be able to. (Line 332, *sikkh°* = desid., want to be able, *i.e.,* train oneself.)

sakuṇa (m.), bird.

sakkhi (adv.), directly, face to face; *lit.* = with one's own eyes.

sakya (m.) *name of a people; Gotama's clan.* (Line 20, *sakyaputta,* can be personal name.)

saṅkiliṭṭha (ppp. √*kilis* + *saṃ*), corrupted, stained.

saṅkhadhama (m.), trumpeter, *lit.,* conch-blower.

saṅkhalikhita (adj.), *fig.*, resplendent, bright, perfect; *tech.*, polished or carved (*likhita*) like a shell or mother-of-pearl (*saṅkha*).

saṅgha (m.), group, assembly, community.

saṅghāṭī (f.), type of robe.

sacca (adj.; n.), real, actual, verifiable; reality, actuality, fact.

sacchikata (ppp. √*kar* + *sa* [with] + *akkha* [eyes]), realized directly.

saññin (adj.), conscious, cognizant, aware.

sata (num.), one hundred.

sata (ppp. √*sar*), remembering, conscious, aware.

sati (f.), present-moment awareness, presence of mind, reflective clarity, non-interfering consciousness, lucidity; *lit.* memory; *tech.*, memory-in-the-present.

sattama (num.), seven.

sattha (n.), sword, weapon.

satthar (ag.n.), teacher.

sadda (m.), sound.

saddhā (f.), confidence, trust.

saddhiṃ (part.), together; in company with.

santa (prap.), being.

santuṭṭha (ppp. √*tus* + *saṃ*), contented, pleased.

santuṭṭhi (f.), contentment, satisfaction.

santosa (m.), contentment.

sandha (m.), connection, union.

sandhātar (ag. n.), conciliator, uniter.

sabba (adj.), all, every.

sabbattatā (f.), ubiquitousness.

sabbadhi (part.), everywhere.

sabbāvant (adj.), all, entire.

samagga (adj.), harmonious.

samaṇa (m.), seeker, wanderer, ascetic.

samatittika (adj.), *lit.*, even (*sama*) with the river bank (*tittha*).

samanupassata (ppp. √*pas* + *saṃ* + *anu*), realized, gained insight into, thorougly perceived, comprehensively recognized.

samannāgata (adj.), endowded with.

samaya (m.), time, occasion.

samiñjita (ppp. √*iñj* + *saṃ*), bending.

samihita = *saṃhita*

samosaraṇa (n.), convergence, merging, junction.

sampajañña (n.), attention, attentiveness.

sampajāna (adj.), attentive, deliberate, conscientious.

sampanna (ppp. √*pad* + *saṃ*), endowed with, possessing, abounding in, perfected in.

sampha (adj.), frivolous, foolish.

sambahula (adj.), many.

sambādha (m.), pressure, crowding, difficulty.

sambuddha (ppp. √*budh* + *saṃ*), fully awakened, completely understood.

sammā (part.), thoroughly, completely, perfectly; sound, right, proper.

sayaṃ (part.), oneself, by oneself.

saraṇa (n.), shelter, refuge.

sahagata (adj.), accompanied by, concomitant with.

sahabyatā (f.), companionship, communion, commonality.

sahabyūpaga (m.), becoming a companion, coming into union.

sahita (ppp. √*dhā* + *saṃ*), united, kept together.

sā (f. dem. pron.), that, the, *etc.*

sāttha, see attha.

sādhu (part.), expression of approval.

sādhuka (adv.), thoroughly, completely.

sāpadesa (adj.), reasonable, principled.

sāma (adj.), brown.

√*sā,* to taste.

sāyita (ppp. √*sā*), tasting.

sāraṇīya (adj.), polite.

sārathi (m.), trainer.

sikkhati = √*sak*

sikkhāpada (n.), training course; *tech.,* keeping ten precepts.

siyā = √*as*

sīd° = √*sad*

sīla (n.), integrity, morality.

sīsa (n.), head.

√*su,* to hear, to listen.

su, prefix denoting well, completely, very.

sukara (adj.), easy.

sukkha (adj.), dry.

sukha (n.; adj.), ease, serenity, harmony, happiness, pleasure; gratifying, pleasant, agreeable, harmonious.

sugata (adj.), well, happy; *lit.,* well-faring; epithet of Gotama.

suci (adj), clean, bright, pure.

suta (ppp. √*su*), heard.

sutta (n.), discourse, dialogue, text; *lit.,* thread, stitching, textile.

sutta (ppp. √*sup*), sleeping.

sudaṃ (part.), just, even.

sudda (m.), class designation: the lowest, most underpriviledged, class.

susāna (n.), cemetery.

sūriya (n.), sun.

senāsana (n.), dwelling, lodging.

seyyathidaṃ (part.), as follows, namely.

seyyathā (part.), for example, as if, just as.

so (m. dem. pron.), he, that, the, *etc.*

sota (n.), ear.

soma (m.), *name of a Vedic deity.*

h

hadaya (m.), heart.

hassa (adj.), laughable, ridiculous.

hita (ppp. √*dhā;* n.), friendly; welfare.

hetu (adv.; m.), on account of, by reason of; cause, reason.

hoti = √*bhū.*

Sutta 4

Kesamuttisuttaṃ

(Aṅguttaranikāya 3.2.2.5.66.)

Evaṃ me sutaṃ – ekaṃ samayaṃ bhagavā kosalesu cārikaṃ caramāno mahatā bhikkhusaṅghena saddhiṃ yena kesamuttaṃ nāma kālāmānaṃ nigamo tadavasari. Assosuṃ kho kesamuttiyā kālāmā – "samaṇo khalu, bho, gotamo sakyaputto sakyakulā pabbajito kesamuttaṃ anuppatto. Taṃ kho pana bhavantaṃ gotamaṃ evaṃ kalyāṇo kittisaddo abbhuggato – 'itipi so bhagavā...pe... sādhu kho pana tathārūpānaṃ arahataṃ dassanaṃ hotī'"ti.

Atha kho kesamuttiyā kālāmā yena bhagavā tenupasaṅkamiṃsu; upasaṅkamitvā appekacce bhagavantaṃ abhivādetvā ekamantaṃ nisīdiṃsu, appekacce bhagavatā saddhiṃ sammodiṃsu, sammodanīyaṃ kathaṃ sāraṇīyaṃ vītisāretvā ekamantaṃ nisīdiṃsu, appekacce yena bhagavā tenañjaliṃ paṇāmetvā ekamantaṃ nisīdiṃsu, appekacce nāmagottaṃ sāvetvā ekamantaṃ nisīdiṃsu, appekacce tuṇhībhūtā ekamantaṃ nisīdiṃsu. Ekamantaṃ nisinnā kho te kesamuttiyā kālāmā bhagavantaṃ etadavocuṃ –

"Santi, bhante, eke samaṇabrāhmaṇā kesamuttaṃ āgacchanti. Te sakaṃyeva vādaṃ dīpenti jotenti, parappavādaṃ pana khuṃsenti vambhenti paribhavanti omakkhiṃ karonti. Aparepi, bhante, eke samaṇabrāhmaṇā kesamuttaṃ āgacchanti. Tepi sakaṃyeva vādaṃ dīpenti jotenti, parappavādaṃ pana khuṃsenti vambhenti paribhavanti omakkhiṃ karonti. Tesaṃ no, bhante, amhākaṃ hoteva kaṅkhā hoti vicikicchā – 'ko su nāma imesaṃ bhavataṃ

samaṇabrāhmaṇānaṃ saccaṃ āha, ko musā'"ti? "Alañhi vo, kālāmā, kaṅkhituṃ alaṃ vicikicchituṃ. Kaṅkhanīyeva pana vo ṭhāne vicikicchā uppannā."

"Etha tumhe, kālāmā, mā anussavena, mā paramparāya, mā itikirāya, mā piṭakasampadānena, mā takkahetu, mā nayahetu, mā ākāraparivitakkena, mā diṭṭhinijjhānakkhantiyā, mā bhabbarūpatāya, mā samaṇo no garūti. Yadā tumhe, kālāmā, attanāva jāneyyātha – 'ime dhammā akusalā, ime dhammā sāvajjā, ime dhammā viññugarahitā, ime dhammā samattā samādinnā ahitāya dukkhāya saṃvattantī'"ti, atha tumhe, kālāmā, pajaheyyātha.

"Taṃ kiṃ maññatha, kālāmā, lobho purisassa ajjhattaṃ uppajjamāno uppajjati hitāya vā ahitāya vā"ti?

"Ahitāya, bhante."

"Luddho panāyaṃ, kālāmā, purisapuggalo lobhena abhibhūto pariyādinnacitto pāṇampi hanati, adinnampi ādiyati, paradārampi gacchati, musāpi bhaṇati, parampi tathattāya samādapeti, yaṃ sa hoti dīgharattaṃ ahitāya dukkhāyā"ti.

"Evaṃ, bhante."

"Taṃ kiṃ maññatha, kālāmā, doso purisassa ajjhattaṃ uppajjamāno uppajjati hitāya vā ahitāya vā"ti?

"Ahitāya, bhante."

"Duṭṭho panāyaṃ, kālāmā, purisapuggalo dosena abhibhūto pariyādinnacitto pāṇampi hanati, adinnampi ādiyati, paradārampi gacchati, musāpi bhaṇati, parampi tathattāya samādapeti, yaṃ sa hoti dīgharattaṃ ahitāya dukkhāyā"ti.

"Evaṃ, bhante."

"Taṃ kiṃ maññatha, kālāmā, moho purisassa ajjhattaṃ uppajjamāno uppajjati hitāya vā ahitāya vā"ti?

"Ahitāya, bhante."

"Mūḷho panāyaṃ, kālāmā, purisapuggalo mohena abhibhūto pariyādinnacitto pāṇampi hanati, adinnampi ādiyati, paradārampi gacchati, musāpi bhaṇati, parampi tathattāya samādapeti, yaṃ sa hoti dīgharattaṃ ahitāya dukkhāyā"ti.

"Evaṃ, bhante."

"Taṃ kiṃ maññatha, kālāmā, ime dhammā kusalā vā akusalā vā"ti?

"Akusalā, bhante."

"Sāvajjā vā anavajjā vā"ti?

"Sāvajjā, bhante."

"Viññugarahitā vā viññuppasatthā vā"ti?

"Viññugarahitā, bhante."

"Samattā samādinnā ahitāya dukkhāya saṃvattanti, no vā? Kathaṃ vā ettha hotī"ti?

"Samattā, bhante, samādinnā ahitāya dukkhāya saṃvattantīti. Evaṃ no ettha hotī"ti.

"Iti kho, kālāmā, yaṃ taṃ avocumhā – 'etha tumhe, kālāmā! Mā anussavena, mā paramparāya, mā itikirāya, mā piṭakasampadānena, mā takkahetu, mā nayahetu, mā ākāraparivitakkena, mā diṭṭhinijjhānakkhantiyā, mā bhabbarūpatāya, mā samaṇo no garūti. Yadā tumhe kālāmā attanāva jāneyyātha – 'ime dhammā akusalā, ime dhammā sāvajjā, ime dhammā viññugarahitā, ime dhammā samattā samādinnā ahitāya dukkhāya saṃvattantīti, atha tumhe, kālāmā, pajaheyyāthā'ti, iti yaṃ taṃ vuttaṃ, idametaṃ paṭicca vuttaṃ.

"Etha tumhe, kālāmā, mā anussavena, mā paramparāya, mā itikirāya, mā piṭakasampadānena, mā takkahetu, mā nayahetu, mā ākāraparivitakkena, mā diṭṭhinijjhānakkhantiyā, mā bhabbarūpatāya, mā samaṇo no garūti. Yadā tumhe, kālāmā, attanāva jāneyyātha – 'ime dhammā kusalā, ime dhammā anavajjā, ime dhammā viññuppasatthā, ime dhammā samattā samādinnā hitāya sukhāya saṃvattantī'ti, atha tumhe, kālāmā, upasampajja vihareyyātha.

"Taṃ kiṃ maññatha, kālāmā, alobho purisassa ajjhattaṃ uppajjamāno uppajjati hitāya vā ahitāya vā"ti?

"Hitāya, bhante."

"Aluddho panāyaṃ, kālāmā, purisapuggalo lobhena anabhibhūto apariyādinnacitto neva pāṇaṃ hanati, na adinnaṃ ādiyati, na paradāraṃ gacchati, na musā bhaṇati, na parampi tathattāya samādapeti, yaṃ sa hoti dīgharattaṃ hitāya sukhāyā"ti.

"Evaṃ, bhante."

"Taṃ kiṃ maññatha, kālāmā, adoso purisassa ajjhattaṃ uppajjamāno uppajjati…pe… amoho purisassa ajjhattaṃ uppajjamāno uppajjati…pe… hitāya sukhāyā"ti.

"Evaṃ bhante."

"Taṃ kiṃ maññatha, kālāmā, ime dhammā kusalā vā akusalā vā"ti?

"Kusalā, bhante."

"Sāvajjā vā anavajjā vā"ti?

"Anavajjā, bhante."

"Viññugarahitā vā viññuppasatthā vā"ti?

"Viññuppasatthā, bhante."

"Samattā samādinnā hitāya sukhāya saṃvattanti no vā? Kathaṃ vā ettha hotī"ti?

"Samattā, bhante, samādinnā hitāya sukhāya saṃvattanti. Evaṃ no ettha hotī"ti.

"Iti kho, kālāmā, yaṃ taṃ avocumhā – 'etha tumhe, kālāmā! Mā anussavena, mā paramparāya, mā itikirāya, mā piṭakasampadānena, mā takkahetu, mā nayahetu, mā ākāraparivitakkena, mā diṭṭhinijjhānakkhantiyā, mā bhabbarūpatāya, mā samaṇo no garūti. Yadā tumhe, kālāmā, attanāva jāneyyātha – ime dhammā kusalā, ime dhammā anavajjā, ime dhammā viññuppasatthā, ime dhammā samattā samādinnā hitāya sukhāya saṃvattantīti, atha tumhe, kālāmā, upasampajja vihareyyāthā'ti, iti yaṃ taṃ vuttaṃ idametaṃ paṭicca vuttaṃ.

"Sa kho so, kālāmā, ariyasāvako evaṃ vigatābhijjho vigatabyāpādo asammūḷho sampajāno patissato mettāsahagatena cetasā ekaṃ disaṃ pharitvā viharati, tathā dutiyaṃ, tathā tatiyaṃ, tathā catutthaṃ, iti uddhamadho tiriyaṃ sabbadhi sabbattatāya sabbāvantaṃ lokaṃ mettāsahagatena cetasā vipulena mahaggatena appamāṇena averena abyāpajjhena pharitvā viharati. Karuṇāsahagatena cetasā ... pe... muditāsahagatena cetasā...pe... upekkhāsahagatena cetasā ekaṃ disaṃ pharitvā viharati, tathā dutiyaṃ, tathā tatiyaṃ, tathā catutthaṃ, iti uddhamadho tiriyaṃ sabbadhi sabbattatāya sabbāvantaṃ lokaṃ upekkhāsahagatena cetasā vipulena mahaggatena appamāṇena averena abyāpajjhena pharitvā viharati.

"Sa kho so, kālāmā, ariyasāvako evaṃ averacitto evaṃ abyāpajjhacitto evaṃ asaṅkiliṭṭhacitto evaṃ visuddhacitto. Tassa diṭṭheva dhamme cattāro assāsā adhigatā honti. 'Sace kho pana atthi paro loko, atthi sukatadukkaṭānaṃ kammānaṃ phalaṃ vipāko, athāhaṃ kāyassa bhedā paraṃ maraṇā sugatiṃ saggaṃ lokaṃ upapajjissāmī'ti, ayamassa paṭhamo assāso adhigato hoti.

"'Sace kho pana natthi paro loko, natthi sukatadukkaṭānaṃ kammānaṃ phalaṃ vipāko, athāhaṃ diṭṭheva dhamme averaṃ abyāpajjhaṃ anīghaṃ sukhiṃ attānaṃ pariharāmī'ti, ayamassa dutiyo assāso adhigato hoti.

"'Sace kho pana karoto karīyati pāpaṃ, na kho panāhaṃ kassaci pāpaṃ cetemi. Akarontaṃ kho pana maṃ pāpakammaṃ kuto dukkhaṃ phusissatī'ti, ayamassa tatiyo assāso adhigato hoti.

"'Sace kho pana karoto na karīyati pāpaṃ, athāhaṃ ubhayeneva visuddhaṃ attānaṃ samanupassāmī'ti, ayamassa catuttho assāso adhigato hoti.

"Sa kho so, kālāmā, ariyasāvako evaṃ averacitto evaṃ abyāpajjhacitto evaṃ asaṅkiliṭṭhacitto evaṃ visuddhacitto. Tassa diṭṭheva dhamme ime cattāro assāsā adhigatā hontī"ti.

"Evametaṃ, bhagavā, evametaṃ, sugata! Sa kho so, bhante, ariyasāvako evaṃ averacitto evaṃ abyāpajjhacitto evaṃ asaṅkiliṭṭhacitto evaṃ visuddhacitto. Tassa diṭṭheva dhamme cattāro assāsā adhigatā honti. 'Sace kho pana atthi paro loko, atthi sukatadukkaṭānaṃ kammānaṃ phalaṃ vipāko, athāhaṃ kāyassa bhedā paraṃ maraṇā sugatiṃ saggaṃ lokaṃ upapajjissāmī'ti, ayamassa paṭhamo assāso adhigato hoti.

"'Sace kho pana natthi paro loko, natthi sukatadukkaṭānaṃ kammānaṃ phalaṃ vipāko, athāhaṃ diṭṭheva dhamme averaṃ abyāpajjhaṃ anīghaṃ sukhiṃ attānaṃ pariharāmī'ti, ayamassa dutiyo assāso adhigato hoti.

"Sace kho pana karoto karīyati pāpaṃ, na kho panāhaṃ – kassaci pāpaṃ cetemi, akarontaṃ kho pana maṃ pāpakammaṃ kuto dukkhaṃ phusissatī"ti, ayamassa tatiyo assāso adhigato hoti.

"'Sace kho pana karoto na karīyati pāpaṃ, athāhaṃ ubhayeneva visuddhaṃ attānaṃ samanupassāmī'ti, ayamassa catuttho assāso adhigato hoti.

"Sa kho so, bhante, ariyasāvako evaṃ averacitto evaṃ abyāpajjhacitto evaṃ asaṅkiliṭṭhacitto evaṃ visuddhacitto. Tassa diṭṭheva dhamme ime cattāro assāsā adhigatā honti.

"Abhikkantaṃ, bhante...pe... ete mayaṃ, bhante, bhagavantaṃ saraṇaṃ gacchāma dhammañca bhikkhusaṅghañca. Upāsake no, bhante, bhagavā dhāretu ajjatagge pāṇupete saraṇaṃ gate"ti.

Sutta 4 ♦ Glossary

a

a = *negative prefix* (*an* before vowel): non°, un°, not, without, lacking, *etc.*

akusala (adj.; n.), detrimental, unskillful, bad; *tech., a quality or an action that is disadvantageous to well being.*

ajjatagge (part.), henceforth, from this day on.

ajjhattaṃ (part.), in, inner, subjective, within oneself.

añjali (m.), *a gesture of placing the hands palm to palm at the forehead, signifying respect.*

attan (m.), self, oneself.

atha (part.), then.

atha kho (part.), now, then.

adhigata (ppp. √*gam* + *adhi*), realized, acquired, attained.

adho (part.), below.

an° = *a*.

anīgha (adj.), calm, undisturbed.

anuppatta (ppp. √*āp* + *anu*), reached, arrived at.

anussava (m.), hearsay, unconfirmed claim, what has been heard.

apara (pr. adj.), other; furthermore.

appamāṇa (adj.), boundless, immeasurable.

appekacca (adj.), some.

abyāpajjha (adj.), friendly, kind.

abbhuggata (ppp. √*gam* + *abhi*), preceded, spread, gone out.

abhikkanta (adj.), wonderful.

abhijjhā (f.), desire, longing.

abhibhūta (ppp. √*bhū* + *abhi*), overpowered, overwhelmed.

abhi + √*vand*, to greet respectfully, to salute.

amhākaṃ (1st pers. per. pron.), to us, *etc.*

ayaṃ (m.f. dem. pron.), this, *etc.*

arahant (adj.), worthy.

ariya (adj.), noble, preëminent, superlative; Buddhist.

alaṃ (part.), certainly, alas, enough.

avajja (adj.), blameable, faulty.

ava + √*sar*, to go, to leave, to withdraw to.

avera (adj.), without hostility, peaceful.

√*as*, to be.

asaṅkiliṭṭha (adj.), clear, unblemished.

assāsa (m.), confidence, consolation, comfort; *lit.*, exhaling.

√*ah*, to say, to speak. (Line 20, *āha*, is a rare perfect tense, formed by reduplication, *a* + *ah* + 3rd pers. sing. ending *a*.)

ahaṃ (1st pers. per. pron.), I.ahita (adj.; n.), harmful; harm.

ā

ākāra (m.), form, appearance; deceptive appearance.

ā + √gam, to come.

ā + √dā, to take, to appropriate, to seize. (Line 32, *ādiyati* = 3rd pers. sing. indic.)

i

√*i*, to go.

iti (part.), here, in this/that case; *marks quotation of speech or thought.*

itikirā (f.), hearsay.

idaṃ (n. dem. pron), this, *etc.*

ime (m. dem. pron.), these, *etc.*

imesaṃ (m.n. dem. pron.), among them, *etc.*

u

uddha (part.), above.

upa + √*pad*, to arise, to appear, to be produced, to come into being.

upa + *saṃ* + √*kam*, to approach, to come near.

upa + *saṃ* +

pad, to take up, to take upon oneself. (Line 71, *upasampajja* = abs.)

upāsaka (m.), lay follower.

upekkhā (f.), equanimity.

uppanna (ppp. √*pad* + *ud*), arisen, come into being.

ubhaya (adj.), both.

e

eka (num.; adj.), one; a certain, some.

ekamantaṃ (adv.), to one side.

etaṃ (m.f.n. dem. pron.), this, *etc.* (Line 13, n. *etad* before vowel.)

ete (m. dem. pron.), these, *etc.*

ettha (part.), here, in this case.

etha = √*i.*

eva (part.), *adds emphasis to preceding term*; so, just, even; for sure, with certainty, certainly.

evaṃ, (part.), thus, so, such, in this way; yes.

o

opapakkhi (adj.), rejected, weakened.

omakkhi = *opapakkhi.*

k

√*kaṅkh*, to doubt, to be uncertain, to be unsettled.

kaṅkhā (f.), doubt.

kathaṃ (part), how?

kathā (f.), speech, conversation.

kamma (n.), action, behavior, deed.

√*kar*, to do, to make, to act, to perform. (Line 118, *karīyati* = pass.)

karont (prap. √*kar*), doing, acting, performing.

karuṇā (f.), compassion, care, concern.

kalyāṇa (adj.), good, fine, excellent, favorable, beautiful.

kassaci (indef. pron.), to anyone, of anyone, *etc.*

kāya (m.), body.

kālāma (m.), *name of peoples.*

kiṃ (n. interrog. pron.), what?

kittī (f.), report, reputation; praise.

kuto (part.) from where? how?

kula (n.), family, clan, peoples.

kusala (adj.; n.), beneficial, skillful, good; *tech., a quality or an action that is conducive to well being.*

kesamutta (m.), *place name.*

kesamuttī (f.) = *kesamutta.*

ko (m. interg. pron.), who, which, what?

kosala (m.), *place and peoples' name.*

kh

khanti (f.), forbearance, toleration; predilection, preference.

khalu (part.), *emphatic, stressing preceding word*; *indicating that X was heard, or reported.*

√*khuṃs*, to curse.

kho (encl. part.), indeed, clearly, surely, certainly.

kho pana (part.), *marks continuation of narrative*; *emphasizes preceeding.*

g

√*gam*, to go; to approach.

garahita (ppp. √*garah*), blameworthy, censurable.

garu (m.), teacher.

gotama (m.), *family name of the Buddha.*

gotta (n.), family lineage, clan.

c

catuttha (ord. num.), fourth.

catur (num.), four.

√*car*, go, to wander, to walk, to go on rounds.

cārikā (f.), wandering, walk, rounds.

citta (n.), mind, discursive thought, discursive mind.

√*cet*, to think.

cetas (n.), mind.

j

√*jān*, to know, to realize.

√*jot*, to shine; *cause.*, to lluminate, to make clear.

ñ

√*ñā,* to know, to realize.

ṭh

ṭhāna (n.), occasion, situation.

t

taṃ (m.f.n. dem. pron.), him, her, it, that, this, the, *etc.*

taṃ (part.), then, now, so.

takkahetu (m.), logical reasoning.

tatiya (ord. num.), third.

tathatta (n.), that-itself, the same, such as that.

tathā (part.), that, thus, in that manner; such, so.

tathārūpa (adj.), such, such like, of this or that kind.

tassa (m.n. dem. pron.), for him, for that one, *etc.*

ti (part.), marks end of direct speech, a thought, or quoted term. (Note: A short vowel preceding *ti* is lengthened, and *ṃ* is converted to *n.*)

tiriyaṃ (part.), across, horizontally.

tuṇhī (part.), silence.

tumhe (2nd pers. per. pron.), you, *etc.*

te (2nd pers. per. pron.; m. dem. pron.), by you, yours, to you (sg.); those, them, *etc.*

tesaṃ (m.n., dem. pron.), of these, *etc.*

d

dassana (n.), seeing; sight of, appearance.

dāra (f.), wife.

diṭṭha (ppp. √*das*), seen, visible, known. (Line 111, *diṭṭhe dhamme*, in this world, here and now, in the present.)

diṭṭhi (f.), theory, speculative view, opinion, dogma.

dinna (ppp. √*dā*), given, granted.

√*dip*, shine; *caus.*, to illustrate, to elucidate, to explain.

disā (f.), direction; region.

dīgharattaṃ (part.), a long time.

dukkaṭa (adj.), negative, poorly done.

dukkha (n.), unease, distress, trouble, unhappiness, pain.

duṭṭha (ppp. √*dus*), corrupted, spoiled.

dutiya (ord. num.), second.

dosa (m.), hostility, anger.

dh

dhamma (m.), teaching; quality. (Line 111, *diṭṭhe dhamme*, in this world.)

√*dhār*, *caus.*, accept, admit, allow.

n

nayahetu (m.), inferential reasoning.

nāma (part.), by name, called; indeed, certainly.

nāman (n.), name.

nigama (m.), town.

nijjhāna (n.), indulgence, pleasure, delight.

ni + √*sad*, to sit down. (Line 8, *nisīdiṃsu* = aor.)

nisinna (ppp. √*sad* + *ni*), sat down.

no (1st pers. per. pron.), us, to us, our, *etc.*

no (part.), no, not.

p

pa + √*āp*, to attain, to get, to reach.

paṭicca (abs. √*i* + *paṭi*), because, on account of, for this (*etaṃ*) reason.

paṭhama (ord. num.), first.

patissata (ppp. √*sar* + *pati*), mindful, conscientious.

pana (encl. part.), but, however; moreover; now (*continuing particle*).

pa + √*nam*, to bow, to bend, to raise.

pabbajita (ppp. √*vaj* + *pa*), wandered forth; *tech.*, left the householder life for the training life.

para (adj.; n.), other, another; others.

paraṃ (part.), beyond, after.

paramparā (f.), tradition.

pari + √*bhū*, to despise, to treat with contempt.

pariyādinna (ppp. √*dā* + *pari* + *ā*), overcome, controlled, mastered.

parivitakka (m.), reflection, consideration, thought.

pari + √*har*, take care of, attend to.

pavāda (m.), disputation, doctrine.

pasattha (ppp. √*saṃs* + *pa*), praised, approved.

pa + √*hā*, to abandon, to reject. (Line 65, *pajaheyyātha* = opt.].

pāṇa (m.), sentient being; life; breath.

pāpa (n.), detrimental act, harmful act.

pi (encl. part.), even, also, just so, too; but; *adds emphasis to preceding term.*

piṭakasampadāna (n.), textual authority, scripture.

puggala (m.), person.

putta (m.), son.

purisa (m.), man, person, people.

pe (part.), abridgement of *peyyāla*: repetition, etcetera.

ph

phala (n.), result, fruit.

√*phar*, to suffuse, to saturate.

√*phus*, touch.

b

byāpāda (m.), hostility, anger, ill-will, antagonism.

brāhmaṇa (m.), *class designation*: Brahmin; *Vedic religious authority.*

bh

bhagavant (adj.), fortunate, illustrious, honorable; fortunate one: *epithet of Gotama.*

√*bhaṇ*, to speak.

bhante (ind.), *form of respectful address, like E.* sir.

bhabba (adj.), possible, plausible.

bhavant (adj.), *synonomous with bhagavant.* (Line 19, *bhavataṃ* = gen. pl.)

√bhū, to be, to become; to cultivate, to nurture, to develop.

bhūta (ppp. √*bhū*), became.

bho (part.), friend, comrade.

bhikkhu (m.), mendicant; *lit.* beggar.

bheda (m.), breaking, breach, dissolution.

m

maṃ (pers. pron.), me, to me, *etc.*

maññ° = √*man.*

√*man*, to think.

mayaṃ (1st pers. per. pron.), we, *etc.*

maraṇa (n.), death.

mahaggata (adj.), expansive, extensive, great.

mahant (adj.), large, great, extensive.

mā (part.), not, do not.

muditā (f.), joy.

musā (part.), falsely, wrongly.

mūḷha (ppp. √*muh*), deluded, confused.

me (1st pers. per. pron.), to me, *etc.*

mettā (f.), friendliness, kindness, love, concern.

moha (m.), delusion, confusion, mental dullness.

y

yaṃ (mfn. rel. pron.), that which, *etc.*

yadā (part.), when.

yena (part.), where, to where, at which place; *with tena* = where (*yena*) X was, there (*tena*) he went.

yeva = *eva*.

r

rūpatā (f.), appearance.

l

luddha (ppp. √*lubh*), desirous, infatuated, greedy.

loka (m.), world.

lobha (m.), wanting, greed, longing, infatuation.

v

va = *eva* after a long vowel.

√*vac*, to speak. (Line 13, *avocuṃ* = *aor.*; line 59, *avocumhā* = aor.)

√*vambh*, to revile.

vā (encl. part.), or.

vāda (m.), doctrine, viewpoint, opinion.

vi + *ati* + √*sar*, to greet, to address, to converse.

vigata (ppp. √*gam* + *vi*), devoid of, ceased; without.

vicikicchā (f.), uncertainty, perplexity.

viññū (adj.), intelligent, wise.

vipāka (m.), fruit, fruition, result, consequence.

vipula (adj.), extensive, expansive, abundant.

visuddha (ppp. √*sudh* + *vi*), clean, clear, bright, pure, unblemished, untainted.

vi + √*har*, to live, to dwell, to abide.

vutta (ppp. √*vac*), spoken, said.

vo (2nd pers. per. pron.), you, etc.

s

sa (m. pers. pron.), he, *etc.*

saṃ + *anu* + √*pas*, to view, to see.

saṃ + *ā* + √*dā*, *caus.*, to incite, to provoke.

saṃ + √*mud*, to greet politely, to welcome.

saṃ + √*vatt*, to lead to.

saka (adj.), own, one's own.

sakya (m.), *name of peoples.*

saṅgha (m.), group, assembly, community.

sagga (m.), replendance, luster; sky, heaven.

sace (part.), if.

sacca (adj.; n.), real, actual, verifiable; reality, actuality, fact.

sadda (m.), sound; mention, remark, report.

saddhiṃ (part.), together; in company with.

santi = *as.*

sabbattatā (f.), universally.

sabbadhi (part.), everywhere.

sabbāvant (adj.), entire.

samaṇa (m.), seeker, wanderer, ascetic

samatta (ppp. √*āp* + *saṃ*), accomplished, brought to fruition, completed.

samaya (m.), time, occasion.

samādinna (ppp. √*dā* + *saṃ* + *ā*), taken up, undertaken, embarked on.

sampajāna (adj.), attentive, conscientious, thoughtful, fully comprehending.

sammūḷha (ppp. √*muh* + *saṃ*), confused, bewildered.

saraṇa (n.), shelter, refuge.

sahagata (adj.), accompanied by, concomitant with.

sādhu (adj.; part.), good; *expression of approval.*

sāraṇīya (adj.), friendly, polite.

sāvaka (m.), student, disciple, practitioner.

√*su*, to hear; *caus.*, to announce, to tell. (Line 3, *assosuṃ* = aor.)

su (interog. part.), *added to interog. pron., sometimes expressing emphasis.*

sugata (adj.), well, happy; *lit.*, well-faring; *epithet of Gotama.*

sugati (f.), favorable, happy.

sukata (adj.), well done, positive.

sukhin (adj.), at ease, happy, well.

suta (ppp. √*su*), heard.

sutta (n.), discourse, dialogue, text; *lit.*, thread, stitching, textile.

so (m. dem. pron.), he, that, the, *etc.*

h

√*han*, hurt, destroy, kill.

hi (part.), surely, indeed.

hita (ppp. √*dhā*; adj.; n.), beneficial, helpful.; welfare.

hoti, *honti* = √*bhū*.

Sutta 5

Sabbasuttaṃ

(Saṃyuttanikāya 4.1.3.1.23)

Sāvatthinidānaṃ. "Sabbaṃ vo, bhikkhave, desessāmi. Taṃ suṇātha. Kiñca, bhikkhave, sabbaṃ? Cakkhuñceva rūpā ca, sotañca saddā ca, ghānañca gandhā ca, jivhā ca rasā ca, kāyo ca phoṭṭhabbā ca, mano ca dhammā ca – idaṃ vuccati, bhikkhave, sabbaṃ. Yo, bhikkhave, evaṃ vadeyya – 'ahametaṃ sabbaṃ paccakkhāya aññaṃ sabbaṃ paññāpessāmī'ti, tassa vācāvatthukamevassa; puṭṭho ca na sampāyeyya, uttariñca vighātaṃ āpajjeyya. Taṃ kissa hetu? Yathā taṃ, bhikkhave, avisayasmi"nti.

Sutta 5 ♦ Glossary

a

a = *negative prefix* (*an* before vowel): non°, un°, not, without, lacking, *etc.*

añña (pr. adj.), other, another.

avatthuka (adj.), groundless.

avisaya (m.), habitat, domain, sensorium.

ahaṃ (1st pers. per. pron.), I.

ā

ā + √*pad*, to meet with, to exhibit. (Line 6, *āpajjeyya* = *pass.*)

i

idaṃ (n. dem. pron), this, *etc.*

u

uttariṃ (part.), moreover, further, besides.

e

etaṃ (m.f.n. dem. pron.), this, *etc.*

eva (part.), *adds emphasis to preceding term*; so, just, even.

evaṃ, (part.), thus, so, such, in this way.

k

kāya (m.), body.

kiṃ (n. interrog. pron.), what?

kissa (m.n. interrog. pron.), for what?, *etc.*

g

gandha (m.), scent.

gh

ghāna (n.), nose.

c

ca (encl. part.), and.

cakkhu (n.), eye.

j

jivhā (f.), tongue.

t

taṃ (m.f.n. dem. pron.), him, her, it, that, this, the, *etc.*

tassa (m.n. dem. pron.), therefore, because of that, etc.

ti (part.), marks end of direct speech, a thought, or quoted term. (Note: A short vowel preceding *ti* is lengthened, and *ṃ* is converted to *n.*)

d

dhamma (m.), thought.

√*dis*, to teach, to instruct.

n

na (part.), not.

nidāna (n.), occasion; originating in.

p

pa + √*ñā*, caus. to declare, to define.

paṭi + *ā* + √*khā*, to refute, to reject.

puṭṭha (ppp. √*pucch*), asked.

ph

phoṭṭhabba (n.), tactile feeling, touch.

bh

bhikkhu (m.), mendicant; *lit.* beggar.

m

mano (n.), mind.

y

yathā (part.), as.

yo (m. rel. pron.), he who, *etc.*

r

rasa (m.), taste.

rūpa (n.), form, appearance, body, object.

v

√*vac*, to speak. (Line 3, *vuccati* = *pass.*)

√*vad*, to say, to speak.

vācā (f.), speech.

vighāta (adj.), distress, trouble.

vo (2nd pers. per. pron.), you, *etc.*

s

saṃ + *pa* + *ā* + √*yā*, to explain.

sadda (m.), sound.

sabba (adj.; n.), all; the all.

sāvatthi (f.), *name of a city.*

√*su*, to hear, to listen.

sutta (n.), discourse, dialogue, text; *lit.*, thread, stitching, textile.

sota (n.), ear.

h

hetu (adv; m.), on account of, by reason of; cause, reason.

Sutta 6

Pheṇapiṇḍūpamasuttaṃ

(Saṃyuttanikāya 3.1.10.3.95)

Ekaṃ samayaṃ bhagavā ayujjhāyaṃ viharati gaṅgāya nadiyā tīre. Tatra kho bhagavā bhikkhū āmantesi:

Seyyathāpi, bhikkhave, ayaṃ gaṅgā nadī mahantaṃ pheṇapiṇḍaṃ āvaheyya. Tamenaṃ cakkhumā puriso passeyya nijjhāyeyya yoniso upaparikkheyya. Tassa taṃ passato nijjhāyato yoniso upaparikkhato rittakaññeva khāyeyya, tucchakaññeva khāyeyya, asārakaññeva khāyeyya. Kiñhi siyā, bhikkhave, pheṇapiṇḍe sāro? Evameva kho, bhikkhave, yaṃ kiñci rūpaṃ atītānāgatapaccuppannaṃ ajjhattaṃ vā bahiddhā vā oḷārikaṃ vā sukhumaṃ vā hīnaṃ vā paṇītaṃ vā yaṃ dūre santike vā taṃ bhikkhu passati nijjhāyati yoniso upaparikkhati. Tassa taṃ passato nijjhāyato yoniso upaparikkhato rittakaññeva khāyati, tucchakaññeva khāyati, asārakaññeva khāyati. Kiñhi siyā, bhikkhave, rūpe sāro?

Seyyathāpi, bhikkhave, saradasamaye thullaphusitake deve vassante udake udakapubbuḷaṃ uppajjati ceva nirujjhati ca. Tamenaṃ cakkhumā puriso passeyya nijjhāyeyya yoniso upaparikkheyya. Tassa taṃ passato nijjhāyato yoniso upaparikkhato rittakaññeva khāyeyya, tucchakaññeva khāyeyya, asārakaññeva khāyeyya. Kiñhi siyā, bhikkhave, udakapubbuḷe sāro? Evameva kho, bhikkhave, yā kāci vedanā atītānāgatapaccuppannā ajjhattaṃ vā bahiddhā vā oḷārikaṃ vā sukhumaṃ vā hīnaṃ vā paṇītaṃ vā yā dūre santike vā taṃ

bhikkhu passati āyati yoniso upaparikkhati. Tassa taṃ passato nijjhāyato yoniso upaparikkhato rittakaññeva khāyati, tucchakaññeva khāyati, asārakaññeva khāyati. Kiñhi siyā, bhikkhave, vedanāya sāro?

Seyyathāpi, bhikkhave, gimhānaṃ pacchime māse ṭhite majjhantike kāle marīcikā phandati. Tamenaṃ cakkhumā puriso passeyya nijjhāyeyya yoniso upaparikkheyya. Tassa taṃ passato nijjhāyato yoniso upaparikkhato rittakaññeva khāyeyya, tucchakaññeva khāyeyya , asārakaññeva khāyeyya. Kiñhi siyā, bhikkhave, marīcikāya sāro? Evameva kho, bhikkhave, yā kāci saññā atītānāgatapaccuppannā ajjhattaṃ vā bahiddhā vā oḷārikaṃ vā sukhumaṃ vā hīnaṃ vā paṇītaṃ vā yā dūre santike vā taṃ bhikkhu passati nijjhāyati yoniso kkhati. Tassa taṃ passato nijjhāyato yoniso upaparikkhato rittakaññeva khāyati, tucchakaññeva khāyati, asārakaññeva khāyati. Kiñhi siyā, bhikkhave, saññāya sāro?

Seyyathāpi, bhikkhave, puriso sāratthiko sāragavesī sārapariyesanaṃ caramāno tiṇhaṃ kuṭhāriṃ ādāya vanaṃ paviseyya. So tattha passeyya mahantaṃ kadalikkhandhaṃ ujuṃ navaṃ akukkukajātaṃ. Tamenaṃ mūle chindeyya; mūle chetvā agge chindeyya, agge chetvā pattavaṭṭiṃ vinibbhujeyya. So tassa pattavaṭṭiṃ vinibbhujanto pheggumpi nādhigaccheyya, kuto sāraṃ! Tamenaṃ cakkhumā puriso passeyya nijjhāyeyya yoniso upaparikkheyya. Tassa taṃ passato nijjhāyato yoniso upaparikkhato rittakaññeva khāyeyya, tucchakaññeva āyeyya, asārakaññeva khāyeyya. Kiñhi siyā, bhikkhave, kadalikkhandhe sāro? Evameva kho, bhikkhave, ye keci saṅkhārā atītānāgatapaccuppannā vā bahiddhā vā oḷārikaṃ vā sukhumaṃ vā hīnaṃ vā paṇītaṃ vā ye dūre santike vā taṃ bhikkhu passati nijjhāyati yoniso upaparikkhati. Tassa taṃ passato nijjhāyato yoniso upaparikkhato rittakaññeva khāyati, tucchakaññeva khāyati, asārakaññeva āyati. Kiñhi siyā, bhikkhave, saṅkhāresu sāro?

"Seyyathāpi, bhikkhave, māyākāro vā māyākārantevāsī vā catumahāpathe māyaṃ vidaṃseyya. Tamenaṃ cakkhumā puriso passeyya nijjhāyeyya yoniso upaparikkheyya. Tassa taṃ passato nijjhāyato yoniso upaparikkhato rittakaññeva khāyeyya, tucchakaññeva khāyeyya, asārakaññeva khāyeyya. Kiñhi siyā, bhikkhave, māyāya sāro? Evameva kho, bhikkhave, yaṃ kiñci viññāṇaṃ atītānāgatapaccuppannaṃ vā bahiddhā vā oḷārikaṃ vā sukhumaṃ vā hīnaṃ vā paṇītaṃ vā yaṃ dūre santike vā, taṃ bhikkhu passati nijjhāyati yoniso upaparikkhati. Tassa taṃ passato nijjhāyato yoniso upaparikkhato rittakaññeva khāyati, tucchakaññeva khāyati, asārakaññeva khāyati. Kiñhi siyā, bhikkhave, viññāṇe sāro?

"Evaṃ passaṃ, bhikkhave, sutavā ariyasāvako rūpasmimpi nibbindati, vedanāyapi nibbindati, saññāyapi nibbindati, saṅkhāresupi nibbindati, viññāṇasmimpi nibbindati. Nibbindaṃ virajjati; virāgā vimuccati. Vimuttasmiṃ vimuttamiti ñāṇaṃ hoti: 'khīṇā jāti, vusitaṃ brahmacariyaṃ, kataṃ karaṇīyaṃ, nāparaṃ itthattāyā'ti pajānātī"ti.

Idamavoca bhagavā. Idaṃ vatvāna sugato athāparaṃ etadavoca satthā:

"Pheṇapiṇḍūpamaṃ rūpaṃ, vedanā bubbuḷūpamā;
Marīcikūpamā saññā, saṅkhārā kadalūpamā;
Māyūpamañca viññāṇaṃ, desitādiccabandhunā.

"Yathā yathā nijjhāyati, yoniso upaparikkhati;
Rittakaṃ tucchakaṃ hoti, yo naṃ passati yoniso.

"Imañca kāyaṃ ārabbha, bhūripaññena desitaṃ;
Pahānaṃ tiṇṇaṃ dhammānaṃ, rūpaṃ passatha chaḍḍitaṃ.

"Āyu usmā ca viññāṇaṃ, yadā kāyaṃ jahantimaṃ;
Apaviddho tadā seti, parabhattaṃ acetanaṃ.

"Etādisāyaṃ santāno, māyāyaṃ bālalāpinī;
Vadhako esa akkhāto, sāro ettha na vijjati.

"Evaṃ khandhe avekkheyya, bhikkhu āraddhavīriyo;
Divā vā yadi vā rattiṃ, sampajāno paṭissato.

"Jaheyya sabbasaṃyogaṃ, kareyya saraṇattano;
Careyyādittasīsova, patthayaṃ accutaṃ pada"nti.

Sutta 6 ♦ Glossary

a

a = *negative prefix* (*an* vowel): non°, un°, not, without, lacking, *etc.*

akukkukajāta (adj.), of enormous growth.

akkhāta (ppp. √*khā* + *ā*), proclaimed, called, declared.

agga (n.), top.

ajjhatta (prep.), within, inside.

accuta (adj., n.), steady, resolute; *tech.* = *nibbāna.*

atīta (adj.; ppp. √*i* + *ati*), past, former; passed away.

attan (m.), self, oneself.

atthika (adj.), wanting, desirous.

atha (part.), then.

adhi + √*gam,* find, to acquire, to understand, to realize; to experience.

anāgata (adj.; ppp. √*gam* + *an* + *ā*), future; not come.

antevāsin (m.), student, apprentice.

apa + √*ikkh,* to regard, to consider.

aparaṃ (part.), further, furthermore, besides, again.

api (part.), *adds emphasis to preceding term;* even, even though, also; but.

ayaṃ (m.f. dem. pron.), this, *etc.*

ayujjhā (f.), name of a city.

ariya (adj.), noble, preëminent, superlative.

avekkh°, see apa + √*ikkh.*

√*as,* to be.

asāraka (adj.), insubstantial.

ā

ādāya (abs. *ā* + √*dā*), having taken.

ādicca (m.), the sun.

āditta (ppp. √*dip* + *ā*), blazing, burning, on fire.

ā + √*man,* to address, to speak to.

āyu (n.), life, vitality.

āraddha (ppp. √*rabh* + *ā*), resolved, begun, undertaken.

ā + √*rabh,* begin, undertake. (Line 67, *ārabbha* = abs. used as prep. with acc. = concerning, with reference to, about.)

ā + √*vah,* to produce, to bring forth.

i

itthatta (n.), this state, present condition.

idaṃ (n. dem. pron), this, *etc.*

imaṃ (m.f.n. dem. pron.), this, *etc.*

u

uju (adj.), straight, upright.

ud + √*pad,* to arise, to appear.

udaka (n.), water.

upa + *pari* + √*ikkha,* to investigate, to examine.

upaparikkhant (prap. √*khā* + *upa* + *pari*), investigating, examining.

upama (adj.), like.

usmā (f.), heat.

e

eka (num.; adj.), one; a certain, some.

etaṃ (m.f.n. dem. pron.), this, *etc.* (Line 61, n. *etad* before vowel.)

etādisa (adj.), such, like, of this kind.

ettha (part.), here, in this case.

enaṃ (m.f.n. dem. pron.), him, her, it, that, this, the, *etc.*

eva (part.), *adds emphasis to preceding term;* so, just, even; for sure, with certainty, certainly. (Line 5, *ñeva* = after nasal.)

evaṃ, (part.), thus, so, such, in this way.

esa (m. dem. pron.), this, *etc.*

o

oḷārika (adj.), massive, solid, extensive.

k

kata (ppp. √*kar*), made, done, accomplished.

kadalī (f.), plantain tree. (Line 35, *kadali*°= in compound.)

√*kar,* to do, to make. (Line 59, *karaṇīya* = fpp.)

kāci (f. indef. pron.), whatever, *etc.*

kāya (m.), body.

kuto (part.) from where? how? how then?

kiñci (n. indef. pron.), certain, whatever, *etc.*

kiṃ (n. interrog. pron.), what?, *etc.*

kuṭhārī (f.), ax.

kh

khandha (m.), trunk; complex, bulk, mass, accumulation; *tech.,* the five existential functions of the human being (namely, materialty, sensation, perception, conceptualization, consciousness).

√*khā,* to tell; pass., to seem, to appear.

khīṇa (ppp. √*khi*), destroyed.

kho (encl. part.), indeed, clearly, surely, certainly.

g

gaṇgā (f.), name of a river.

gavesin (adj.), seeking, looking for.

gimha (m.), summer.

c

ca (encl. part.), and.

cakkhumant (adj.), having eyes.

catumahāpatha (m.), town square.

√*car,* to live.

caramāna (prmp.), going, wandering.

cetanā (f.), intention, will, cognizance, mentality.

ch

√*chaḍḍ,* to cast aside, to reject, to leave behind, to throw away.

√*chid,* to cut.

j

jaha°, jaheyya, *see* √hā

jāti (f.), birth, generation.

ñ

ñāṇa (n.), knowledge, recognition, discernment.

ṭh

ṭhita (ppp. √*ṭhā*), stood, standing.

t

taṃ (m.f.n. dem. pron.), him, her, it, that, this, the, *etc.*

taṃ (part.), then, now, so.

tattha (part.), there, that place.

tatra (part.), there.

tadā (part.), then, there.

tassa (m.n. dem. pron.), his, etc.

ti (part.), *marks end of direct speech, a thought, or quoted term.* (Note: A short vowel preceding *ti* is lengthened, and *ṃ* is converted to *n*.)

ti (num.), three. (Line 68, *tiṇṇaṃ* = m.n.gen.)

tiṇha (adj.), sharp.

tīra (n.), bank, shore.

tucchaka (adj.), empty, hollow.

th

thulla (adj.), big, massive.

d

√*das,* to see; *caus.,* to show. (Line 47, *vidaṃs*° = *vidasse*°.)

divā (part.), by day.

dūra (adj.), distant, remote.

deva (m.), rain cloud.

desita (ppp. caus. √*dis*), taught, shown, pointed out, expounded.

dh

dhamma (m.), phenomenon, thing; quality, mental quality, thought; nature; teaching; standard.

n

na (part.), no, not.

naṃ (mfn. dem. pron.), that, *etc.*

nadī (f.), river.

nava (adj.), new, fresh.

ni + √*jhā,* to reflect on.

nibbind° = *ni* + √*vid.*

ni + √*rudh,* to break, to dissolve. (Line 14, *nirujjhati* = pass.)

ni + √*vid,* to be or become disenchanted, weary, disgusted.

p

paccuppanna (adj.), present, existing.

pacchima (adj.), late, last.

pa + √*jān,* to know, to realize.

pañña (adj.), possessing wisdom, endowed with insight.

paṭissata (ppp. √*sar* + *paṭi*), thoughtful, attentive.

paṇīta (ppp. √*nī*), exalted, excellent.

pattavaṭṭi (f.), outer bark (*lit.,* bowl exterior).

√*patth,* to yearn for, to have nostalgia for. (Line 76, *patthaya* = prap.)

pada (n.), path, way, course.

para (adj.; n.), other, another; others.

pariyesanā (f.), search.

paviddha (ppp. √*vyadh* + *pa*), abandoned, thrown down, given up.

pa + √*vis,* to enter, to go.

√*pas,* to see.

pahāna (n.), abandonment, rejection, reliquishment.

pi (encl. part.), even, also, just so, too; but; *adds emphasis to preceding term.*

piṇḍa (m.), ball, round mass.

pubbuḷa (m.), bubble.

purisa (m.), man, person.

pe (part.), abridgement of *peyyāla*: repetition, etcetera.

ph

√*phand,* to shimmer, to vibrate.

phusitaka (m.), rain drop.

pheggu (m.), soft wood, inferior wood.

pheṇa (m.), foam, froth.

b

bandhu (m.), a relative, kinsman. (Line 64, *ādiccabandhunā* = epithet of Gotama.)

bāla (m.), child, fool.

bahiddhā (prep.), external, outside.

bubbuḷa (m.), bubble.

brahmacariya (n.), life of training, the expansive life.

bh

bhagavant (adj.), fortunate, illustrious, honorable; fortunate one: *epithet of Gotama.*

bhatta (m.), food, nourishment, meal.

bhikkhu (m.), mendicant; *tech.*, beggar.

√*bhū,* be, to become; to cultivate, to nurture, to develop.

bhūri (adj.), extensive, abundant, much, vast.

m

majjhantika (m.), mid-day, noon.

marīcikā (f.), mirage.

mahant (adj.), large, great, extensive.

māyā (f.), trick, illusion, deception.

māyākāra (m.), magician.

māsa (m.), month.

mūla (n.), root.

y

yaṃ (mfn. rel. pron.), that which, *etc.*

yathā (part.), as.

yadā (part.), when.

yadi (part.), if.

yā (f. rel. pron.), which, that which, *etc.*

yo (m. rel. pron.), he who, that which, *etc.*

yoniso (part.), thoroughly, carefully, judiciously.

r

ratti (f.), night.

rittaka (adj.), empty, void.

rūpa (n.), form, appearance, body, object.

l

lāpin (adj.), talking foolishly, talking charmingly.

v

√*vac,* to speak. (Line 61, *avoca* = aor.; *vatvāna* = abs.)

vatvāna, see √*vac.*

vadhaka (m.), killer.

vana (n.), grove, wood.

√*vass,* to rain.

vā (encl. part.), or.

viññāṇa, (n.), cognizance, consciousness, cognition.

√*vid,* to find; to be. (Line 72, *vijjati*= pass.)

vidaṃseyya, see √das.

vi + *ni* + √*bhuj,* to cut, to remove, to separate.

vi + √*muc,* to be liberated, to be released, to be freed.

vimutta (ppp. √*muc* + *vi*), liberated, released, freed.

vi + √*raj,* to disengage, to free; *tech*., discard infatuation (*rāga*).

virāga (m.), dispassion, detachment.

vi + √*har,* to live, to stay, to dwell, to abide.

vīriya (n.), vigor, virility, energy, effort.

vusita (ppp. √*vas*), lived.

vedanā (f.), feeling, sensation.

s

saṃyoga (m.), restraint, bond, fetter, attachment, limitation.

saṅkhāra (m.), mental formation, conceptual fabrication; volition, will; anything made, conditioned, fashioned, constructed or put together.

satthar (ag.n.), teacher

santāna (m.), continuum, continuity, extension.

santika (adj.), near, at hand.

sabba (adj.), all, every.

samaya (m.), time, occasion.

sampajāna (adj.), attentive, conscientious, thoughtful, fully comprehending.

sarada (m.), autumn.

saraṇa (n.), shelter, refuge.

sāra (m.), substance, essence; heartwood.

sāvaka (m.), student, disciple, practitioner.

siyā, see √as.

√*sī,* to lie.

sīsa (n.), head.

sukhuma (adj.), subtle, minute, fine.

sugata (adj.), well, happy; *lit*., well-faring; *epithet of Gotama.*

sutavant (adj.), learned.

sutta (n.), discourse; *lit.,* thread, stitching, textile.

seyyathā (part.), as if, just as.

so (m. dem. pron.), he, that, the, *etc.*

h

√*hā,* to leave, to abandon, to give up, to be devoid of.

hi (part.), surely, indeed.

hīna (adj.; ppp. √*hā*), lowly, inferior.

hoti = √*bhū.*

Sutta 7

Anattalakkhaṇasuttaṃ

(Saṃyuttanikāya 3.1.6.7.59)

Ekaṃ samayaṃ bhagavā bārāṇasiyaṃ viharati isipatane migadāye. Tatra kho bhagavā pañcavaggiye bhikkhū āmantesi – "bhikkhavo"ti. "Bhadante"ti te bhikkhū bhagavato paccassosuṃ. Bhagavā etadavoca –

"Rūpaṃ, bhikkhave, anattā. Rūpañca hidaṃ, bhikkhave, attā abhavissa, nayidaṃ rūpaṃ ābādhāya saṃvatteyya, labbhetha ca rūpe – 'evaṃ me rūpaṃ hotu, evaṃ me rūpaṃ mā ahosī'ti. Yasmā ca kho, bhikkhave, rūpaṃ anattā, tasmā rūpaṃ ābādhāya saṃvattati, na ca labbhati rūpe – 'evaṃ me rūpaṃ hotu, evaṃ me rūpaṃ mā ahosī'"ti. "Vedanā anattā. Vedanā ca hidaṃ, bhikkhave, attā abhavissa, nayidaṃ vedanā ābādhāya saṃvatteyya, labbhetha ca vedanāya – 'evaṃ me vedanā hotu, evaṃ me vedanā mā ahosī'ti. Yasmā ca kho, bhikkhave, vedanā anattā, tasmā vedanā ābādhāya saṃvattati, na ca labbhati vedanāya – 'evaṃ me vedanā hotu, evaṃ me vedanā mā ahosī'"ti.

"Saññā anattā...pe... saṅkhārā anattā. Saṅkhārā ca hidaṃ, bhikkhave, attā abhavissaṃsu, nayidaṃ saṅkhārā ābādhāya saṃvatteyyuṃ, labbhetha ca saṅkhāresu – 'evaṃ me saṅkhārā hontu, evaṃ me saṅkhārā mā ahesu'nti. Yasmā ca kho, bhikkhave, saṅkhārā anattā, tasmā saṅkhārā ābādhāya saṃvattanti, na ca labbhati saṅkhāresu – 'evaṃ me saṅkhārā hontu, evaṃ me saṅkhārā mā ahesu'"nti.

"Viññāṇaṃ anattā. Viññāṇañca hidaṃ, bhikkhave, attā abhavissa, nayidaṃ viññāṇaṃ ābādhāya saṃvatteyya, labbhetha ca viññāṇe – 'evaṃ me viññāṇaṃ hotu, evaṃ me viññāṇaṃ mā ahosī'ti. Yasmā ca kho, bhikkhave, viññāṇaṃ anattā, tasmā viññāṇaṃ ābādhāya saṃvattati, na ca labbhati viññāṇe – 'evaṃ me viññāṇaṃ hotu, evaṃ me viññāṇaṃ mā ahosī'"ti.

"Taṃ kiṃ maññatha, bhikkhave, rūpaṃ niccaṃ vā aniccaṃ vā"ti? "Aniccaṃ, bhante". "Yaṃ panāniccaṃ dukkhaṃ vā taṃ sukhaṃ vā"ti? "Dukkhaṃ, bhante". "Yaṃ panāniccaṃ dukkhaṃ vipariṇāmadhammaṃ, kallaṃ nu taṃ samanupassituṃ – 'etaṃ mama, esohamasmi, eso me attā'"ti? "No hetaṃ, bhante". "Vedanā... saññā... saṅkhārā... viññāṇaṃ niccaṃ vā aniccaṃ vā"ti? "Aniccaṃ, bhante". "Yaṃ panāniccaṃ dukkhaṃ vā taṃ sukhaṃ vā"ti? "Dukkhaṃ, bhante". "Yaṃ panāniccaṃ dukkhaṃ vipariṇāmadhammaṃ, kallaṃ nu taṃ samanupassituṃ – 'etaṃ mama, esohamasmi, eso me attā'"ti? "No hetaṃ, bhante".

"Tasmātiha, bhikkhave, yaṃ kiñci rūpaṃ atītānāgatapaccuppannaṃ ajjhattaṃ vā bahiddhā vā oḷārikaṃ vā sukhumaṃ vā hīnaṃ vā paṇītaṃ vā yaṃ dūre santike vā, sabbaṃ rūpaṃ – 'netaṃ mama, nesohamasmi, na meso attā'ti evametaṃ yathābhūtaṃ sammappaññāya daṭṭhabbaṃ. Yā kāci vedanā atītānāgatapaccuppannā ajjhattā vā bahiddhā vā...pe... yā dūre santike vā, sabbā vedanā – 'netaṃ mama, nesohamasmi, na meso attā'ti evametaṃ yathābhūtaṃ sammappaññāya daṭṭhabbaṃ.

"Yā kāci saññā...pe... ye keci saṅkhārā atītānāgatapaccuppannā ajjhattaṃ vā bahiddhā vā...pe... ye dūre santike vā, sabbe saṅkhārā – 'netaṃ mama, nesohamasmi, na meso attā'ti evametaṃ yathābhūtaṃ sammappaññāya daṭṭhabbaṃ.

"Yaṃ kiñci viññāṇaṃ atītānāgatapaccuppannaṃ ajjhattaṃ vā bahiddhā vā oḷārikaṃ vā sukhumaṃ vā hīnaṃ vā paṇītaṃ vā yaṃ dūre santike vā,

sabbaṃ viññāṇaṃ – 'netaṃ mama, nesohamasmi, na meso attā'ti evametaṃ yathābhūtaṃ sammappaññāya daṭṭhabbaṃ.

"Evaṃ passaṃ, bhikkhave, sutavā ariyasāvako rūpasmimpi nibbindati, vedanāyapi nibbindati, saññāyapi nibbindati, saṅkhāresupi nibbindati, viññāṇasmimpi nibbindati. Nibbindaṃ virajjati; virāgā vimuccati. Vimuttasmiṃ vimuttamiti ñāṇaṃ hoti. 'Khīṇā jāti, vusitaṃ brahmacariyaṃ, kataṃ karaṇīyaṃ, nāparaṃ itthattāyā'ti pajānātī"ti.

Idamavoca bhagavā. Attamanā pañcavaggiyā bhikkhū bhagavato bhāsitaṃ abhinanduṃ.

Imasmiñca pana veyyākaraṇasmiṃ bhaññamāne pañcavaggiyānaṃ bhikkhūnaṃ anupādāya āsavehi cittāni vimucciṃsūti.

Sutta 7 ♦ Glossary

a

ajjhattaṃ (part.), in, inner, subjective, within oneself.

atīta (adj.; ppp. √*i* + *ati*), past, former; passed away.

attan (m.), self, oneself.

attamana (m.), exalted, upraised mind.

anattan (m.; adj.) self; insubstantial, lacking essence.

anāgata (adj.; ppp. √*gam* + *an* + *ā*), future; not come.

anicca (adj.), inconstant, unstable, impermanent.

an + *upa* + *ā* + √*dā,* to let go, not to take, not to grasp.

apara (pr. adj.), other, another.

abhavissa, see√*bhū.*

abhi + √*nand,* to rejoice at, to delight in, to enjoy oneself, to approve of.

ariya (adj., n.), noble, ideal, excellent, preëminent; noble one.

√*as,* to be.

ahaṃ (1stpers. per. pron.), I.

ahosi, see √*bhū.*

ā

ābādha (m.), affliction, distress, disease.

ā + √*mant,* to address, to advise.

āsava (m.), habitual impulse, effluent, toxin.

i

√*i,* to go.

itthatta (n.), this state, present condition.

idaṃ (n. dem. pron.), this, etc.

idaṃ (part.), here, now.

isipatana (m.), place name.

iha (part.), here, in this case, in this instance.

e

eka (num.; adj.), one; a certain, some.

etaṃ (m.f.n. dem. pron.), this, *etc.* (Line 3, n. *etad* before vowel.)

evaṃ, (part.), thus, so, such, in this way; yes.

esa (m. dem. pron.), this, etc. (Usually before a personal pron.; e.g. *esoham.*)

o

oḷārika (adj.), massive, solid, extensive.

k

kata (ppp. √*kar*), made, done, created.

√*kar,* to do, to make. (Line 52, *karaṇīya* = fpp.)

kallaṃ nu (part.), is it correct?

kāci (f. indef. pron.), whatever, *etc.*

kiṃ (n. interrog. pron.), who? which? what?, *etc.*

kiṃ (part.) = *question marker.*

kiñci (n. indef. pron.), whatever, somewhat, *etc.;* with negation = nothing whatsoever, not at all, *etc.*

kh

√*khi,* to destroy.

khīṇa (ppp. √*khi*), destroyed.

kho (encl. part.), indeed, clearly, surely, certainly.

g

√*gam,* to go.

c

ca (encl. part.), and.

citta (n.), mind, discursive thought, discursive mind.

j

jāti (f.), generation, birth.

ñ

āṇa (n.), knowledge, recognition, discernment.

t

taṃ (part.), now, so, then.

taṃ (m.f.n. dem. pron.), him, her, it, that, this, the, *etc.*

tatra (part.), there.

tasmā (part.), therefore. (Note: *t* before following vowel: *tasmāt.*)

ti (part.), *marks end of direct speech, a thought, or quoted term.* (Note: A short vowel preceding *ti* is lengthened, and *ṃ* is converted to *n.*)

te (2nd pers. per. pron.; m. dem. pron.), by you, yours, to you (sg.); those, them, *etc.*

d

√*das,* to see. (Line 37, *daṭṭhabba* = fpp.)

√*dā,* to give.

dāya (m.), grove, park.

dukkha (n.; adj.), unease, distress, trouble, unhappiness, pain; distressful, painful, troublesome.

dūra (adj.), distant.

dh

dhamma (m.), thing, object, phenomenon; teaching; right, correct.

n

na (part.), not, no. (Line 5: *nayidaṃ,* euphonic *y.*)

nicca (adj.), constant, stable, permanent.

nibbind° = *ni* + √*vid.*

ni + √*vid,* to be/become disenchanted, to be/become weary, to be/become disgusted.

√*nī,* to lead.

no hi (part.), indeed not.

p

pacca + √*su,* to respond.

paccuppanna (ppp. √*pad* +*paṭi* + *ud*), present, existing.

pa + √*ñā,* to know, to understand.

pañca (num.) five.

paṇīta (ppp. √*nī*), exalted, excellent.

pana (encl. part.), but, however; moreover; now (continuing particle).

√*pas,* to see.

pi (encl. part.), even, also, just so, too; but; *adds emphasis to preceding term.*

pe (part.), abridgement of *peyyāla*: repetition, etcetera.

b

bahiddhā (part.), outside, externally.

bārāṇasī (f.), place name: Varanasi/Benaras.

brahmacariya (n.), worthy life, exalted life, expansive life, life lived according to Gotama's teachings.

bh

bhagavant (adj.), fortunate, illustrious, honorable; fortunate one: *epithet of Gotama.*

bhadante (ind.), *form of respectful address, like E.* sir.

√*bhaṇ,* to speak (Line 56, *bhaññamāna* = prpp.)

bhante (ind.), *form of respectful address, like E.* sir.

√*bhās,* to speak.

bhāsita (n.), speech, words.

bhikkhu (m.), mendicant; *tech.,* beggar.

√*bhū,* be, to become; to cultivate, to nurture, to develop. (Line 5, *abhavissa* = cond.)

m

√*man,* to think, to consider.

mama (1st pers. per. pron.), mine, etc.

mā (part.), not, no.

miga (m.), deer, wild animal.

me (1st pers. per. pron.), me, my, mine, *etc.*

y

yaṃ (n. rel. pron.), that, which, that which, etc.

yathābhūtaṃ (part.), as is; in reality.

yasmā (part.), because, since.

yā (f. rel. pron.), who, which, that, etc.

r

rasa (m.), taste.

rūpa (n.), form, appearance, body.

l

lakkhaṇa (n.), sign, quality, feature, characteristic.

√*labh,* to obtain, to acquire, to get; pass. *labbha* = be possible.

v

vaggiya (m.; adj.), group.

√*vac,* to say, to speak. (Line 3, *avoca* = aor.)

√*vas,* to live, to dwell.

vā (encl. part.), or.

viññāṇa, (n.), cognizance, consciousness, cognition.

vipariṇāma (m.), change.

vi + √*muc,* to be liberated, to be released, to be freed.

vimutta (ppp. √*muc* + *vi*), liberated, released, freed.

vi + √*raj,* to be free from, to detach oneself from, to be disinterested in.

virāga (m.), dispassion, disinterest, lack of desire, detatchment.

vi + √*har,* dwell, to live, to stay.

vusita (ppp. √*vas*), lived.

vedanā (f.), feeling, sensation.

veyyākaraṇa (n.), exposition, discourse.

s

saṃ + *anu* + √*pas,* to see, to regard.

saṃ + √*vatt,* lead.

saṅkhāra (m.), mental formation, conceptual fabrication; volition, will; anything made, conditioned, fashioned, constructed or put together.

saññā (f.), perception.

santika (adj.), near at hand, present.

sabba (adj.), every, all, entire.

samaya (m.), time, occasion.

sammappaññā (f.), sound knowledge.

sammā (part.), sound, right, correct, thorough, complete. (Note: *ā* > *a* before short vowel, with insertion of *d* or doubling of consonant.)

sāvaka (m.), student, disciple, practitioner.

sukha (n.; adj.), ease, serenity, harmony, happiness, pleasure; gratifying, pleasurable, harmonious.

sukhuma (adj.), subtle, minute, fine.

sutavant (adj. m.), trained, learned.

sutta (n.), discourse; *lit.,* thread, stitching, textile.

h

hi (part.), because, indeed, for. (With *idaṃ* = *hidaṃ*.)

hīna (adj.; ppp. √*hā*), inconsequential, lowly, inferior.

hoti, hotu, see √*bhū.*

Sutta 8

Bhārasuttaṃ

(*Saṃyuttanikāya* 3.1.3.1.22)

Evaṃ me sutaṃ – ekaṃ samayaṃ bhagavā sāvatthiyaṃ viharati jetavane anāthapiṇḍikassa ārāme. Tatra kho bhagavā bhikkhū āmantesi – "bhikkhavo"ti: "bhārañca vo, bhikkhave, desessāmi bhārahārañca bhārādānañca bhāranikkhepanañca. Taṃ suṇātha. Katamo ca, bhikkhave, bhāro? Pañcupādānakkhandhā tissa vacanīyaṃ. Katame pañca? Rūpupādānakkhandho, vedanupādānakkhandho, saññupādānakkhandho, saṅkhārupādānakkhandho, viññāṇupādānakkhandho; ayaṃ vuccati, bhikkhave, bhāro."

"Katamo ca, bhikkhave, bhārahāro? Puggalo tissa vacanīyaṃ. Yvāyaṃ āyasmā evaṃnāmo evaṃgotto; ayaṃ vuccati, bhikkhave, bhārahāro.

"Katamañca, bhikkhave, bhārādānaṃ? Yāyaṃ taṇhā ponobhavikā nandīrāgasahagatā tatratatrābhinandinī, seyyathidaṃ – kāmataṇhā, bhavataṇhā, vibhavataṇhā. Idaṃ vuccati, bhikkhave, bhārādānaṃ.

"Katamañca, bhikkhave, bhāranikkhepanaṃ? Yo tassāyeva taṇhāya asesavirāganirodho cāgo paṭinissaggo mutti anālayo. Idaṃ vuccati, bhikkhave, bhāranikkhepana"nti.

Idamavoca bhagavā. Idaṃ vatvāna sugato athāparaṃ etadavoca satthā –

“Bhārā have pañcakkhandhā, bhārahāro ca puggalo;
Bhārādānaṃ dukhaṃ loke, bhāranikkhepanaṃ sukhaṃ.

“Nikkhipitvā garuṃ bhāraṃ, aññaṃ bhāraṃ anādiya;
Samūlaṃ taṇhamabbuyha, nicchāto parinibbuto.”

Sutta 8 ♦ Glossary

a

añña (pr. adj.), other, another.

an = *negative prefix* (*a* before consonant): non°, un°, not, without, lacking, *etc.*

anāthapiṇḍika (m.), *personal name.*

anālaya (m.n.), non-attachment, detachment, doing away with, letting go.

abbuyha, see ā + √*barh.*

abhi + √*nand*, to rejoice, to take delight, to be glad.

ayaṃ (m.f. dem. pron.), this, *etc.*

asesa (adj.), without remainder, complete, whole, entire.

ā

ā + √*dā*, to take hold, to grasp, to take up. (Line 19, °*ādiya* = abs.)

ādāna (n.), taking, grasping, seizing, clinging to, attachment.

ā + √*barh*, to pull out, to lift away, to take away. (Line 20, *abbuyha* = abs.)

ā + √*man*, to address, to speak to.

āyasmant (adj.), venerable.

ārāma (m.), park, garden.

i

idaṃ (n. dem. pron), this, *etc.*

u

upādā (f.), grasping, clenching, taking.

e

eka (num.; adj.), one; a certain, some.

etaṃ (m.f.n. dem. pron.), this, *etc.* (Line 16, n. *etad* before vowel.)

evaṃ, (part.), thus, so, such, in this way; yes.

k

katama (m.f.n. interg. pron.), which (of several)?, *etc.*

kāma (m.n.), desire, sensory pleasure, passion.

kh

khandha (m.), trunk; complex, bulk, mass, accumulation; *tech.*, the five existential functions of the human being (namely, materialty, sensation, perception, conceptualization, consciousness).

kho (encl. part.), indeed, clearly, surely, certainly.

g

garu (adj.), heavy.

gotta (n.), family lineage, clan.

c

ca (encl. part.), and.

cāga (m.), abandoning, giving up, renunciation.

j

jeta (m.), *personal name.*

t

taṃ (m.f.n. dem. pron.), him, her, it, that, this, the, *etc.*

taṇhā (f.), thirst, craving, compulsive longing.

tatra (part.), there.

tassāya (f. dem. pron.), to this, of this, *etc.*.

ti (part.), marks end of direct speech, a thought, or quoted term.

d

√*dis*, to show; *caus.* to teach, to declare; to point to, to point out.

dukha (adj.), painful, troublesome, unreliable, upsetting.

n

nandī (f.), enjoyment, pleasure, delight.

nāma (n.), name; *tech.* mental functions, e.g. feeling, perception, conceptualization, intention, attentiveness.

ni + √*khip*, to put down, to throw down, to abandon, to eliminate.

nikkhepa (m.), putting dowm, laying down, discarding, abandoning, eliminating.

nikkhepana (n.) putting down, laying down, discarding, abandoning, eliminating.

nicchāta (adj.), stilled, satisfied, having no cravings, having no hunger, sated.

nirodha (m.), cessation, ending, stopping.

p

pañca (num.), five.

paṭinissagga (m.), giving up, relinquishment, renunciation, forsaking.

parinibbuta (adj.), at peace, completely calmed, cooled, released.

puggala (m.), person.

ponobhavika (adj.), leading to further becoming, leading to rebirth.

bh

bhagavant (adj.), fortunate, illustrious, honorable; fortunate one: *epithet of Gotama.*

bhava (m.), becoming, being, existence, life.

bhāra (m.), load, burden, enumbrance.

bhikkhu (m.), mendicant; *lit.* beggar.

m

mutti (f.), freedom, liberation, release.

mūla (n.), root.

me (1st pers. per. pron.), me, by me, *etc.*

y

yā (f. rel. pron.), which, that which, *etc.*

yo (m. rel. pron.), who, he who, one who, *etc.* (Line 8, *yvāyaṃ* = *yo ayaṃ*.)

r

rāga (m.), passion, excitement, infatuation, lust.

rūpa (n.), form, appearance, body, object.

l

loka (m.), world.

v

√*vac*, to speak. (Line 5, *vacanīya* = fpp.; line 7, *vuccati* = pass.; line 16, *avoca* = aor.; line 16, *vatvāna* = abs.)

vana (n.), grove, wood.

viññāṇa, (n.), cognizance, consciousness, cognition.

vibhava (m.), non-existence, annihilation, cessation of life.

virāga (m.), dispassion, detatchment.

vi + √*har*, to live, to stay, to dwell, to abide.

vedanā (f.), feeling, sensation.

vo (2nd pers. per. pron.), you, *etc.*

s

sa (m. pers. pron.), he, it, that, *etc.*

sa, *prefix denoting* with, possessed of, having, together with.

saṅkhāra (m.), mental formation, conceptual fabrication; volition, will; anything made, conditioned, fashioned, constructed or put together.

saññā (f.), perception.

satthar (ag.n.), teacher.

samaya (m.), time, occasion.

sahagata (adj.), accompanying, concomitant with, connected with, associated with.

sāvatthi (f.), *place name.*

√*su*, to hear, to listen.

sukha (n.; adj.), ease, serenity, harmony, happiness, pleasure; gratifying, pleasant, agreeable, harmonious.

sugata (adj.), well, happy; *lit.*, well-faring; *epithet of Gotama.*

suta (ppp. √*su*), heard.

sutta (n.), discourse, dialogue, text; *lit.*, thread, stitching, textile.

seyyathidaṃ (part.), as follows, namely.

h

have (part.), indeed, certainly, *adds emphasis to preceeding word.*

hāra (m.), (in compound with *bhāra*) carrier, bearer, holder, possessor.

Sutta 9

Dhammacakkappavattanasuttaṃ

(*Saṃyuttanikāya* 5.12.2.1.1081)

Ekaṃ samayaṃ bhagavā bārāṇasiyaṃ viharati isipatane migadāye. Tatra kho bhagavā pañcavaggiye bhikkhū āmantesi – "dveme, bhikkhave, antā pabbajitena na sevitabbā. Katame dve? Yo cāyaṃ kāmesu kāmasukhallikānuyogo hīno gammo pothujjaniko anariyo anatthasaṃhito, yo cāyaṃ attakilamathānuyogo dukkho anariyo anatthasaṃhito. Ete kho, bhikkhave, ubho ante anupagamma majjhimā paṭipadā tathāgatena abhisambuddhā cakkhukaraṇī ñāṇakaraṇī upasamāya abhiññāya sambodhāya nibbānāya saṃvattati."

"Katamā ca sā, bhikkhave, majjhimā paṭipadā tathāgatena abhisambuddhā cakkhukaraṇī ñāṇakaraṇī upasamāya abhiññāya sambodhāya nibbānāya saṃvattati? Ayameva ariyo aṭṭhaṅgiko maggo, seyyathidaṃ – sammādiṭṭhi sammāsaṅkappo sammāvācā sammākammanto sammāājīvo sammāvāyāmo sammāsati sammāsamādhi. Ayaṃ kho sā, bhikkhave, majjhimā paṭipadā tathāgatena abhisambuddhā cakkhukaraṇī ñāṇakaraṇī upasamāya abhiññāya sambodhāya nibbānāya saṃvattati.

"Idaṃ kho pana, bhikkhave, dukkhaṃ ariyasaccaṃ – jātipi dukkhā, jarāpi dukkhā, byādhipi dukkho, maraṇampi dukkhaṃ, appiyehi sampayogo dukkho, piyehi vippayogo dukkho, yampicchaṃ na labhati tampi dukkhaṃ – saṅkhittena pañcupādānakkhandhā dukkhā. Idaṃ kho pana, bhikkhave, dukkhasamudayaṃ ariyasaccaṃ – yāyaṃ taṇhā ponobbhavikā nandirāgasahagatā

tatratatrābhinandinī, seyyathidaṃ – kāmataṇhā, bhavataṇhā, vibhavataṇhā. Idaṃ kho pana, bhikkhave, dukkhanirodhaṃ ariyasaccaṃ – yo tassāyeva taṇhāya asesavirāganirodho cāgo paṭinissaggo mutti anālayo. Idaṃ kho pana, bhikkhave, dukkhanirodhagāminī paṭipadā ariyasaccaṃ – ayameva ariyo aṭṭhaṅgiko maggo, seyyathidaṃ – sammādiṭṭhi...pe... sammāsamādhi.

"'Idaṃ dukkhaṃ ariyasacca'nti me, bhikkhave, pubbe ananussutesu dhammesu cakkhuṃ udapādi, ñāṇaṃ udapādi, paññā udapādi, vijjā udapādi, āloko udapādi. 'Taṃ kho panidaṃ dukkhaṃ ariyasaccaṃ pariññeyya'nti me, bhikkhave, pubbe...pe... udapādi. 'Taṃ kho panidaṃ dukkhaṃ ariyasaccaṃ pariññāta'nti me, bhikkhave, pubbe ananussutesu dhammesu cakkhuṃ udapādi, ñāṇaṃ udapādi, paññā udapādi, vijjā udapādi, āloko udapādi.

"'Idaṃ dukkhasamudayaṃ ariyasacca'nti me, bhikkhave, pubbe ananussutesu dhammesu cakkhuṃ udapādi, ñāṇaṃ udapādi, paññā udapādi, vijjā udapādi, āloko udapādi. 'Taṃ kho panidaṃ dukkhasamudayaṃ ariyasaccaṃ pahātabba'nti me, bhikkhave, pubbe...pe... udapādi. 'Taṃ kho panidaṃ dukkhasamudayaṃ ariyasaccaṃ pahīna'nti me, bhikkhave, pubbe ananussutesu dhammesu cakkhuṃ udapādi, ñāṇaṃ udapādi, paññā udapādi, vijjā udapādi, āloko udapādi.

"'Idaṃ dukkhanirodhaṃ ariyasacca'nti me, bhikkhave, pubbe ananussutesu dhammesu cakkhuṃ udapādi, ñāṇaṃ udapādi, paññā udapādi, vijjā udapādi, āloko udapādi. 'Taṃ kho panidaṃ dukkhanirodhaṃ ariyasaccaṃ sacchikātabba'nti me, bhikkhave, pubbe...pe... udapādi. 'Taṃ kho panidaṃ dukkhanirodhaṃ ariyasaccaṃ sacchikata'nti me, bhikkhave, pubbe ananussutesu dhammesu cakkhuṃ udapādi, ñāṇaṃ udapādi, paññā udapādi, vijjā udapādi, āloko udapādi.

"'Idaṃ dukkhanirodhagāminī paṭipadā ariyasacca'nti me, bhikkhave, pubbe ananussutesu dhammesu cakkhuṃ udapādi, ñāṇaṃ udapādi, paññā udapādi,

vijjā udapādi, āloko udapādi. Taṃ kho panidaṃ dukkhanirodhagāminī paṭipadā ariyasaccaṃ bhāvetabba'nti me, bhikkhave, pubbe ...pe... udapādi. 'Taṃ kho panidaṃ dukkhanirodhagāminī paṭipadā ariyasaccaṃ bhāvita'nti me, bhikkhave, pubbe ananussutesu dhammesu cakkhuṃ udapādi, ñāṇaṃ udapādi, paññā udapādi, vijjā udapādi, āloko udapādi.

"'Yāvakīvañca me, bhikkhave, imesu catūsu ariyasaccesu evaṃ tiparivaṭṭaṃ dvādasākāraṃ yathābhūtaṃ ñāṇadassanaṃ na suvisuddhaṃ ahosi, neva tāvāhaṃ, bhikkhave, sadevake loke samārake sabrahmake sassamaṇabrāhmaṇiyā pajāya sadevamanussāya 'anuttaraṃ sammāsambodhiṃ abhisambuddho'ti paccaññāsiṃ.

"'Yato ca kho me, bhikkhave, imesu catūsu ariyasaccesu evaṃ tiparivaṭṭaṃ dvādasākāraṃ yathābhūtaṃ ñāṇadassanaṃ suvisuddhaṃ ahosi, athāhaṃ, bhikkhave, sadevake loke samārake sabrahmake sassamaṇabrāhmaṇiyā pajāya sadevamanussāya 'anuttaraṃ sammāsambodhiṃ abhisambuddho'ti paccaññāsiṃ. Ñāṇañca pana me dassanaṃ udapādi – 'akuppā me vimutti, ayamantimā jāti, natthidāni punabbhavo'"ti. Idamavoca bhagavā. Attamanā pañcavaggiyā bhikkhū bhagavato bhāsitaṃ abhinandunti.

Imasmiñca pana veyyākaraṇasmiṃ bhaññamāne āyasmato koṇḍaññassa virajaṃ vītamalaṃ dhammacakkhuṃ udapādi – "yaṃ kiñci samudayadhammaṃ, sabbaṃ taṃ nirodhadhamma"nti.

Pavattite ca pana bhagavatā dhammacakke bhummā devā saddamanussāvesuṃ – "etaṃ bhagavatā bārāṇasiyaṃ isipatane migadāye anuttaraṃ dhammacakkaṃ pavattitaṃ appaṭivattiyaṃ samaṇena vā brāhmaṇena vā devena vā mārena vā brahmunā vā kenaci vā lokasmi"nti. Bhummānaṃ devānaṃ saddaṃ sutvā cātumahārājikā devā saddamanussāvesuṃ – "etaṃ bhagavatā bārāṇasiyaṃ isipatane migadāye anuttaraṃ dhammacakkaṃ pavattitaṃ, appaṭivattiyaṃ samaṇena vā brāhmaṇena vā devena vā mārena vā brahmunā vā kenaci

vā lokasmi"nti. Cātumahārājikānaṃ devānaṃ saddaṃ sutvā tāvatiṃsā devā ...pe... yāmā devā ...pe... tusitā devā ...pe... nimmānaratī devā ...pe... paranimmitavasavattī devā...pe... brahmakāyikā devā saddamanussāvesuṃ – "etaṃ bhagavatā bārāṇasiyaṃ isipatane migadāye anuttaraṃ dhammacakkaṃ pavattitaṃ appaṭivattiyaṃ samaṇena vā brāhmaṇena vā devena vā mārena vā brahmunā vā kenaci vā lokasmi"nti.

Itiha tena khaṇena tena layena tena muhuttena yāva brahmalokā saddo abbhuggacchi. Ayañca dasasahassilokadhātu saṅkampi sampakampi sampavedhi, appamāṇo ca uḷāro obhāso loke pāturahosi atikkamma devānaṃ devānubhāvanti.

Atha kho bhagavā imaṃ udānaṃ udānesi – "aññāsi vata, bho, koṇḍañño, aññāsi vata, bho, koṇḍañño"ti! Iti hidaṃ āyasmato koṇḍaññassa 'aññāsikoṇḍañño' tveva nāmaṃ ahosīti.

Sutta 9 ♦ Glossary

a

a = *negative prefix* (*an* before vowel): non°, un°, not, without, lacking, *etc.*

akuppa (adj.; fpp. √*kup* + *a*), sure, safe, steadfast, immoveable; not to be shaken.

aṭṭha (num.), eight.

aṅgika (adj.), °fold, consisting of parts.

atikkamma (adj.), difficult to exceed, hard to pass.

atta (m.; reflexive pron.), self; oneself.

attamana (adj.), delighted, pleased, content.

atthasaṃhita (adj.), beneficial, profitable, meaningful.

atthi, see √*as.*

atha (part.), then.

an = *negative prefix* (*a* before consonant): non°, un°, not, without, lacking, *etc.*

anuttara (adj.), unsurpassed, unexcelled, excellent, supreme.

anu +√*bhū*, to experience, to attain, to enjoy, to share in, to partake of.

anuyoga (m.), question, examination, enquiry; application, devotion to, practice, pursuit.

anu +√*su*, *caus.* = to cry out, to proclaim to speak repeatedly. (Line 67, *sāvesuṃ* = aor.)

anussuta (adj.), heard of, known, identified.

antima (adj.), last, final.

anta (m.), end, opposite, extreme, goal.

appamāṇa (adj.), immeasurable, limitless, boundless, all-permeating.

appaṭivattiya (adj., neg. fpp. √*vatt* + *paṭi*), not to be turned back, not to be rolled back, not to be blocked, unpreventable, irresistible.

abhi + *ud* +√*gam*, to go forth, to go out, to rise, to spread about.

abhiññā (f.), direct knowledge, wisdom.

abhi + √*nand*, to rejoice, to take delight, to be glad.

abhinandin (adj.), rejoicing at, taking pleasure in, finding delight in.

abhisambuddha (ppp. √*budh* + *abhi* + *saṃ*), completely understood, thoroughly realized, attained full awakening.

ayaṃ (m.f. dem. pron.), this, *etc.*

ariya (adj.), noble, preëminent, superlative, praiseworthy.

√*as*, to be. (Line 62, *natthi*° = *na* + *atthi.*)

ahaṃ (1st pers. per. pron.), I.

ahosi, *see* √*bhū*.

ā

ājiva (m.), livelihood, occupation, means of subsistence.

ā + √*mant*, to address, to advise.

āyasmant (adj.), venerable.

ālaya (m.n.), holding, clinging, attachment.

āloka (m.), seeing, vision, understanding.

i

icchā (f.), wish, want, desire, long for.

itiha (part.), thus, so it seems, according to tradition.

idaṃ (n. dem. pron.), this, *etc.*

idāni (adv.), now.

imaṃ (m.f.n. dem. pron.), this, *etc.*

imasmiṃ (m.n. dem. pron.), in this, while this, *etc.*

ime (m. dem. pron.), these, *etc.*

isipatana (m.), *place name.*

u

udāna (m.n.), *inspired comment, joyful utterance, stirring speech.* (Line 84, *udānesi* = aor. of denominative of *udāna*: to utter joyfully, *etc.*)

ud + √*pad*, to arise, to originate, to come into existence, to occur. (Line 26, *udapādi* = aor.)

upa + √*gam*, to participate in, to enter on, to make the choice of. (Line 5, °*upagamma* = abs.)

upādāna (n.), taking, grasping, appropriating; material support, fuel.

upasama (m.), calmness, peace, tranquility.

ubho (adj.), both.

uḷāra (adj.) great, magnificent, excellent.

e

eka (num.; adj.), one; a certain, some.

ete (m. dem. pron.), these, *etc.*

eva (part.), *adds emphasis to preceding term*; so, just, even.

o

obhāsa (m.), light, luster, splendor, effulgence.

k

ka, *a suffix designating a group, forming an adjective, or added to bahuvrīhi compounds.*

katama (m.f.n. interg. pron.), which? what?, *etc.*

kammanta (m.), action, feat, business.

karaṇī (f.), making, doing, effecting, causing, creating.

kāma (m.n.), desire, sensory pleasure, passion.

kāra (m.), *marks grammatical, phonetic, or numerical itemization.*

kiñci (n. indef. pron.), certain, some, *etc.*; *with negation*, whatsoever, *etc.*

kilamatha (m.), exhaustion, over-exertion, mortification.

kīva (adv.), how.

kenaci (m.n. indef. pron.), by whatever, by whomever, *etc.*

koṇḍañña (m.), personal name.

kh

khaṇa (m.), a moment, an instant.

khandha (m.), trunk; complex, bulk, mass, accumulation; *tech.*, the five existential functions of the human being (namely, materialty, sensation, perception, conceptualization, consciousness).

kho (encl. part.), indeed, clearly, surely, certainly.

kho pana (part.), *marks continuation of narrative; emphasizes preceeding.*

g

gamma (adj.), common, ordinary, provincial, belonging to the village.

gāmin (adj.), going toward, leading to.

c

ca (encl. part.), and.

cakka (n.), wheel, discus, cycle, instrument.

cakkhu (n.), insight, understanding, recognition [of reality], vision; *lit.* the eye.

catu(r) (num.), four.

cātumahārājika (adj.), *name of a class of deva.*

cāga (m.), abandoning, giving up, renunciation.

j

jāti (f.), birth, generation.

jarā (f.), aging.

ñ

√*ñā*, to know, to realize. (Line 84, *aññāsi* = aor.)

ñāṇa (n.), knowledge, recognition, discernment, insight.

t

taṃ (m.f.n. dem. pron.), him, her, it, that, this, the, *etc.*

taṇhā (f.), thirst, craving, compulsive longing.

tatra (part.), there. (Line 20, *tatratatra*, here and there, everywhere.)

tathāgata (adj.; m.), come to [know] reality, come to suchness; *epithet of Gotama.*

tassa (m.n. dem. pron.), of that, *etc.*

tāva (part.), until, so long.

tāvatiṃsa (adj.), *name of a class of deva.*

ti (num.), three.

tu (part.), indeed.

tusita (adj.), *name of a class of deva.*

d

dasasahassi (adj.), ten-thousandfold.

dassana (n.), seeing, vision; sight of, appearance.

dāya (m.), grove, park.

diṭṭhi (f.), view, outlook, point of view.

dukkha (n.; adj.), unease, distress, trouble, unhappiness, pain;

distressful, painful, troublesome.

deva (m.), resplendent being; god.

dvādasa (num.), twelve .

dvi (num.), two.

dh

dhamma (m.), phenomenon, thing; quality, mental quality, thought; nature; teaching; standard, custom, way; justice, righteousness, goodness.

n

na (part.), no, not.

nandi (m.), enjoyment, pleasure, delight.

nāma (n.), name; *tech.* mental functions, e.g. feeling, perception, conceptualization, intention, attentiveness.

nibbāna (n.), extinguishing, unbinding, letting go, releasing.

nimmānarati (adj.), *name of a class of deva.*

nirodha (m.), cessation, ending, stopping.

neva = *na eva* (part.), certainly not, indeed not.

p

pajā (f.), progeny, offspring, beings, people, mankind.

pañca (num.), five.

paññā (f.), intelligence, insight, recognition, wisdom.

paṭi +√*ñā*, to acknowledge, to admit, to agree to,

paṭinissagga (m.), giving up, relinquishment, renunciation, forsaking.

paṭipadā (f.), path, course, practice, way.

pātur + √*bhū*, to appear, to become manifest. (Line 82, °*ahosi* = aor.)

pana (encl. part.), but, however; moreover; now (*continuing particle*).

pabbajita (ppp. √*vaj* + *pa*), wandered forth; *tech.*, left the hosuholder life for the training life.

paranimmitavasavatti (adj.), *name of a class of deva.*

pari + √*ñā*, to understand completely, to know thoroughly. (Line 27, *pariññeyya* = fpp.)

parivaṭṭa (m.), succession, sequence, series, progression.

pavattana (n.), performance, execution, carrying out, setting in motion, inaugurating.

pavattita (ppp. √*vatt* + *pa*), carried out, set in motion, inaugurated.

pa +√*hā*, to reject, to abandon, to give up, to avoid. (Line 35, *pahīna* = ppp.)

pi (encl. part.), even, also, just so, too; but; *adds emphasis to preceding term.*

piya (adj.; n.), dear, beloved, pleasant; pleasantry, pleasure.

punabbhava (m.), further becoming, repeated existence, rebirth.

pubba (adj.), previous, former, before.

pe (part.), abridgement of *peyyāla*: repetition, etcetera.

pothujjanika (adj.), common, ordinary, mediocre.

ponobbhavika (adj.), leading to further becoming, leading to rebirth.

b

bārāṇasiyā (f.), *place name*: Varanasi/ Benaras.

byādhi (m.), sickness, illness, disease.

brahmakāyika (adj.), *name of a class of deva.*

brahman (n.), Brahma, *name of Vedic creator deity;* God; the ideal; possessing exceptional integrity.

brahmaloka (m.), *roughly equivalent to to E.* "heaven."

brāhmaṇī (f.), *class designation*: Brahmin.

bh

bhagavant (adj.), fortunate, illustrious, honorable; fortunate one: *epithet of Gotama.*

√*bhaṇ*, to speak, to say. (Line 64, *bhaññamāna* = prmp.)

bhava (m.), becoming, being, existence, life.

√*bhās*, to speak, to say.

bhāsita (ppp. √*bhās*; n.), spoken, speeking; speech, talk.

bhikkhu (m.), mendicant; *lit.* beggar.

bhumma (adj.), belonging to the earth, terrestrial, earthly.

√*bhū*, to be, to become; to cultivate, to nurture, to develop. (Line 53, *ahosi* = aor.)

bho (part.), friend, comrade.

m

magga (m.), road, path, course, way.

majjhima (adj.), medium, middle.

manussa (m.), human being.

maraṇa (n.), death.

māra (m.), death; Mara, *the personification of mortality.*

miga (m.), deer, wild animal.

mutti (f.), freedom, liberation, release.

muhutta (m.), a moment, a second.

me (1st pers. per. pron.), to me, for me, *etc.*

y

yaṃ (mfn. rel. pron.), that which, *etc.*

yato (part.), when; since, because.

yathābhūtaṃ (part.), as is; in reality.

yampicchaṃ (adv.), that which is desirable, wanted, wished for, pleasant.

yā (f. rel. pron.), which, that which, *etc.*

yāma (adj.), *name of a class of deva.*

yāva (part.), as long as, to the extent that, as far as.

yo (m. rel. pron.), he who, that which, *etc.*

r

rāga (m.), passion, excitement, infatuation, lust.

l

√*labh*, to gain, to get, to aquire.

laya (m.), *a brief moment of time.*

loka (m.), world.

lokadhātu (f.), world, world-realm, universe, cosmos.

v

vaggiya (adj.), forming a group, a party of, belonging to a group.

√*vac*, to speak, to say. (Line 62, *avoca* = aor.)

vata (encl. part.), *exclamation*: indeed! of course! surely!

vā (encl. part.), or.

vācā (f.), speech.

vāyāma (m.), effort, exertion, endeavor, striving.

vijjā (f.), knowledge, comprehension, understanding.

vippayoga (m.), disconnection, separation.

vibhava (m.), non-existence, annihilation, cessation of life.

vimutti (f.), freedom, liberation, release.

viraja (adj.), stainless, pure, unblemished.

virāga (m.), dispassion, detatchment.

visuddha (ppp. √*sudh* + *vi*), clean, clear, bright, pure, unblemished, untainted.

vi + √*har*, to live, to stay, to dwell, to abide.

vītamala (adj), without blemish, stainless, free of dust, clear, clean,.

veyyākaraṇa (n.), exposition, discourse.

s

sa, *prefix denoting* with, possessed of, having.

saṃ + √*kamp*, to tremble, to shake. (Line 81, *saṅkampi* = aor.)

saṃ + *pa* + √*kamp*, to tremble, to shake. (Line 81, *sampakampi* = aor.)

saṃ + *pa* + √*vedh*, to shake violently, to affect deeply. (Line 82, *sampavedhi* = aor.)

saṃ + √*vatt*, to lead to, to be conducive to.

saṅkappa (m.), intention, proclivity, inclination, though.

saṅkhittena (part.), in short, in brief, concisely.

sacca (adj.; n.), real, actual, verifiable; reality, actuality, fact.

sacchi + √*kar*, to realize, to see for oneself, to know directly.

sati (f.), present-moment awareness, presence of mind, reflective clarity, non-interfering consciousness, lucidity; *lit.* memory; *tech.*, memory-in-the-present.

sadda (m.), sound, noise, report.

sabba (adj.), all, every.

samaṇa (m.), seeker, wanderer, ascetic.

samaya (m.), time, occasion.

samādhi (m.), concentration, collectedness, composure, mental intentness.

samudaya (m.), origin, arising, source.

sampayoga (m.), connection, union, association.

sambodha (m.), complete awakening.

sambodhi (f.), complete awakening.

sammā (part.), thoroughly, completely, perfectly; sound, right, proper.

sahagata (adj.), accompanied by, concomitant with.

sā (f. pers. pron.), she, that, *etc.*

su, *prefix denoting* well, completely, very.

√*su*, to hear, to listen.

sukhallikānuyoga (adj.), luxurious living, hedonistic.

sutta (n.), discourse, dialogue, text; *lit.*, thread, stitching, textile.

seyyathidaṃ (part.), as follows, namely.

√*sev*, to serve, to resort to.

sesa (n.), remainder, residue, left over.

h

hi (part.), because, indeed, for. (With *idaṃ* = *hidaṃ*.)

hīna (adj.; ppp. √*hā*), lowly, inferior.

Sutta 10

Gotamasuttaṃ

(*Saṃyuttanikāya* 2.1.1.10.10)

"Pubbeva me, bhikkhave, sambodhā anabhisambuddhassa bodhisattasseva sato etadahosi – 'kicchaṃ vatāyaṃ loko āpanno jāyati ca jīyati ca mīyati ca cavati ca upapajjati ca. Atha ca panimassa dukkhassa nissaraṇaṃ nappajānāti jarāmaraṇassa. Kudāssu nāma imassa dukkhassa nissaraṇaṃ paññāyissati jarāmaraṇassā'"ti?

"Tassa mayhaṃ, bhikkhave, etadahosi – 'kimhi nu kho sati jarāmaraṇaṃ hoti, kiṃpaccayā jarāmaraṇa'nti? Tassa mayhaṃ, bhikkhave, yoniso manasikārā ahu paññāya abhisamayo – 'jātiyā kho sati jarāmaraṇaṃ hoti, jātipaccayā jarāmaraṇa'"nti.

"Tassa mayhaṃ bhikkhave etadahosi: 'kimhi nu kho sati jāti hoti? Kimpaccayā jātī'ti? Tassa mayhaṃ bhikkhave, yoniso manasikārā ahu paññāyā abhisamayo: 'bhave kho sati jāti hoti, bhavapaccayā jātī'"ti.

"Tassa mayhaṃ bhikkhave, etadahosi: 'kimhi nu kho sati bhavo hoti? Kimpaccayā bhavo'ti? Tassa mayhaṃ bhikkhave, yoniso manasikārā ahu paññāya abhisamayo: 'upādāne kho sati bhavo hoti, upādānapaccayā bhavo'"ti.

"Tassa mayhaṃ bhikkhave, etadahosi: 'kimhi nu kho sati upādānaṃ hoti? Kimpaccayā upādāna'nti. Tassa mayhaṃ bhikkhave, yoniso manasikārā

ahu paññāya abhisamayo: 'taṇhāya kho sati upādānaṃ hoti. Taṇhāpaccayā upādāna'"nti.

"Tassa mayhaṃ bhikkhave, etadahosi: 'kimhi nu kho sati taṇhā hoti? Kimpaccayā taṇhā'ti. Tassa mayhaṃ bhikkhave, yoniso manasikārā ahu paññāya abhisamayo: 'vedanāya kho sati taṇhā hoti. Vedanāpaccayā taṇhā'"ti.

"Tassa mayhaṃ bhikkhave, etadahosi: 'kimhi nu kho sati vedanā hoti? Kimpaccayā vedanā'ti. Tassa mayhaṃ bhikkhave, yoniso manasikārā ahu paññāya abhisamayo: 'phasse kho sati vedanā hoti. Phassapaccayā vedanā'"ti.

"Tassa mayhaṃ bhikkhave, etadahosi: 'kimhi nu kho sati phasso hoti? Kimpaccayā phasso'ti. Tassa mayhaṃ bhikkhave, yoniso manasikārā ahu paññāya abhisamayo: 'saḷāyatane kho sati phasso hoti. Saḷāyatanapaccayā phasso'"ti.

"Tassa mayhaṃ bhikkhave, etadahosi: 'kimhi nu kho sati saḷāyatanaṃ hoti? Kimpaccayā saḷāyatana'nti. Tassa mayhaṃ bhikkhave, yoniso manasikārā ahu paññāya abhisamayo: 'nāmarūpe kho sati saḷāyatanaṃ hoti. Nāmarūpapaccayā saḷāyatana'"nti.

"Tassa mayhaṃ bhikkhave etadahosi: 'kimhi nu kho sati nāmarūpaṃ hoti? Kimpaccayā nāmarūpa'nti. Tassa mayhaṃ bhikkhave, yoniso manasikārā ahu paññāya abhisamayo: 'viññāṇe kho sati nāmarūpaṃ hoti. Viññāṇapaccayā nāmarūpa'"nti.

"Tassa mayhaṃ bhikkhave etadahosi: 'kimhi nu kho sati viññāṇaṃ hoti? Kimpaccayā viññāṇa'nti. Tassa mayhaṃ bhikkhave, yoniso manasikārā ahu paññāya abhisamayo: 'saṅkhāresu kho sati viññāṇaṃ hoti. Saṅkhārapaccayā viññāṇa'"nti.

"Tassa mayhaṃ bhikkhave etadahosi: 'kimhi nu kho sati saṅkhārā honti.

Kimpaccayā saṅkhārā'ti? Tassa mayhaṃ bhikkhave, yoniso manasikārā ahu paññāya abhisamayo: 'avijjāya kho sati saṅkhārā honti. Avijjāpaccayā saṅkhārā'"ti.

"Iti hidaṃ avijjāpaccayā saṅkhārā. Saṅkhārapaccayā viññāṇaṃ. Viññāṇapaccayā nāmarūpaṃ. Nāmarūpapaccayā saḷāyatanaṃ. Saḷāyatanapaccayā phasso. Phassapaccayā vedanā. Vedanāpaccayā taṇhā. Taṇhāpaccayā upādānaṃ. Upādānapaccayā bhavo. Bhavapaccayā jāti. Jātipaccayā jarāmaraṇaṃ, sokaparidevadukkhadomanassūpāyāsā sambhavanti. Evametassa kevalassa dukkhakkhandhassa samudayo hoti.

"'Samudayo samudayo'ti kho me bhikkhave pubbe ananussutesu dhammesu cakkhuṃ udapādi. Ñāṇaṃ udapādi. Paññā udapādi. Vijjā udapādi. Āloko udapādi.

"Tassa mayhaṃ bhikkhave, etadahosi: 'kimhi nu kho asati jarāmaraṇaṃ na hoti? Kissa nirodhā jarāmaraṇanirodho?'ti. Tassa mayhaṃ bhikkhave, yoniso manasikārā ahu paññāya abhisamayo: 'jātiyā kho asati jarāmaraṇaṃ na hoti. Jarāmaraṇanirodho'"ti.

"Tassa mayhaṃ bhikkhave, etadahosi: 'kimhi nu kho asati jāti na hoti? Kissa nirodhā jātinirodho?'ti. Tassa mayhaṃ bhikkhave, yoniso manasikārā ahu paññāya abhisamayo: 'bhave kho asati jāti na hoti. Bhavanirodhā jātinirodho'"ti.

"Tassa mayhaṃ bhikkhave etadahosi: 'kimhi nu kho asati bhavo na hoti? Kissa nirodhā bhavanirodho?'ti. Tassa mayhaṃ bhikkhave, yoniso manasikārā ahu paññāya abhisamayo: 'upādāne kho asati bhavo na hoti. Upādānanirodhā bhavanirodho'"ti.

"Tassa mayhaṃ bhikkhave etadahosi: 'kimhi nu kho asati upādānaṃ na hoti? Kissa nirodhā upādānanirodho?'ti. Tassa mayhaṃ bhikkhave, yoniso

manasikārā ahu paññāya abhisamayo: 'taṇhāya kho asati upādānaṃ na hoti. Taṇhānirodhā upādānanirodho'"ti.

"Tassa mayhaṃ bhikkhave etadahosi: 'kimhi nu kho asati taṇhā na hoti? Kissa nirodhā taṇhānirodho?'ti. Tassa mayhaṃ bhikkhave, yoniso manasikārā ahu paññāya abhisamayo: 'vedanāya kho asati taṇhā na hoti. Vedanānirodhā taṇhānirodho'"ti.

"Tassa mayhaṃ bhikkhave etadahosi: 'kimhi nu kho asati vedanā na hoti? Kissa nirodhā vedanānirodho?'ti. Tassa mayhaṃ bhikkhave, yoniso manasikārā ahu paññāya abhisamayo: 'phasse kho asati vedanā na hoti. Phassanirodhā vedanānirodho'"ti.

"Tassa mayhaṃ bhikkhave etadahosi: 'kimhi nu kho asati phasso na hoti? Kissa nirodhā phassanirodho?'ti. Tassa mayhaṃ bhikkhave, yoniso manasikārā ahu paññāya abhisamayo: 'saḷāyatane kho asati phasso na hoti. Saḷāyatananirodhā phassanirodho'"ti.

"Tassa mayhaṃ bhikkhave, etadahosi: 'kimhi nu kho asati saḷāyatanaṃ na hoti. Kissa nirodhā saḷāyatananirodho?'ti. Tassa mayhaṃ bhikkhave, yoniso manasikārā ahu paññāya abhisamayo: 'nāmarūpe kho asati saḷāyatanaṃ na hoti. Nāmarūpanirodhā saḷāyatananirodho'"ti.

"Tassa mayhaṃ bhikkhave, etadahosi: 'kimhi nu kho asati nāmarūpaṃ na hoti. Kissa nirodhā nāmarūpanirodho?'ti. Tassa mayhaṃ bhikkhave, yoniso manasikārā ahu paññāya abhisamayo: 'viññāṇe kho asati nāmarūpaṃ na hoti. Viññāṇanirodhā nāmarūpanirodho'"ti.

"Tassa mayhaṃ bhikkhave, etadahosi: 'kimhi nu kho asati viññāṇaṃ na hoti. Kissa nirodhā viññāṇanirodho?'ti. Tassa mayhaṃ bhikkhave, yoniso manasikārā ahu paññāya abhisamayo: 'saṅkhāresu kho asati viññāṇaṃ na hoti. Saṅkhāranirodhā viññāṇanirodho'"ti.

"Tassa mayhaṃ bhikkhave etadahosi: 'kimhi nu kho asati saṅkhārā na honti. Kissa nirodhā saṅkhāranirodho?'ti. Tassa mayhaṃ bhikkhave, yoniso manasikārā ahu paññāya abhisamayo: 'avijjāya kho asati saṅkhārā na honti. Avijjānirodhā saṅkhāranirodho'"ti.

"Iti hidaṃ avijjānirodhā saṅkhāranirodho. Saṅkhāranirodhā viññāṇanirodho. Viññāṇanirodhā nāmarūpanirodho. Nāmarūpanirodhā saḷāyatananirodho. Saḷāyatananirodhā phassanirodho. Phassanirodhā vedanānirodho. Vedanānirodhā taṇhānirodho. Taṇhānirodhā upādānanirodho. Upādānanirodhā bhavanirodho. Bhavanirodhā jātinirodho. Jātinirodhā jarāmaraṇaṃ, sokaparidevadukkhadomanassupāyāsā nirujjhanti. Evametassa kevalassa dukkhakkhandhassa nirodho hoti.

"'Nirodho, nirodho'ti kho me bhikkhave, pubbe ananussutesu dhammesu cakkhuṃ udapādi. Ñāṇaṃ udapādi. Paññā udapādā. Vijjā udapādi. Āloko udapādī'ti."

Sutta 10 ♦ Glossary

a

atha (part.), then.

an = *negative prefix* (*a* before consonant): non°, un°, not, without, lacking, *etc.*

ananussuta (adj.), unheard of.

abhisamaya (m.), penetration into, insight into, grasp, comprehension, realization, clear understanding.

abhisambuddha (ppp. √*budh* + *abhi* + *saṃ*), completely understood, thoroughly realized, attained full awakening.

ayaṃ (m.f. dem. pron.), this, *etc.*

√*as*, to be.

ahu, see √*bhū.*

ahosi, see √*bhū.*

ā

āpanna (ppp. √*pad* + *ā*), possessed of, entered on, having, reached; in trouble.

āyatana (n.), resting place, abode; source; region, field, sphere; *tech.* the perceptual sphere, the sensorium: the six sense organs and their respective objects (including mind and thoughts).

āloka (m.), seeing, vision, understanding.

i

iti (part.), here, in this/that case; *marks quotation of speech or thought.*

idaṃ (n. dem. pron), this, *etc.*

imassa (m.n. dem. pron.), of this, *etc.*

u

ud + √*pad*, to arise, to originate, to come into existence, to occur. (Line 53, *udapādi* = aor.)

upa + √*pad*, to arise, to appear, to be produced, to come into being.

upādāna (n.), taking, grasping, appropriating; material support, fuel.

upāyāsa (m.), trouble, unrest, turbulence, disturbance, unsettled condition.

e

etaṃ (m.f.n. dem. pron.), this, *etc.* (Line 1, n. *etad* before vowel.)

etassa (m.n. dem. pron.), of him, of this, to this, to that one, *etc.*

eva (part.), *adds emphasis to preceding term*; so, just, even.

evaṃ, (part.), thus, so, such, in this way.

k

kiṃ (part.) = *question marker.*

kiccha (adj.), troubled, distressed, causing trouble, attended with pain.

kimhi (m.n. interrog. pron.), in whom/what/which? being whom/what/which? *etc.*

kissa (m.n. interrog. pron.), for what?, from what?, *etc.*

kudā (part.), when?

kevala (adj.), whole, entire, complete, all.

kh

khandha (m.), trunk; complex, bulk, mass, accumulation; *tech.*, the five existential functions of the human being (namely, materialty, sensation, perception, conceptualization, consciousness).

kho (encl. part.), indeed, clearly, surely, certainly.

g

gotama (m.), *family name of the Buddha.*

c

ca (encl. part.), and.

cakkhu (n.), eye; insight, understanding, recognition [of reality], vision.

√*cu*, to move, to shift, to pass from one condition to another, to disappear.

ch

cha (num.), six.

j

√*jan*, to create, to produce, to generate, to be born.

√*jar*, to crush, to pound; *pass.*, to suffer destruction, to decay.

jarā (f.), aging.

jāti (f.), birth, generation.

jāy° = √*jan.*

jīy° = *pass. of* √*jar.*

ñ

ñāṇa (n.), knowledge, recognition, discernment.

t

taṇhā (f.), thirst, craving, compulsive longing.

tassa (m.n. dem. pron.), therefore, because of that, from that, *etc.*

ti (part.), marks end of direct speech, a thought, or quoted term. (Note: A short vowel preceding *ti* is lengthened, and *ṃ* is converted to *n.*)

d

domanassa (n.), heavy heartedness, depression, abjection.

dukkha (n.; adj.), unease, distress, trouble, unhappiness, pain; distressful, painful, troublesome.

n

na (part.), no, not.

nāma (n.), name; *tech.* mental functions, e.g. feeling, perception, conceptualization, intention, attentiveness. (Line 32, °*rūpa* = *tech.* the person, a human being; the mind-body continuum.)

nirodha (m.), cessation, ending, stopping.

nissaraṇa (n.), giving up, leaving behind, escape.

nu (part.), *emphasizes preceeding term*: now, then, now then, *etc.*

p

paccaya (m.), cause, ground, basis, reason, condition, motive.

pa + √*ñā*, to know, to realize. *caus.*to declare, to proclaim.

paññā (f.), intelligence, insight, recognition, wisdom.

pana (encl. part.), but, however; moreover; now (*continuing particle*).

parideva (m.), grief, lamentation, heartache.

pubba (adj.), previous, former, before.

ph

phassa (m.), contact, touch; *tech.* sense impression.

b

bodhisatta (m.), *tech.* a person still working toward awakening; Gotama's status prior to awakening.

bh

bhava (m.), becoming, being, existence, life.

bhikkhu (m.), mendicant; *tech.*, beggar.

√*bhū*, to be, to become; to cultivate, to nurture, to develop. (Line 2, *ahosi* = aor.; line 8, *ahu* = aor.)

m

manasikāra (n.), attention, attentiveness, consideration, fixed thought.

mayhaṃ (1st pers. per. pron.), to me, *etc.*

√*mar*, to die.

maraṇa (n.), death.

mīy° = √*mar*.

me (1st pers. per. pron.), to me, *etc.*

y

yoniso (part.), thoroughly, carefully, judiciously.

r

rūpa (n.), form, appearance, body, object; *tech.* elemental physical properties of matter and, specifically, human beings; namely, earth (solidity), water (cohesion), fire (heat), and air (distension).

l

loka (m.), world.

v

vata (encl. part.), *exclamation*: indeed! of course! surely!

vijjā (f.), knowledge, comprehension, understanding.

viññāṇa, (n.), cognizance, consciousness, cognition.

vedanā (f.), feeling, sensation.

s

saṃ + √*bhū*, to be produced, to arise, to manifest.

saṅkhāra (m.), mental formation, conceptual fabrication; volition, will; anything made, conditioned, fashioned, constructed or put together.

sat (prap. √*as*), being.

samudaya (m.), origin, arising, source.

sambodha (m.), awakening.

saḷ = *cha*.

sutta (n.), discourse, dialogue, text; *lit.*, thread, stitching, textile.

soka (m.), sorrow, sadness, grief, mourning.

h

hi (part.), surely, indeed. (With *idaṃ* = *hidaṃ*.)

hoti = √*bhū*.

Sutta 11

Parāyanasuttaṃ

(*Saṃyuttanikāya* 4.9.2.33.409)

"Parāyanañca vo, bhikkhave, desessāmi parāyanagāmiñca maggaṃ. Taṃ suṇātha. Katamañca, bhikkhave, parāyanaṃ? Yo, bhikkhave, rāgakkhayo dosakkhayo mohakkhayo – idaṃ vuccati, bhikkhave, parāyanaṃ. Katamo ca, bhikkhave, parāyanagāmī maggo? Kāyagatāsati. Ayaṃ vuccati, bhikkhave, parāyanagāmimaggo. Iti kho, bhikkhave, desitaṃ vo mayā parāyanaṃ, desito parāyanagāmimaggo. Yaṃ, bhikkhave, satthārā karaṇīyaṃ sāvakānaṃ hitesinā anukampakena anukampaṃ upādāya, kataṃ vo taṃ mayā. Etāni, bhikkhave, rukkhamūlāni, etāni suññāgārāni. Jhāyatha, bhikkhave, mā pamādattha; mā pacchā vippaṭisārino ahuvattha. Ayaṃ vo amhākaṃ anusāsanī"ti.

Sutta 11 ♦ Glossary

a

anukampaka (m.), kind, caring, compassionate.

anukampā (f.), kindness, care, compassion.

anusāsanī (f.), teaching, instruction, admonition, advice..

amhākaṃ (1st pers. per. pron.), our, to us, *etc.*; (can be used to indicate singular "my," *etc.*).

ayaṃ (m.f. dem. pron.), this, *etc.*

ahuvattha, *see* √*bhū.*

ā

āgāra (n.), house, dwelling, place, spot.

i

iti (part.), here, in this/that case; *marks quotation of speech or thought.*

idaṃ (n. dem. pron), this, *etc.*

u

upa + *ā* + √*dā* , to take as one's own, to appropriate, to serve as a support. (Line 6, *upādāya* = abs.)

e

etāni (n. dem. pron.), there are, here are, these, *etc.*

k

kata (ppp. √*kar*), made, done, created.

katama (m.f.n. interg. pron.), which (of several)? what?, *etc.*

√*kar*, to do, to make. (Line 6, *karaṇīya* = fpp.)

kāyagatā (adj.), relating to the body, directed toward the body.

kh

khaya (m.), wearing away, diminution, exhaustion, destruction, ending.

kho (encl. part.), indeed, clearly, surely, certainly.

g

gāmin (adj.), leading to, going toward.

c

ca (encl. part.), and.

jh

√*jhā*, to meditate.

t

taṃ (m.f.n. dem. pron.), him, her, it, that, this, the, *etc.*

d

√*dis*, to show, to point toward, to indicate.

desita (ppp. *caus.* √*dis*), taught, shown, pointed out, expounded.

dosa (m.), hostility, anger.

p

pacchā (adv.), behind.

pa + √*mad*, to be careless, to be negligent, to be remiss.

parāyana (n.), goal, destination, final end.

b

bhikkhu (m.), mendicant; *lit.* beggar.

√*bhū*, to be, to become; to cultivate, to nurture, to develop. (Line 8, *ahuvattha* = aor.)

m

magga (m.), path, road, way.

mayā (1st pers. per. pron.), by me, *etc.*

mā (part.), not, do not.

mūla (n.), root.

moha (m.), delusion, confusion, mental dullness.

y

yaṃ (mfn. rel. pron.), that which, *etc.*

yo (m. rel. pron.), he who, that which, *etc.*

r

rāga (m.), passion, excitement, infatuation, lust.

rukkha (m.), tree.

v

√*vac*, to speak. (Line 3, *vuccati* = pass.)

vippaṭisārin (adj.), remorseful, regretful.

vo (2nd pers. per. pron.), you, *etc.*

s

sati (f.), present-moment awareness, presence of mind, reflective clarity, non-interfering consciousness, lucidity; *lit.* memory; *tech.*, memory-in-the-present.

satthar (ag.n.), teacher.

sāvaka (m.), student, disciple, practitioner.

√*su*, to hear, to listen.

suñña (adj.), empty, uninhabited.

sutta (n.), discourse, dialogue, text; *lit.*, thread, stitching, textile.

h

hita (ppp. √*dhā*; n.), friendly; welfare.

hitesin (adj.), desiring another's welfare, well-wishing.

Sutta 12

Nibbutasuttaṃ

(*Aṅguttaranikāya* 3.2.1.5.56)

Atha kho jāṇussoṇi brāhmaṇo yena bhagavā tenupasaṅkami; upasaṅkamitvā bhagavantaṃ abhivādetvā ekamantaṃ nisīdi. Ekamantaṃ nisinno kho jāṇussoṇi brāhmaṇo bhagavantaṃ etadavoca – "sandiṭṭhikaṃ nibbānaṃ sandiṭṭhikaṃ nibbāna'nti, bho gotama, vuccati. Kittāvatā nu kho, bho gotama, sandiṭṭhikaṃ nibbānaṃ hoti akālikaṃ ehipassikaṃ opaneyyikaṃ paccattaṃ veditabbaṃ viññūhī"ti?

"Ratto kho, brāhmaṇa, rāgena abhibhūto pariyādinnacitto attabyābādhāyapi ceteti, parabyābādhāyapi ceteti, ubhayabyābādhāyapi ceteti, cetasikampi dukkhaṃ domanassaṃ paṭisaṃvedeti. Rāge pahīne nevattabyābādhāyapi ceteti, na parabyābādhāyapi ceteti, na ubhayabyābādhāyapi ceteti, na cetasikampi dukkhaṃ domanassaṃ paṭisaṃvedeti. Evampi kho, brāhmaṇa, sandiṭṭhikaṃ nibbānaṃ hoti.

"Duṭṭho kho, brāhmaṇa, dosena abhibhūto pariyādinnacitto attabyābādhāyapi ceteti, parabyābādhāyapi ceteti, ubhayabyābādhāyapi ceteti, cetasikampi dukkhaṃ domanassaṃ paṭisaṃvedeti. Dose pahīne nevattabyābādhāyapi ceteti, na parabyābādhāyapi ceteti, na ubhayabyābādhāyapi ceteti, na cetasikaṃ dukkhaṃ domanassaṃ paṭisaṃvedeti. Evampi kho, brāhmaṇa, sandiṭṭhikaṃ nibbānaṃ hoti.

"Mūḷho kho, brāhmaṇa, mohena abhibhūto pariyādinnacitto attabyābādhāyapi ceteti, parabyābādhāyapi ceteti, ubhayabyābādhāyapi ceteti, cetasikampi dukkhaṃ domanassaṃ paṭisaṃvedeti. Mohe pahīne nevattabyābādhāyapi ceteti, na parabyābādhāyapi ceteti, na ubhayabyābādhāyapi ceteti, na cetasikaṃ dukkhaṃ domanassaṃ paṭisaṃvedeti. Evampi kho, brāhmaṇa, sandiṭṭhikaṃ nibbānaṃ hoti.

"Yato kho ayaṃ, brāhmaṇa anavasesaṃ rāgakkhayaṃ paṭisaṃvedeti, anavasesaṃ dosakkhayaṃ paṭisaṃvedeti, mohakkhayaṃ paṭisaṃvedeti; evaṃ kho, brāhmaṇa, sandiṭṭhikaṃ nibbānaṃ hoti akālikaṃ ehipassikaṃ opaneyyikaṃ paccattaṃ veditabbaṃ viññūhī"ti.

Sutta 12 ♦ Glossary

a

a = *negative prefix* (*an* before vowel): non°, un°, not, without, lacking, *etc.*

atta (m.; reflexive pron.), self; oneself.

atha kho (part.), now, then, moreover; *beginning or continuation of narrative.*

anavasesa (adj.), having nothing left over, without remainder; wholly, completely.

abhibhūta (ppp. √*bhū* + *abhi*), overpowered, overwhelmed.

abhi + √*vad*, to greet, to address.

ayaṃ (m.f. dem. pron.), this, *etc.*

i

√*i*, to come. (Line 5, *ehi* = 2nd pers. sg. imper; *ehipassika* = adj., come and see!)

u

upa + *saṃ* + √*kam*, to approach.

ubhaya (adj.), both.

e

ekamantaṃ (adv.), on one side, beside.

etaṃ (m.f.n. dem. pron.), this, *etc.* (Line 3, n. *etad* before vowel.)

evaṃ, (part.), thus, so, such, in this way; yes.

o

opaneyyika (adj.), fit for bringing near, deserving to be used.

k

kālika (adj), dependent on time, relating to a particular time, belonging to the future.

kittāvatā (ind.), how? in what way? by virtue of what attributes? defined how?

kh

khaya (m.), wearing away, diminution, exhaustion, destruction, ending.

kho (encl. part.), indeed, clearly, surely, certainly.

g

gotama (m.), *family name of the Buddha.*

c

citta (n.), mind, discursive thought, discursive mind.

√*cet*, to appear, to perceive, to consider.

cetasika (adj.; m.), related to the mind; mental properties.

j

jāṇussoṇi (m.), *personal name.*

t

ti (part.), marks end of direct speech, a thought, or quoted term

tena, *see yena*.

d

duṭṭha (ppp. √*dus*), offensive, hateful, corrupted, spoiled.

dukkha (n.; adj.), unease, distress, trouble, unhappiness, pain; distressful, painful, troublesome.

domanassa (n.), heavy heartedness, depression, abjection.

dosa (m.), hostility, antagonism, anger, hatred.

n

nibbāna (n.), extinguishing, unbinding, letting go, releasing.

nibbuta (adj.), at peace, calmed, cooled, released.

ni + √*sad*, to sit down. (Line 2, *nisīdi* = aor).

nisinna (ppp. √*sad* + *ni*), seated.

nu (part.), *emphasizes preceeding term*: now, then, now then, *etc.*

neva = *na eva* (part.), certainly not, indeed not. (Line 9, *neva* ... *na* ... *na* = *neither* ... *nor*.)

p

paccattaṃ (adv.), individually, singly, personally, separately.

paṭi + *saṃ* + √*vid*, to experience, to feel, to undergo.

para (adj.; n.), other, another; others.

pariyādinna (ppp. √*dā* + *pari* + *ā*), overcome, controlled, mastered.

passika, *see* √*i* .

pahīna (ppp. √*hā*), abandoned, eliminated, put down, left alone.

pi (encl. part.), even, also, just so, too; but; *adds emphasis to preceding term.*

pe (part.), abridgement of *peyyāla*: repetition, etcetera.

b

byābādha (m.), injury, harm, wrong.

brāhmaṇa (m.), *class designation*: Brahmin.

bh

bhagavant (adj.), fortunate, illustrious, honorable; fortunate one: *epithet of Gotama.*

bho (part.), friend, comrade.

m

mūḷha (ppp. √*muh*), become confused, get lost, go astray.

moha (m.), delusion, confusion, mental dullness.

y

yato (part.), when; since, because.

yena (part.), where, to where, at which place; *with tena* = where (*yena*) X was, there (*tena*) he went.

r

ratta (ppp. √*rañj*), excited, infatuated, impassioned.

rāga (m.), passion, excitement, infatuation, lust.

v

√*vac*, to speak. (Line 3, *avoca* = aor.; line 4, *vuccati* = pass.)

viññū (adj.), intelligent, wise.

√*vid*, to know, to experience.

s

sandiṭṭhika (adj.), visible, conspicuous, manifest,

sutta (n.), discourse, dialogue, text; *lit.*, thread, stitching, textile.

h

hoti = √*bhū*

Sutta 13

Saṅkhatalakkhaṇasuttaṃ

(*Aṅguttaranikāya* 3.1.5.7.47)

"Tīṇimāni, bhikkhave, saṅkhatassa saṅkhatalakkhaṇāni. Katamāni tīṇi? Uppādo paññāyati, vayo paññāyati, ṭhitassa aññathattaṃ paññāyati. Imāni kho, bhikkhave, tīṇi saṅkhatassa saṅkhatalakkhaṇānī"ti.

Sutta 13 ♦ Glossary

a

aññathatta (n.), change, alteration.

i

imāni (n. dem. pron.), these, those, *etc.*

u

uppāda (m.), coming into being, appearance, production, manifestation, arising.

k

katama (m.f.n. interg. pron.), which (of several)? what?, *etc.*

kh

kho (encl. part.), indeed, clearly, surely, certainly.

ṭh

ṭhita (ppp. √*ṭhā*; m.), stood, standing; abiding, endurance, persistence.

t

ti (num.), three.

ti (part.), marks end of direct speech, a thought, or quoted term. (Note: A short vowel preceding *ti* is lengthened, and *ṃ* is converted to *n*.)

p

pa + √*ñā*, to know, to realize. *caus.*to declare, to proclaim.

bh

bhikkhu (m.), mendicant; *lit.* beggar.

l

lakkhaṇa (n.), sign, quality, feature, characteristic.

v

vaya (m.), loss, decay, perishing, disappearance.

s

saṅkhata (ppp. √*kar* + *saṃ*), put together, fashioned, fabricated, compounded, constructed, created.

sutta (n.), discourse, dialogue, text; *lit.*, thread, stitching, textile.

Sutta 14

Asaṅkhatalakkhaṇasuttaṃ

(*Aṅguttaranikāya* 3.1.5.8.48)

"Tīṇimāni, bhikkhave, asaṅkhatassa asaṅkhatalakkhaṇāni. Katamāni tīṇi? Na uppādo paññāyati, na vayo paññāyati, na ṭhitassa aññathattaṃ paññāyati. Imāni kho, bhikkhave, tīṇi asaṅkhatassa asaṅkhatalakkhaṇānī"ti.

Sutta 14 ♦ Glossary

a

a = *negative prefix* (*an* before vowel): non°, un°, not, without, lacking, *etc.*

aññathatta (n.), change, alteration.

i

imāni (n. dem. pron.), these, those, *etc.*

u

uppāda (m.), coming into being, appearance, production, manifestation, arising.

k

katama (m.f.n. interg. pron.), which (of several)? what?, *etc.*

kh

kho (encl. part.), indeed, clearly, surely, certainly.

ṭh

ṭhita (ppp. √*ṭhā*; m.), stood, standing; abiding, endurance, persistence.

t

ti (num.), three.

ti (part.), marks end of direct speech, a thought, or quoted term. (Note: A short vowel preceding *ti* is lengthened, and *ṃ* is converted to *n.*)

n

na (part.), no, not.

p

pa + √*ñā*, to know, to realize. *caus.*to declare, to proclaim.

bh

bhikkhu (m.), mendicant; *lit.* beggar.

l

lakkhaṇa (n.), sign, quality, feature, characteristic.

v

vaya (m.), loss, decay, perishing, disappearance.

s

saṅkhata (ppp. √*kar* + *saṃ*), put together, fashioned, fabricated, compounded, constructed, created.

sutta (n.), discourse, dialogue, text; *lit.*, thread, stitching, textile.

Sutta 15

Ānāpānasatisuttaṃ

(*Majjhimanikāya* 3.2.8.144)

Evaṃ me sutaṃ – ekaṃ samayaṃ bhagavā sāvatthiyaṃ viharati pubbārāme migāramātupāsāde sambahulehi abhiññātehi abhiññātehi therehi sāvakehi saddhiṃ – āyasmatā ca sāriputtena āyasmatā ca mahāmoggallānena āyasmatā ca mahākassapena āyasmatā ca mahākaccāyanena āyasmatā ca mahākoṭṭhikena āyasmatā ca mahākappinena āyasmatā ca mahācundena āyasmatā ca anuruddhena āyasmatā ca revatena āyasmatā ca ānandena, aññehi ca abhiññātehi abhiññātehi therehi sāvakehi saddhiṃ.

Tena kho pana samayena therā bhikkhū nave bhikkhū ovadanti anusāsanti. Appekacce therā bhikkhū dasapi bhikkhū ovadanti anusāsanti, appekacce therā bhikkhū vīsampi bhikkhū ovadanti anusāsanti, appekacce therā bhikkhū tiṃsampi bhikkhū ovadanti anusāsanti, appekacce therā bhikkhū cattārīsampi bhikkhū ovadanti anusāsanti. Te ca navā bhikkhū therehi bhikkhūhi ovadiyamānā anusāsiyamānā uḷāraṃ pubbenāparaṃ visesaṃ jānanti.

Tena kho pana samayena bhagavā tadahuposathe pannarase pavāraṇāya puṇṇāya puṇṇamāya rattiyā bhikkhusaṅghaparivuto abbhokāse nisinno hoti. Atha kho bhagavā tuṇhībhūtaṃ tuṇhībhūtaṃ bhikkhusaṅghaṃ anuviloketvā bhikkhū āmantesi – "āraddhosmi, bhikkhave, imāya paṭipadāya; āraddhacittosmi, bhikkhave, imāya paṭipadāya. Tasmātiha, bhikkhave, bhiyyosomattāya vīriyaṃ ārabhatha appattassa pattiyā, anadhigatassa adhigamāya, asacchikatassa

sacchikiriyāya. Idhevāhaṃ sāvatthiyaṃ komudiṃ cātumāsiniṃ āgamessāmī"ti. Assosuṃ kho jānapadā bhikkhū – "bhagavā kira tattheva sāvatthiyaṃ komudiṃ cātumāsiniṃ āgamessatī"ti. Te jānapadā bhikkhū sāvatthiyaṃ osaranti bhagavantaṃ dassanāya. Te ca kho therā bhikkhū bhiyyosomattāya nave bhikkhū ovadanti anusāsanti. Appekacce therā bhikkhū dasapi bhikkhū ovadanti anusāsanti, appekacce therā bhikkhū vīsampi bhikkhū ovadanti anusāsanti, appekacce therā bhikkhū tiṃsampi bhikkhū ovadanti anusāsanti, appekacce therā bhikkhū cattārīsampi bhikkhū ovadanti anusāsanti. Te ca navā bhikkhū therehi bhikkhūhi ovadiyamānā anusāsiyamānā uḷāraṃ pubbenāparaṃ visesaṃ jānanti.

Tena kho pana samayena bhagavā tadahuposathe pannarase komudiyā cātumāsiniyā puṇṇāya puṇṇamāya rattiyā bhikkhusaṅghaparivuto abbhokāse nisinno hoti. Atha kho bhagavā tuṇhībhūtaṃ tuṇhībhūtaṃ bhikkhusaṅghaṃ anuviloketvā bhikkhū āmantesi – "apalāpāyaṃ, bhikkhave, parisā; nippalāpāyaṃ, bhikkhave, parisā; suddhā sāre patiṭṭhitā. Tathārūpo ayaṃ, bhikkhave, bhikkhusaṅgho; tathārūpā ayaṃ, bhikkhave, parisā yathārūpā parisā āhuneyyā pāhuneyyā dakkhiṇeyyā añjalikaraṇīyā anuttaraṃ puññakkhettaṃ lokassa. Tathārūpo ayaṃ, bhikkhave, bhikkhusaṅgho; tathārūpā ayaṃ, bhikkhave, parisā yathārūpāya parisāya appaṃ dinnaṃ bahu hoti, bahu dinnaṃ bahutaraṃ. Tathārūpo ayaṃ, bhikkhave, bhikkhusaṅgho; tathārūpā ayaṃ, bhikkhave, parisā yathārūpā parisā dullabhā dassanāya lokassa. Tathārūpo ayaṃ, bhikkhave, bhikkhusaṅgho; tathārūpā ayaṃ, bhikkhave, parisā yathārūpaṃ parisaṃ alaṃ yojanagaṇanāni dassanāya gantuṃ puṭosenāpi."

"Santi, bhikkhave, bhikkhū imasmiṃ bhikkhusaṅghe arahanto khīṇāsavā vusitavanto katakaraṇīyā ohitabhārā anuppattasadatthā parikkhīṇabhavasaṃyojanā sammadaññāvimuttā – evarūpāpi, bhikkhave, santi bhikkhū imasmiṃ bhikkhusaṅghe. Santi, bhikkhave, bhikkhū imasmiṃ bhikkhusaṅghe pañcannaṃ orambhāgiyānaṃ saṃyojanānaṃ parikkhayā

opapātikā tattha parinibbāyino anāvattidhammā tasmā lokā – evarūpāpi, bhikkhave, santi bhikkhū imasmiṃ bhikkhusaṅghe. Santi, bhikkhave, bhikkhū imasmiṃ bhikkhusaṅghe tiṇṇaṃ saṃyojanānaṃ parikkhayā rāgadosamohānaṃ tanuttā sakadāgāmino sakideva imaṃ lokaṃ āgantvā dukkhassantaṃ karissanti – evarūpāpi, bhikkhave, santi bhikkhū imasmiṃ bhikkhusaṅghe. Santi, bhikkhave, bhikkhū imasmiṃ bhikkhusaṅghe tiṇṇaṃ saṃyojanānaṃ parikkhayā sotāpannā avinipātadhammā niyatā sambodhiparāyanā – evarūpāpi, bhikkhave, santi bhikkhū imasmiṃ bhikkhusaṅghe.

"Santi, bhikkhave, bhikkhū imasmiṃ bhikkhusaṅghe catunnaṃ satipaṭṭhānānaṃ bhāvanānuyogamanuyuttā viharanti – evarūpāpi, bhikkhave, santi bhikkhū imasmiṃ bhikkhusaṅghe. Santi, bhikkhave, bhikkhū imasmiṃ bhikkhusaṅghe catunnaṃ sammappadhānānaṃ bhāvanānuyogamanuyuttā viharanti...pe... catunnaṃ iddhipādānaṃ... pañcannaṃ indriyānaṃ... pañcannaṃ balānaṃ... sattannaṃ bojjhaṅgānaṃ... ariyassa aṭṭhaṅgikassa maggassa bhāvanānuyogamanuyuttā viharanti – evarūpāpi, bhikkhave, santi bhikkhū imasmiṃ bhikkhusaṅghe. Santi, bhikkhave, bhikkhū imasmiṃ bhikkhusaṅghe mettābhāvanānuyogamanuyuttā viharanti... karuṇābhāvanā nuyogamanuyuttā viharanti... muditābhāvanānuyogamanuyuttā viharanti... upekkhābhāvanānuyogamanuyuttā viharanti... asubhabhāvanānuyogamanuyutt ā viharanti... aniccasaññābhāvanānuyogamanuyuttā viharanti – evarūpāpi, bhikkhave, santi bhikkhū imasmiṃ bhikkhusaṅghe. Santi, bhikkhave, bhikkhū imasmiṃ bhikkhusaṅghe ānāpānassatibhāvanānuyogamanuyuttā viharanti. Ānāpānassati, bhikkhave, bhāvitā bahulīkatā mahapphalā hoti mahānisaṃsā. Ānāpānassati, bhikkhave, bhāvitā bahulīkatā cattāro satipaṭṭhāne paripūreti. Cattāro satipaṭṭhānā bhāvitā bahulīkatā satta bojjhaṅge paripūrenti. Satta bojjhaṅgā bhāvitā bahulīkatā vijjāvimuttiṃ paripūrenti.

"Kathaṃ bhāvitā ca, bhikkhave, ānāpānassati kathaṃ bahulīkatā mahapphalā hoti mahānisaṃsā? Idha, bhikkhave, bhikkhu araññagato vā rukkhamūlagato

vā suññāgāragato vā nisīdati pallaṅkaṃ ābhujitvā ujuṃ kāyaṃ paṇidhāya parimukhaṃ satiṃ upaṭṭhapetvā. So satova assasati satova passasati.

"Dīghaṃ vā assasanto 'dīghaṃ assasāmī'ti pajānāti, dīghaṃ vā passasanto 'dīghaṃ passasāmī'ti pajānāti; rassaṃ vā assasanto 'rassaṃ assasāmī'ti pajānāti, rassaṃ vā passasanto 'rassaṃ passasāmī'ti pajānāti; 'sabbakāyapaṭisaṃvedī assasissāmī'ti sikkhati, 'sabbakāyapaṭisaṃvedī passasissāmī'ti sikkhati; 'passambhayaṃ kāyasaṅkhāraṃ assasissāmī'ti sikkhati, 'passambhayaṃ kāyasaṅkhāraṃ passasissāmī'ti sikkhati.

"'Pītipaṭisaṃvedī assasissāmī'ti sikkhati, 'pītipaṭisaṃvedī passasissāmī'ti sikkhati; 'sukhapaṭisaṃvedī assasissāmī'ti sikkhati, 'sukhapaṭisaṃvedī passasissāmī'ti sikkhati; 'cittasaṅkhārapaṭisaṃvedī assasissāmī'ti sikkhati, 'cittasaṅkhārapaṭisaṃvedī passasissāmī'ti sikkhati; 'passambhayaṃ cittasaṅkhāraṃ assasissāmī'ti sikkhati, 'passambhayaṃ cittasaṅkhāraṃ passasissāmī'ti sikkhati.

"'Cittapaṭisaṃvedī assasissāmī'ti sikkhati, 'cittapaṭisaṃvedī passasissāmī'ti sikkhati; 'abhippamodayaṃ cittaṃ assasissāmī'ti sikkhati, 'abhippamodayaṃ cittaṃ passasissāmī'ti sikkhati; 'samādahaṃ cittaṃ assasissāmī'ti sikkhati, 'samādahaṃ cittaṃ passasissāmī'ti sikkhati; 'vimocayaṃ cittaṃ assasissāmī'ti sikkhati, 'vimocayaṃ cittaṃ passasissāmī'ti sikkhati.

"'Aniccānupassī assasissāmī'ti sikkhati, 'aniccānupassī passasissāmī'ti sikkhati; 'virāgānupassī assasissāmī'ti sikkhati, 'virāgānupassī passasissāmī'ti sikkhati; 'nirodhānupassī assasissāmī'ti sikkhati, 'nirodhānupassī passasissāmī'ti sikkhati; 'paṭinissaggānupassī assasissāmī'ti sikkhati, 'paṭinissaggānupassī passasissāmī'ti sikkhati. Evaṃ bhāvitā kho, bhikkhave, ānāpānassati evaṃ bahulīkatā mahapphalā hoti mahānisaṃsā.

"Kathaṃ bhāvitā ca, bhikkhave, ānāpānassati kathaṃ bahulīkatā cattāro satipaṭṭhāne paripūreti? Yasmiṃ samaye, bhikkhave, bhikkhu dīghaṃ vā

assasanto 'dīghaṃ assasāmī'ti pajānāti, dīghaṃ vā passasanto 'dīghaṃ passasāmī'ti pajānāti; rassaṃ vā assasanto 'rassaṃ assasāmī'ti pajānāti, rassaṃ vā passasanto 'rassaṃ passasāmī'ti pajānāti; 'sabbakāyapaṭisaṃvedī assasissāmī'ti sikkhati, 'sabbakāyapaṭisaṃvedī passasissāmī'ti sikkhati; 'passambhayaṃ kāyasaṅkhāraṃ assasissāmī'ti sikkhati, 'passambhayaṃ kāyasaṅkhāraṃ passasissāmī'ti sikkhati; kāye kāyānupassī, bhikkhave, tasmiṃ samaye bhikkhu viharati ātāpī sampajāno satimā vineyya loke abhijjhādomanassaṃ. Kāyesu kāyaññatarāhaṃ, bhikkhave, evaṃ vadāmi yadidaṃ – assāsapassāsā. Tasmātiha, bhikkhave, kāye kāyānupassī tasmiṃ samaye bhikkhu viharati ātāpī sampajāno satimā vineyya loke abhijjhādomanassaṃ.

"Yasmiṃ samaye, bhikkhave, bhikkhu 'pītipaṭisaṃvedī assasissāmī'ti sikkhati, sikkhati, 'cittasaṅkhārapaṭisaṃvedī passasissāmī'ti sikkhati; 'passambhayaṃ 'pītipaṭisaṃvedī passasissāmī'ti sikkhati; 'sukhapaṭisaṃvedī assasissāmī'ti sikkhati, 'sukhapaṭisaṃvedī passasissāmī'ti sikkhati; 'cittasaṅkhārapaṭisaṃ vedī assasissāmī'ti cittasaṅkhāraṃ assasissāmī'ti sikkhati, 'passambhayaṃ cittasaṅkhāraṃ passasissāmī'ti sikkhati; vedanāsu vedanānupassī, bhikkhave, tasmiṃ samaye bhikkhu viharati ātāpī sampajāno satimā vineyya loke abhijjhādomanassaṃ. Vedanāsu vedanāññatarāhaṃ, bhikkhave, evaṃ vadāmi yadidaṃ – assāsapassāsānaṃ sādhukaṃ manasikāraṃ. Tasmātiha, bhikkhave, vedanāsu vedanānupassī tasmiṃ samaye bhikkhu viharati ātāpī sampajāno satimā vineyya loke abhijjhādomanassaṃ.

"Yasmiṃ samaye, bhikkhave, bhikkhu 'cittapaṭisaṃvedī assasissāmī'ti sikkhati, 'cittapaṭisaṃvedī passasissāmī'ti sikkhati; 'abhippamodayaṃ cittaṃ assasissāmī'ti sikkhati, 'abhippamodayaṃ cittaṃ passasissāmī'ti sikkhati; 'samādahaṃ cittaṃ assasissāmī'ti sikkhati, 'samādahaṃ cittaṃ passasissāmī'ti sikkhati; 'vimocayaṃ cittaṃ assasissāmī'ti sikkhati, 'vimocayaṃ cittaṃ passasissāmī'ti sikkhati; citte cittānupassī, bhikkhave, tasmiṃ samaye bhikkhu viharati ātāpī sampajāno satimā vineyya loke abhijjhādomanassaṃ. Nāhaṃ,

bhikkhave, muṭṭhassatissa asampajānassa ānāpānassatiṃ vadāmi. Tasmātiha, bhikkhave, citte cittānupassī tasmiṃ samaye bhikkhu viharati ātāpī sampajāno satimā vineyya loke abhijjhādomanassaṃ.

"Yasmiṃ samaye, bhikkhave, bhikkhu 'aniccānupassī assasissāmī'ti sikkhati, 'aniccānupassī passasissāmī'ti sikkhati; 'virāgānupassī assasissāmī'ti sikkhati, 'virāgānupassī passasissāmī'ti sikkhati; 'nirodhānupassī assasissāmī'ti sikkhati, 'nirodhānupassī passasissāmī'ti sikkhati; 'paṭinissaggānupassī assasissāmī'ti sikkhati, 'paṭinissaggānupassī passasissāmī'ti sikkhati; dhammesu dhammānupassī, bhikkhave, tasmiṃ samaye bhikkhu viharati ātāpī sampajāno satimā vineyya loke abhijjhādomanassaṃ. So yaṃ taṃ abhijjhādomanassānaṃ pahānaṃ taṃ paññāya disvā sādhukaṃ ajjhupekkhitā hoti. Tasmātiha, bhikkhave, dhammesu dhammānupassī tasmiṃ samaye bhikkhu viharati ātāpī sampajāno satimā vineyya loke abhijjhādomanassaṃ.

"Evaṃ bhāvitā kho, bhikkhave, ānāpānassati evaṃ bahulīkatā cattāro satipaṭṭhāne paripūreti.

"Kathaṃ bhāvitā ca, bhikkhave, cattāro satipaṭṭhānā kathaṃ bahulīkatā satta bojjhaṅge paripūrenti? Yasmiṃ samaye, bhikkhave, bhikkhu kāye kāyānupassī viharati ātāpī sampajāno satimā vineyya loke abhijjhādomanassaṃ, upaṭṭhitāssa tasmiṃ samaye sati hoti asammuṭṭhā. Yasmiṃ samaye, bhikkhave, bhikkhuno upaṭṭhitā sati hoti asammuṭṭhā, satisambojjhaṅgo tasmiṃ samaye bhikkhuno āraddho hoti. Satisambojjhaṅgaṃ tasmiṃ samaye bhikkhu bhāveti, satisambojjhaṅgo tasmiṃ samaye bhikkhuno bhāvanāpāripūriṃ gacchati.

"So tathāsato viharanto taṃ dhammaṃ paññāya pavicinati pavicayati parivīmaṃsaṃ āpajjati. Yasmiṃ samaye, bhikkhave, bhikkhu tathāsato viharanto taṃ dhammaṃ paññāya pavicinati pavicayati parivīmaṃsaṃ āpajjati, dhammavicayasambojjhaṅgo tasmiṃ samaye bhikkhuno āraddho hoti, dhammavicayasambojjhaṅgaṃ tasmiṃ samaye bhikkhu bhāveti,

dhammavicayasambojjhaṅgo tasmiṃ samaye bhikkhuno bhāvanāpāripūriṃ gacchati.

“Tassa taṃ dhammaṃ paññāya pavicinato pavicayato parivīmaṃsaṃ āpajjato āraddhaṃ hoti vīriyaṃ asallīnaṃ. Yasmiṃ samaye, bhikkhave, bhikkhuno taṃ dhammaṃ paññāya pavicinato pavicayato parivīmaṃsaṃ āpajjato āraddhaṃ hoti vīriyaṃ asallīnaṃ, vīriyasambojjhaṅgo tasmiṃ samaye bhikkhuno āraddho hoti, vīriyasambojjhaṅgaṃ tasmiṃ samaye bhikkhu bhāveti, vīriyasambojjhaṅgo tasmiṃ samaye bhikkhuno bhāvanāpāripūriṃ gacchati.

“Āraddhavīriyassa uppajjati pīti nirāmisā. Yasmiṃ samaye, bhikkhave, bhikkhuno āraddhavīriyassa uppajjati pīti nirāmisā, pītisambojjhaṅgo tasmiṃ samaye bhikkhuno āraddho hoti, pītisambojjhaṅgaṃ tasmiṃ samaye bhikkhu bhāveti, pītisambojjhaṅgo tasmiṃ samaye bhikkhuno bhāvanāpāripūriṃ gacchati.

“Pītimanassa kāyopi passambhati, cittampi passambhati. Yasmiṃ samaye, bhikkhave, bhikkhuno pītimanassa kāyopi passambhati, cittampi passambhati, passaddhisambojjhaṅgo tasmiṃ samaye bhikkhuno āraddho hoti, passaddhisambojjhaṅgaṃ tasmiṃ samaye bhikkhu bhāveti, passaddhisambojjhaṅgo tasmiṃ samaye bhikkhuno bhāvanāpāripūriṃ gacchati.

“Passaddhakāyassa sukhino cittaṃ samādhiyati. Yasmiṃ samaye, bhikkhave, bhikkhuno passaddhakāyassa sukhino cittaṃ samādhiyati, samādhisambojjhaṅgo tasmiṃ samaye bhikkhuno āraddho hoti, samādhisambojjhaṅgaṃ tasmiṃ samaye bhikkhu bhāveti, samādhisambojjhaṅgo tasmiṃ samaye bhikkhuno bhāvanāpāripūriṃ gacchati.

“So tathāsamāhitaṃ cittaṃ sādhukaṃ ajjhupekkhitā hoti. Yasmiṃ samaye, bhikkhave, bhikkhu tathāsamāhitaṃ cittaṃ sādhukaṃ ajjhupekkhitā hoti, upekkhāsambojjhaṅgo tasmiṃ samaye bhikkhuno āraddho hoti, upekkhāsambojjhaṅgaṃ tasmiṃ samaye bhikkhu bhāveti, upekkhāsambojjhaṅgo

tasmiṃ samaye bhikkhuno bhāvanāpāripūriṃ gacchati.

"Yasmiṃ samaye, bhikkhave, bhikkhu vedanāsu...pe... citte... dhammesu dhammānupassī viharati ātāpī sampajāno satimā vineyya loke abhijjhādomanassaṃ, upaṭṭhitāssa tasmiṃ samaye sati hoti asammuṭṭhā. Yasmiṃ samaye, bhikkhave, bhikkhuno upaṭṭhitā sati hoti asammuṭṭhā, satisambojjhaṅgo tasmiṃ samaye bhikkhuno āraddho hoti, satisambojjhaṅgaṃ tasmiṃ samaye bhikkhu bhāveti, satisambojjhaṅgo tasmiṃ samaye bhikkhuno bhāvanāpāripūriṃ gacchati.

"So tathāsato viharanto taṃ dhammaṃ paññāya pavicinati pavicayati parivīmaṃsaṃ āpajjati. Yasmiṃ samaye, bhikkhave, bhikkhu tathāsato viharanto taṃ dhammaṃ paññāya pavicinati pavicayati parivīmaṃsaṃ āpajjati, dhammavicayasambojjhaṅgo tasmiṃ samaye bhikkhuno āraddho hoti, dhammavicayasambojjhaṅgaṃ tasmiṃ samaye bhikkhu bhāveti, dhammavicayasambojjhaṅgo tasmiṃ samaye bhikkhuno bhāvanāpāripūriṃ gacchati.

"Tassa taṃ dhammaṃ paññāya pavicinato pavicayato parivīmaṃsaṃ āpajjato āraddhaṃ hoti vīriyaṃ asallīnaṃ. Yasmiṃ samaye, bhikkhave, bhikkhuno taṃ dhammaṃ paññāya pavicinato pavicayato parivīmaṃsaṃ āpajjato āraddhaṃ hoti vīriyaṃ asallīnaṃ, vīriyasambojjhaṅgo tasmiṃ samaye bhikkhuno āraddho hoti, vīriyasambojjhaṅgaṃ tasmiṃ samaye bhikkhu bhāveti, vīriyasambojjhaṅgo tasmiṃ samaye bhikkhuno bhāvanāpāripūriṃ gacchati.

"Āraddhavīriyassa uppajjati pīti nirāmisā. Yasmiṃ samaye, bhikkhave, bhikkhuno āraddhavīriyassa uppajjati pīti nirāmisā, pītisambojjhaṅgo tasmiṃ samaye bhikkhuno āraddho hoti, pītisambojjhaṅgaṃ tasmiṃ samaye bhikkhu bhāveti, pītisambojjhaṅgo tasmiṃ samaye bhikkhuno bhāvanāpāripūriṃ gacchati.

"Pītimanassa kāyopi passambhati, cittampi passambhati. Yasmiṃ

samaye, bhikkhave, bhikkhuno pītimanassa kāyopi passambhati, cittampi passambhati, passaddhisambojjhaṅgo tasmiṃ samaye bhikkhuno āraddho hoti, passaddhisambojjhaṅgaṃ tasmiṃ samaye bhikkhu bhāveti, passaddhisambojjhaṅgo tasmiṃ samaye bhikkhuno bhāvanāpāripūriṃ gacchati.

"Passaddhakāyassa sukhino cittaṃ samādhiyati. Yasmiṃ samaye, bhikkhave, bhikkhuno passaddhakāyassa sukhino cittaṃ samādhiyati, samādhisambojjhaṅgo tasmiṃ samaye bhikkhuno āraddho hoti, samādhisambojjhaṅgaṃ tasmiṃ samaye bhikkhu bhāveti, samādhisambojjhaṅgo tasmiṃ samaye bhikkhuno bhāvanāpāripūriṃ gacchati.

"So tathāsamāhitaṃ cittaṃ sādhukaṃ ajjhupekkhitā hoti. Yasmiṃ samaye, bhikkhave, bhikkhu tathāsamāhitaṃ cittaṃ sādhukaṃ ajjhupekkhitā hoti, upekkhāsambojjhaṅgo tasmiṃ samaye bhikkhuno āraddho hoti, upekkhāsambojjhaṅgaṃ tasmiṃ samaye bhikkhu bhāveti, upekkhāsambojjhaṅgo tasmiṃ samaye bhikkhuno bhāvanāpāripūriṃ gacchati. Evaṃ bhāvitā kho, bhikkhave, cattāro satipaṭṭhānā evaṃ bahulīkatā satta sambojjhaṅge paripūrenti.

"Kathaṃ bhāvitā ca, bhikkhave, satta bojjhaṅgā kathaṃ bahulīkatā vijjāvimuttiṃ paripūrenti? Idha, bhikkhave, bhikkhu satisambojjhaṅgaṃ bhāveti vivekanissitaṃ virāganissitaṃ nirodhanissitaṃ vossaggapariṇāmiṃ. Dhammavicayasambojjhaṅgaṃ bhāveti … pe … vīriyasambojjhaṅgaṃ bhāveti… pītisambojjhaṅgaṃ bhāveti… passaddhisambojjhaṅgaṃ bhāveti… samādhisambojjhaṅgaṃ bhāveti… upekkhāsambojjhaṅgaṃ bhāveti vivekanissitaṃ virāganissitaṃ nirodhanissitaṃ vossaggapariṇāmiṃ. Evaṃ bhāvitā kho, bhikkhave, satta bojjhaṅgā evaṃ bahulīkatā vijjāvimuttiṃ paripūrentī"ti.

Idamavoca bhagavā. Attamanā te bhikkhū bhagavato bhāsitaṃ abhinandunti.

Sutta 15 ♦ Glossary

a

a = *negative prefix* (*an* before vowel): non°, un°, not, without, lacking, *etc.*

aṅga (n.), limb, part, factor, constituent, attribute, quality, determing characteristic.

aṅgika (adj.), °fold, consisting of parts.

ajjhupekkhitar (ag. n.), one who looks on with impartiality, disinterest, detatchment, toleration, *etc.*

añjali (m.), *a gesture of placing the hands palm to palm at the forehead, signifying respect.*

añjalikaraṇīya (adj.), worthy of salutation, deserving of reverence. (*See añjali.*)

añña (pr. adj.), other, another.

aññatara (m.n. pr. adj.), a, a certain.

aññā (f.), knowledge, wisdom, insight.

aṭṭha (num.), eight.

attamana (adj.), mentally uplifted, exalted, pleased, assured, satisfied.

atha (part.), then.

adhigata (ppp. √*gam* + *adhi*), found, acquired; understood, realized; experienced.

adhigama (m.), attainment, acquisition; understanding, realization; experience.

an = *negative prefix* (*a* before consonant): non°, un°, not, without, lacking, *etc.*

anicca (adj.), inconstant, unstable, impermanent.

anuttara (adj.), unsurpassed, unexcelled, excellent, supreme.

anupassin (adj.), observing, viewing, considering.

anuppatta (ppp. √*āp* + *anu*), reached, arrived at.

anuyutta (ppp. √*yuj* + *anu*), applying oneself, intent on, practicing.

anuyoga (m.), question, examination, enquiry; application, devotion to, practice, pursuit.

anuruddha (m.), *personal name.*

anu + *vi* + √*lok*, to look around, to survey.

anu + √*sās*, to teach, to instruct, to lead, to guide, to exhort.

aparaṃ (part.), further, furthermore, besides, again.

apāna (n.), exhalation.

api (part.), *adds emphasis to preceding term*; even, even though, also; but.

appa (adj.), small, insignificant, meager, little.

appekacca (adj.), some.

abbhokāsa (m.), the open, an open space.

abhijjhā (f.), longing, desire.

abhiññāta (ppp. √*ñā* + *abhi*), distinguished, well known, famous.

abhi + √*nand*, to rejoice, to take delight, to be glad. (Line 235, *abhinandum* = aor.)

abhi + *pa* + √*mud*, to please, to make glad. (Line 90, *abhippamodaya* = fpp.)

arañña (n.), forest, wilderness.

arahant (adj.), worthy.

ariya (adj.), noble, preeminent, superlative; Buddhist.

alaṃ (part.), certainly, alas, enough.

√*as*, to be.

asammuṭṭar (ag. n.), one who is not confused, not forgetful, careful, attentive.

asallīna (m.), active, vigorous, steady.

ahaṃ (1st pers. per. pron.), I.

ahan (n.) day. (Line 14, *ahu* = sing. acc., loc.)

ā

ā + √*gam*, to come, to arrive. (Line 51, *āgantvā* = abs.)

āgāra (n.), house, dwelling, place, spot.

ātāpin (adj.), ardent, strenuous, energetic, applying oneself.

āna (n.), inhalation.

ānanda (m.), *personal name.*

ānisaṃsa (m.), profit, advantage, benefit.

ā + √*pad*, to come to, to reach; to enter on, to fall into; to happen, to occur.

ā + √*bhuj*, to bend, to twist.

ā + √*mant*, to address, to advise.

āyasmant (adj.), venerable.

āraddha (ppp. √*rabh* + *ā*), resolved, begun, undertaken; pleased, satisfied.

ā + √*rabh*, to begin, to undertake, to embark on, to initiate.

ārāma (m.), park, garden.

āvatti (adj.), turning toward, being enticed by, being affected by.

āsava (m.), habitual impulse, effluent, toxin.

ā + √*sas*, to inhale, to breathe.

āhuneyya (fpp. √*hu* + *ā*. adj.), to be offered; worthy of offerings.

i

iddhi (f.), power, success, accomplishment.

idha (part.), here, in this connection, now.

indriya (n.), sense faculty; power, strength, faculty.

imaṃ (m.f.n. dem. pron.), this, *etc.*

imasmiṃ (m.n. dem. pron.), in the, in this, *etc.*

imāya (f. dem. pron.), by this; from this, because of this, *etc.*

iha (part.), here, in this case, in this instance.

u

uju (adj.), direct, going in a straight direction; straight, upright.

ud + √*pad*, to arise, to appear, to come into being, to become available.

upa + √*ṭhā*, to establish, to set up; *caus.* to employ, to attend, to bring near, to bring about..

upekkhā (f.), equanimity, balance.

uposatha (m.), a day of intensified practice for Buddhist lay practitioners, in which they undertake eight abstinences and listen to teachings.

uḷāra (adj.) great, magnificent, excellent.

e

eka (num.; adj.), one; a certain, some.

eva (part.), *adds emphasis to preceding term*; so, just, even.

evaṃ, (part.), thus, so, such, in this way; yes.

evarūpa (adj.), of such kind, like this, such a thing.

o

opapātika (adj.), arising spontaneously.

orambhāgiya (adj.), connected with this side of existence, binding to lower states.

o + √*vad*, to instruct, to counsel, to exhort, to admonish.

o + √*sar*, to visit, to procede to.

o + √*har*, to put down, to lay down.

k

kaccāyana (m.), *personal name.*

kata (ppp. √*kar*), made, done, created.

kathaṃ (part), how?

kappina (m.), *personal name.*

√*kar*, to do, to make, to accomplish. (Line 44, *karaṇīya* = fpp.)

kassapa (m.), *personal name.*

karuṇā (f.), compassion, care, concern.

kāya (m.), body.

kira (part.), *emphasizes preceeding term*; then; really, surely.

koṭṭhika (m.), *personal name.*

komudī (f.), white waterlily; moonlight; the full moon day in October/November.

kh

khetta (n.), fertile soil, arable land, cultivated field.

kho pana (part.), *marks continuation of narrative*; *emphasizes preceeding term.*

g

gata (ppp. √*gam*), going, gone.

√*gam*, to go; to arrive at, *hence fig.*, to come to know, to experience, to realize. (Line 42, *gantuṃ* = inf.)

c

ca (encl. part.), and.

catu° = *catur in compound.*

catur (num.), four.

cattārīsa (num.), forty.

citta (n.), mind, discursive thought, discursive mind.

cunda (m.), *personal name.*

j

jānapada (adj.; n.), belonging to the countryside; country person.

√*jān*, to know, to realize.

t

taṃ (m.f.n. dem. pron.), him, her, it, that, this, the, *etc.* [Line 14, n. *tad* before vowel; also, used adverbially = there.]

tattha (part.), there, that place.

tathā (part.), that, thus, in that manner; such, so.

tathārūpa (adj.), such, such like, of this or that kind.

tanutta (n.), attenuation, dimunation, reduction, gradual disappearance.

tasmā (m.n. dem. pron.), from that, *etc.*; because, therefore.

tasmiṃ (m.n. dem. pron.), in that, at that, *etc.*

ti (num.), three. (Line 50, *tiṇṇaṃ* = m.n.gen.)

ti (part.), marks end of direct speech, a thought, or quoted term. (Note: A short vowel preceding *ti* is lengthened, and *ṃ* is converted to *n*.)

tiṃsa (num.), thirty.

tuṇhī (adj.), silent.

te (2nd pers. per. pron.; m. dem. pron.), by you, yours, to you (sg.); those, them, *etc.*

tena (m.n. dem. pron.), at this, with that, *etc.*

th

thera (adj.), senior, venerable, elder.

d

dakkhiṇeyya (adj), worthy of gifts.

dasa (num.), ten.

dassana (n.), sight, appearance, vision, the seeing.

dinna (ppp. √*dā*), given, presented, granted.

√*dis*, to show; *caus.* to teach, to declare; to point to, to point out.

dīgha (adj.), long, tall.

du°, prefix indicating difficulty.

dukkha (n.; adj.), unease, distress, trouble, unhappiness, pain; distressful, painful, troublesome.

domanassa (n.), depression, dejection, mental disturbance.

dosa (m.), hostility, anger.

dh

dhamma (m.), phenomenon, thing; quality, mental quality, thought; nature; teaching; standard.

n

na (part.), no, not.

nava (adj.), new, novice, fresh.

nippalāpa (adj.), free from frivolous talk, free from chatter.

niyata (ppp. √*yam* + *ni*; adj.), restrained, bound to; sure, certain, assured, necessary.

nirāmisa (adj.), *lit.*, fleshless; *fig.*, free from sensual desire, disinterested, immaterial.

nirodha (m.), cessation, ending, stopping.

ni + √*sad*, to sit down.

nisinna (ppp. √*sad* + *ni*), seated.

nisīd° = *ni* + √*sad.*

nissita (adj.), hanging on, depending on, supported by; by means of, on account of.

p

pa + √*jān*, to know, to realize.

pañca (num.), five.

paññā (f.), intelligence, insight, recognition, wisdom.

paṭinissagga (m.), giving up, relinquishment, renunciation, forsaking.

paṭipadā (f.), course, practice, progress, means of reaching a goal.

paṭisaṃvedin (adj.), experiencing, feeling, undergoing.

paṭṭhāna (n.), setting forth, putting forward, establishing, applying.

pa + *ṇi* + √*dhā*, to put down, to apply, to direct, (Line 76, *paṇidhāya* = abs.)

patiṭṭhita (ppp. √*ṭhā* + *pati*), established, set up, fixed, situated.

patta (ppp. √*āp* + *pa*), obtained, acquired, got.

patti (f.), obtainment, acquisition, gain, advantage.

padhāna (n.), exertion, effort, diligence, striving.

pannarasa (num.), fifteen, fifteenth.

parāyana (n.), goal, destination, final end.

parikkhaya (m.), exhaustion, waste, dimunation, decay, loss, end.

parikkhīṇa (ppp. √*khī* + *pari*), exhausted, wasted, destroyed.

pariṇāmin (adj.), ending in, resulting in.

parinibbāyin (m.), one who realizes complete release.

pari + √*pūr*, *caus.*, to make full, to fulfill.

parimukhaṃ (part.), in front, immediately before; *lit.,* around the mouth.

parivīmaṃsa (f.), complete inquiry, thorough examination.

parivuta (ppp. √*var* + *pari*), surrounded by, encircled.

parisā (f.), assembly, group, multitude.

palāpa (m.), frivolous talk, prattle, chatter, nonsense.

pallaṅka (adj.), crossed-legged.

pavāraṇā (f.), a ceremony held in completion of the rainy season retreat, wherein *bhikkhus* make confessions and determinations.

pa + *vi* + √*ci*, to investigate, to ponder, to consider carefully, to examine thoroughly.

pa + √*sas*, to exhale.

passaddha (ppp. √*sambh* + *pa*), calmed, tranquil, at peace.

passaddhi (f.), calmness, tranquility, repose, serenity.

pa + √*sambh*, to calm, to tranquilize. (Line 82, *passambhaya* = prap.)

pahāna (n.), abandonment, rejection, reliquishment.

pāda (m.), base, basis, foundation, footing.

pāripūrī (f.), fulfillment, completion, consummation.

pāsāda (m.), lofty platform, terrace, palace.

pāhuneyya (ppp. √*hu* + *pa* + *ā*; adj.), to be treated hospitably; worthy of reception.

pi (encl. part.), even, also, just so, too; but; *adds emphasis to preceding term.*

pīti (f.), joy, delight, exuberance, bliss.

pītimana (adj.), glad of heart or mind, joyful, exhilarated.

puñña (n.), merit, advantage, value.

puṭosa (m.), travel bag, shoulder bag for carrying provisions.

puṇṇa (ppp. √*pūr*), completed, fulfilled, full, whole.

puṇṇamā (m.), the full moon night.

pubba (adj.), previous, former, before; eastern.

pe (part.), abridgement of *peyyāla*: repetition, etcetera.

ph

phala (n.), result, fruit.

b

bala (n.), strength, power.

bahu (adj.), much, many, great.

bahulīkata (adj.), seriously practiced, continuously engaged.

bojjha (n.), awakening, wisdom, knowledge.

bh

bhagavant (adj.), fortunate, illustrious, honorable; fortunate one: *epithet of Gotama.*

bhava (m.), becoming, being, existence, life.

bhāra (m.), load, burden.

bhāvanā (f.), developing, producing, cultivating, applying; *tech.* cultivating the mind through meditation.

bhāvita (ppp. *caus.* √*bhū*), made to become, cultivated, cultured, developed.

bhāsita (n.), speech, words.

bhiyyoso (part.), still more, more and more.

√*bhū*, to be, to become; to cultivate, to nurture, to develop.

bhūta (ppp. √*bhū*), became, become.

m

magga (m.), path, road, way.

matta (adj.), measured, by measure, as much as; merely, only, not even.

mahant (adj.), great, eminent, prominent, extensive, considerable.

mātar (f.), mother.

māsinī (f.), month.

migāra (m.), *personal name.*

muṭṭha (adj.), forgetful, careless, bewildered. (Line 130, *muṭṭhassatissa* = *muṭṭha* + *sati*.)

muditā (f.), gladness, joy.

mūla (n.), root.

me (1st pers. per. pron.), to me, *etc.*

mettā (f.), friendliness, kindness, love, concern.

moggallāna (m.), *personal name.*

moha (m.), delusion, confusion, mental dullness.

y

yaṃ (mfn. rel. pron.), that which, *etc.*

yathārūpa (adj.), of that kind. (Lines 34-35, *tathārūpa … yathārūpa* = such … that, *etc.*)

yasmiṃ (m.n. rel. pron.), in which, at which, *etc.*

yojana (n.), *a unit of measure, 8-10 miles.*

r

ratti (f.), night.

rassa (adj.), short.

rāga (m.), passion, excitement, infatuation, lust.

rukkha (m.), tree.

rūpa (n.), form, appearance, body, object, figure, matter.

revata (m.), *personal name.*

l

labha (adj.), receiving, to be received, getting, to get.

loka (m.), world.

v

√*vac*, to speak. (Line 235, *avoca* = aor.)

√*vad*, to say, to speak.

vanta (ppp. √*vam*; m.), renounced, given up, left behind; discharge.

vā (encl. part.), or.

vicaya (m.), search, examination, investigation, inquiry into.

vijjā (f.), knowledge, comprehension, understanding.

vinipāta (m.), ruin, destruction, a place of suffering.

vi + √*nī*, to give up, to put down, to remove. (Line 108, *vineyya* = abs.)

vi + √*muc*, to be liberated, to be released, to be freed. (Line 92, *vimocaya* = fpp.)

vimutta (ppp. √*muc* + *vi*), liberated, released, freed.

vimutti (f.), freedom, liberation, release.

virāga (m.), dispassion, detatchment; fading away, dissolution.

viveka (m.), seclusion, separation, withdrawal; discrimination.

visesa (m.), distinction, excellence, eminence, advantage.

vi + √*har*, to live, to stay, to dwell, to abide.

vīriya (n.), vigor, virility, energy, effort.

vīsa (num.), twenty.

vusita (*ppp.* √*vas)*, lived; fulfilled, accomplished.

vedanā (f.), feeling, sensation.

vossagga (m.), letting go, abandoning, relinquishing.

S

saṃ + *ā* + √*dhā*, to put together, to gather, to collect, to compose. (Line 91, *samādaha* = prap.)

saṃyojana (m.), bond, fetter.

√*sak*, can, to be able to. (Line 81, *sikkh°* = desid., want to be able, *i.e.*, train oneself.)

sakadāgāmin (adj.), returning once.

sakid (adv.), once, once more, at once.

saṅkhāra (m.), mental formation, conceptual fabrication; volition, will; anything made, conditioned, fashioned, constructed or put together.

saṅgha (m.), group, assembly, community.

sacchikata (ppp. √*kar* + *sacci*), realized, experienced.

sacchikiriyā, (f.), realization, experiencing.

sat (prap. √*as*), being.

sata (ppp. √*sar*), remembered, established in present-moment awareness. (Line 77, *satova* = *sata* + *eva*.)

sati (f.), present-moment awareness, presence of mind, reflective clarity, non-interfering consciousness, lucidity; *lit.* memory; *tech.*, memory-in-the-present.

satimant (adj.), aware, attentive, watchful.

satta (num.), seven.

sadattha (m.), the ideal, the highest good.

saddhiṃ (part.), together; in company with.

santa (ppp. √*sam*), calmed, quieted, tranquilized, become peaceful.

santi = √*as.*

sabba (adj.), every, all, entire.

samaya (m.), time, occasion.

samādhi (m.), concentration, collectedness, composure, mental intentness.

samāhita (ppp. √*dhā* + *sam* + *ā*), collected, composed, gathered together, concentrated, firm.

sampajāna (adj.), attentive, deliberate, conscientious.

sambahula (adj.), many.

sambojjha = *bojjha.*

sambodhi (f.), complete awakening.

sammā (part.), sound, right, correct, thorough, complete. (Note: *ā* > *a* before short vowel, with insertion of *d* or doubling of consonant.)

sādhuka (adv.), thoroughly, completely.

sāra (m.), substance, essence, core; heartwood.

sāriputta (m.), *personal name.*

sāvaka (m.), student, disciple, practitioner.

sāvatthi (f.), *place name.*

sikkh°, see √sak.

√*su*, to hear. (Line 21, *assosuṃ* = aor.).

sukha (n.; adj.), ease, serenity, harmony, happiness, pleasure; gratifying, pleasant, agreeable, harmonious.

sukhin (adj.), at ease, happy, well.

suñña (adj.), empty, uninhabited.

suta (ppp. √*su*), heard.

sutta (n.), discourse, dialogue, text; *lit.*, thread, stitching, textile.

suddha (ppp. √*sudh*), clean, clear, bright, pure, unblemished, untainted.

subha (adj.; n.), attractive, beautiful, pleasant, pure; pleasantness, purity, beauty, brightness.

so (m. dem. pron.), he, that, that one, the, *etc.*

sotāpanna (m.n.), one who has entered the stream, a convert.

h

hoti = √*bhū.*

Sutta 16

Satipaṭṭhānasuttaṃ

(*Majjhimanikāya* 1.1.10.105)

Evaṃ me sutaṃ – ekaṃ samayaṃ bhagavā kurūsu viharati kammāsadhammaṃ nāma kurūnaṃ nigamo. Tatra kho bhagavā bhikkhū āmantesi – "bhikkhavo"ti. "Bhadante"ti te bhikkhū bhagavato paccassosuṃ. Bhagavā etadavoca –

Uddeso

"Ekāyano ayaṃ, bhikkhave, maggo sattānaṃ visuddhiyā, sokaparidevānaṃ samatikkamāya, dukkhadomanassānaṃ atthaṅgamāya, ñāyassa adhigamāya, nibbānassa sacchikiriyāya, yadidaṃ cattāro satipaṭṭhānā.

"Katame cattāro? Idha, bhikkhave, bhikkhu kāye kāyānupassī viharati ātāpī sampajāno satimā, vineyya loke abhijjhādomanassaṃ; vedanāsu vedanānupassī viharati ātāpī sampajāno satimā, vineyya loke abhijjhādomanassaṃ; citte cittānupassī viharati ātāpī sampajāno satimā, vineyya loke abhijjhādomanassaṃ; dhammesu dhammānupassī viharati ātāpī sampajāno satimā, vineyya loke abhijjhādomanassaṃ.

Uddeso niṭṭhito.

Kāyānupassanā ānāpānapabbaṃ

"Kathañca, bhikkhave, bhikkhu kāye kāyānupassī viharati? Idha, bhikkhave, bhikkhu araññagato vā rukkhamūlagato vā suññāgāragato vā nisīdati, pallaṅkaṃ ābhujitvā, ujuṃ kāyaṃ paṇidhāya, parimukhaṃ satiṃ upaṭṭhapetvā. So satova

assasati, satova passasati. Dīghaṃ vā assasanto 'dīghaṃ assasāmī'ti pajānāti, dīghaṃ vā passasanto 'dīghaṃ passasāmī'ti pajānāti, rassaṃ vā assasanto 'rassaṃ assasāmī'ti pajānāti, rassaṃ vā passasanto 'rassaṃ passasāmī'ti pajānāti, 'sabbakāyapaṭisaṃvedī assasissāmī'ti sikkhati, 'sabbakāyapaṭisaṃvedī passasissāmī'ti sikkhati, 'passambhayaṃ kāyasaṅkhāraṃ assasissāmī'ti sikkhati, 'passambhayaṃ kāyasaṅkhāraṃ passasissāmī'ti sikkhati.

"Seyyathāpi, bhikkhave, dakkho bhamakāro vā bhamakārantevāsī vā dīghaṃ vā añchanto 'dīghaṃ añchāmī'ti pajānāti, rassaṃ vā añchanto 'rassaṃ añchāmī'ti pajānāti; evameva kho, bhikkhave, bhikkhu dīghaṃ vā assasanto 'dīghaṃ assasāmī'ti pajānāti, dīghaṃ vā passasanto 'dīghaṃ passasāmī'ti pajānāti, rassaṃ vā assasanto 'rassaṃ assasāmī'ti pajānāti, rassaṃ vā passasanto 'rassaṃ passasāmī'ti pajānāti; 'sabbakāyapaṭisaṃvedī assasissāmī'ti sikkhati, 'sabbakāyapaṭisaṃvedī passasissāmī'ti sikkhati; 'passambhayaṃ kāyasaṅkhāraṃ assasissāmī'ti sikkhati, 'passambhayaṃ kāyasaṅkhāraṃ passasissāmī'ti sikkhati. Iti ajjhattaṃ vā kāye kāyānupassī viharati, bahiddhā vā kāye kāyānupassī viharati, ajjhattabahiddhā vā kāye kāyānupassī viharati; samudayadhammānupassī vā kāyasmiṃ viharati, vayadhammānupassī vā kāyasmiṃ viharati, samudayavayadhammānupassī vā kāyasmiṃ viharati. 'Atthi kāyo'ti vā panassa sati paccupaṭṭhitā hoti. Yāvadeva ñāṇamattāya paṭissatimattāya anissito ca viharati, na ca kiñci loke upādiyati. Evampi kho , bhikkhave, bhikkhu kāye kāyānupassī viharati.

Ānāpānapabbaṃ niṭṭhitaṃ.

Kāyānupassanā iriyāpathapabbaṃ

"Puna caparaṃ, bhikkhave, bhikkhu gacchanto vā 'gacchāmī'ti pajānāti, ṭhito vā 'ṭhitomhī'ti pajānāti, nisinno vā 'nisinnomhī'ti pajānāti, sayāno vā 'sayānomhī'ti pajānāti. Yathā yathā vā panassa kāyo paṇihito hoti tathā tathā naṃ pajānāti. Iti ajjhattaṃ vā kāye kāyānupassī viharati, bahiddhā vā kāye kāyānupassī viharati, ajjhattabahiddhā vā kāye kāyānupassī viharati; samudayadhammānupassī

vā kāyasmiṃ viharati, vayadhammānupassī vā kāyasmiṃ viharati, samudayavayadhammānupassī vā kāyasmiṃ viharati. 'Atthi kāyo'ti vā panassa sati paccupaṭṭhitā hoti. Yāvadeva ñāṇamattāya paṭissatimattāya anissito ca viharati, na ca kiñci loke upādiyati. Evampi kho, bhikkhave, bhikkhu kāye kāyānupassī viharati.

Iriyāpathapabbaṃ niṭṭhitaṃ.

Kāyānupassanā sampajānapabbaṃ

"Puna caparaṃ, bhikkhave, bhikkhu abhikkante paṭikkante sampajānakārī hoti, ālokite vilokite sampajānakārī hoti, samiñjite pasārite sampajānakārī hoti, saṅghāṭipattacīvaradhāraṇe sampajānakārī hoti, asite pīte khāyite sāyite sampajānakārī hoti, uccārapassāvakamme sampajānakārī hoti, gate ṭhite nisinne sutte jāgarite bhāsite tuṇhībhāve sampajānakārī hoti. Iti ajjhattaṃ vā kāye kāyānupassī viharati...pe... evampi kho, bhikkhave, bhikkhu kāye kāyānupassī viharati.

Sampajānapabbaṃ niṭṭhitaṃ.

Kāyānupassanā paṭikūlamanasikārapabbaṃ

"Puna caparaṃ, bhikkhave, bhikkhu imameva kāyaṃ uddhaṃ pādatalā, adho kesamatthakā, tacapariyantaṃ pūraṃ nānappakārassa asucino paccavekkhati – 'atthi imasmiṃ kāye kesā lomā nakhā dantā taco maṃsaṃ nhāru aṭṭhi aṭṭhimiñjaṃ vakkaṃ hadayaṃ yakanaṃ kilomakaṃ pihakaṃ papphāsaṃ antaṃ antaguṇaṃ udariyaṃ karīsaṃ pittaṃ semhaṃ pubbo lohitaṃ sedo medo assu vasā kheḷo siṅghāṇikā lasikā mutta'nti.

"Seyyathāpi, bhikkhave, ubhatomukhā putoḷi pūrā nānāvihitassa dhaññassa, seyyathidaṃ – sālīnaṃ vīhīnaṃ muggānaṃ māsānaṃ tilānaṃ taṇḍulānaṃ. Tamenaṃ cakkhumā puriso muñcitvā paccavekkheyya – 'ime sālī ime vīhī ime muggā ime māsā ime tilā ime taṇḍulā'ti. Evameva kho, bhikkhave, bhikkhu imameva kāyaṃ uddhaṃ pādatalā, adho kesamatthakā, tacapariyantaṃ pūraṃ

nānappakārassa asucino paccavekkhati – 'atthi imasmiṃ kāye kesā lomā...pe... mutta'nti.

"Iti ajjhattaṃ vā kāye kāyānupassī viharati...pe... evampi kho, bhikkhave, bhikkhu kāye kāyānupassī viharati.

Paṭikūlamanasikārapabbaṃ niṭṭhitaṃ.

Kāyānupassanā dhātumanasikārapabbaṃ

"Puna caparaṃ, bhikkhave, bhikkhu imameva kāyaṃ yathāṭhitaṃ yathāpaṇihitaṃ dhātuso paccavekkhati – 'atthi imasmiṃ kāye pathavīdhātu āpodhātu tejodhātu vāyodhātū'ti.

"Seyyathāpi, bhikkhave, dakkho goghātako vā goghātakantevāsī vā gāviṃ vadhitvā catumahāpathe bilaso vibhajitvā nisinno assa. Evameva kho, bhikkhave, bhikkhu imameva kāyaṃ yathāṭhitaṃ yathāpaṇihitaṃ dhātuso paccavekkhati – 'atthi imasmiṃ kāye pathavīdhātu āpodhātu tejodhātu vāyodhātū'ti. Iti ajjhattaṃ vā kāye kāyānupassī viharati...pe... evampi kho, bhikkhave, bhikkhu kāye kāyānupassī viharati.

Dhātumanasikārapabbaṃ niṭṭhitaṃ.

Kāyānupassanā navasivathikapabbaṃ

"Puna caparaṃ, bhikkhave, bhikkhu seyyathāpi passeyya sarīraṃ sivathikāya chaḍḍitaṃ ekāhamataṃ vā dvīhamataṃ vā tīhamataṃ vā uddhumātakaṃ vinīlakaṃ vipubbakajātaṃ. So imameva kāyaṃ upasaṃharati – 'ayampi kho kāyo evaṃdhammo evaṃbhāvī evaṃanatīto'ti. Iti ajjhattaṃ vā kāye kāyānupassī viharati...pe... evampi kho, bhikkhave, bhikkhu kāye kāyānupassī viharati.

"Puna caparaṃ, bhikkhave, bhikkhu seyyathāpi passeyya sarīraṃ sivathikāya chaḍḍitaṃ kākehi vā khajjamānaṃ kulalehi vā khajjamānaṃ gijjhehi vā khajjamānaṃ kaṅkehi vā khajjamānaṃ sunakhehi vā khajjamānaṃ byagghehi vā khajjamānaṃ dīpīhi vā khajjamānaṃ siṅgālehi vā khajjamānaṃ vividhehi

vā pāṇakajātehi khajjamānaṃ. So imameva kāyaṃ upasaṃharati – 'ayampi kho kāyo evaṃdhammo evaṃbhāvī evaṃanatīto'ti. Iti ajjhattaṃ vā kāye kāyānupassī viharati…pe… evampi kho, bhikkhave, bhikkhu kāye kāyānupassī viharati.

"Puna caparaṃ, bhikkhave, bhikkhu seyyathāpi passeyya sarīraṃ sivathikāya chaḍḍitaṃ aṭṭhikasaṅkhalikaṃ samaṃsalohitaṃ nhārusambandhaṃ…pe… aṭṭhikasaṅkhalikaṃ nimaṃsalohitamakkhitaṃ nhārusambandhaṃ…pe… aṭṭhikasaṅkhalikaṃ apagatamaṃsalohitaṃ nhārusambandhaṃ…pe… aṭṭhikāni apagatasambandhāni disā vidisā vikkhittāni, aññena hatthaṭṭhikaṃ aññena pādaṭṭhikaṃ aññena gopphakaṭṭhikaṃ aññena jaṅghaṭṭhikaṃ aññena ūruṭṭhikaṃ aññena kaṭiṭṭhikaṃ aññena phāsukaṭṭhikaṃ aññena piṭṭhiṭṭhikaṃ aññena khandhaṭṭhikaṃ aññena gīvaṭṭhikaṃ aññena hanukaṭṭhikaṃ aññena dantaṭṭhikaṃ aññena sīsakaṭāhaṃ. So imameva kāyaṃ upasaṃharati – 'ayampi kho kāyo evaṃdhammo evaṃbhāvī evaṃanatīto'ti. Iti ajjhattaṃ vā kāye kāyānupassī viharati…pe… evampi kho, bhikkhave, bhikkhu kāye kāyānupassī viharati.

"Puna caparaṃ, bhikkhave, bhikkhu seyyathāpi passeyya sarīraṃ sivathikāya chaḍḍitaṃ, aṭṭhikāni setāni saṅkhavaṇṇapaṭibhāgāni …pe… aṭṭhikāni puñjakitāni terovassikāni…pe… aṭṭhikāni pūtīni cuṇṇakajātāni. So imameva kāyaṃ upasaṃharati – 'ayampi kho kāyo evaṃdhammo evaṃbhāvī evaṃanatīto'ti. Iti ajjhattaṃ vā kāye kāyānupassī viharati, bahiddhā vā kāye kāyānupassī viharati, ajjhattabahiddhā vā kāye kāyānupassī viharati; samudayadhammānupassī vā kāyasmiṃ viharati, vayadhammānupassī vā kāyasmiṃ viharati, samudayavayadhammānupassī vā kāyasmiṃ viharati. 'Atthi kāyo'ti vā panassa sati paccupaṭṭhitā hoti. Yāvadeva ñāṇamattāya paṭissatimattāya anissito ca viharati, na ca kiñci loke upādiyati. Evampi kho, bhikkhave, bhikkhu kāye kāyānupassī viharati.

Navasivathikapabbaṃ niṭṭhitaṃ.

Cuddasakāyānupassanā niṭṭhitā.

Vedanānupassanā

"Kathañca pana, bhikkhave, bhikkhu vedanāsu vedanānupassī viharati? Idha, bhikkhave, bhikkhu sukhaṃ vā vedanaṃ vedayamāno 'sukhaṃ vedanaṃ vedayāmī'ti pajānāti; dukkhaṃ vā vedanaṃ vedayamāno 'dukkhaṃ vedanaṃ vedayāmī'ti pajānāti; adukkhamasukhaṃ vā vedanaṃ vedayamāno 'adukkhamasukhaṃ vedanaṃ vedayāmī'ti pajānāti; sāmisaṃ vā sukhaṃ vedanaṃ vedayamāno 'sāmisaṃ sukhaṃ vedanaṃ vedayāmī'ti pajānāti; nirāmisaṃ vā sukhaṃ vedanaṃ vedayamāno 'nirāmisaṃ sukhaṃ vedanaṃ vedayāmī'ti pajānāti; sāmisaṃ vā dukkhaṃ vedanaṃ vedayamāno 'sāmisaṃ dukkhaṃ vedanaṃ vedayāmī'ti pajānāti; nirāmisaṃ vā dukkhaṃ vedanaṃ vedayamāno 'nirāmisaṃ dukkhaṃ vedanaṃ vedayāmī'ti pajānāti; sāmisaṃ vā adukkhamasukhaṃ vedanaṃ vedayamāno 'sāmisaṃ adukkhamasukhaṃ vedanaṃ vedayāmī'ti pajānāti; nirāmisaṃ vā adukkhamasukhaṃ vedanaṃ vedayamāno 'nirāmisaṃ adukkhamasukhaṃ vedanaṃ vedayāmī'ti pajānāti; iti ajjhattaṃ vā vedanāsu vedanānupassī viharati, bahiddhā vā vedanāsu vedanānupassī viharati, ajjhattabahiddhā vā vedanāsu vedanānupassī viharati; samudayadhammānupassī vā vedanāsu viharati, vayadhammānupassī vā vedanāsu viharati, samudayavayadhammānupassī vā vedanāsu viharati. 'Atthi vedanā'ti vā panassa sati paccupaṭṭhitā hoti. Yāvadeva ñāṇamattāya paṭissatimattāya anissito ca viharati, na ca kiñci loke upādiyati. Evampi kho, bhikkhave, bhikkhu vedanāsu vedanānupassī viharati.

Vedanānupassanā niṭṭhitā.

Cittānupassanā

"Kathañca pana, bhikkhave, bhikkhu citte cittānupassī viharati? Idha, bhikkhave, bhikkhu sarāgaṃ vā cittaṃ 'sarāgaṃ citta'nti pajānāti, vītarāgaṃ vā cittaṃ 'vītarāgaṃ citta'nti pajānāti; sadosaṃ vā cittaṃ 'sadosaṃ citta'nti pajānāti, vītadosaṃ vā cittaṃ 'vītadosaṃ citta'nti pajānāti; samohaṃ vā cittaṃ 'samohaṃ citta'nti pajānāti, vītamohaṃ vā cittaṃ 'vītamohaṃ citta'nti pajānāti;

saṅkhittaṃ vā cittaṃ 'saṅkhittaṃ citta'nti pajānāti, vikkhittaṃ vā cittaṃ 'vikkhittaṃ citta'nti pajānāti; mahaggataṃ vā cittaṃ 'mahaggataṃ citta'nti pajānāti, amahaggataṃ vā cittaṃ 'amahaggataṃ citta'nti pajānāti; sauttaraṃ vā cittaṃ 'sauttaraṃ citta'nti pajānāti, anuttaraṃ vā cittaṃ 'anuttaraṃ citta'nti pajānāti; samāhitaṃ vā cittaṃ 'samāhitaṃ citta'nti pajānāti, asamāhitaṃ vā cittaṃ 'asamāhitaṃ citta'nti pajānāti; vimuttaṃ vā cittaṃ 'vimuttaṃ citta'nti pajānāti, avimuttaṃ vā cittaṃ 'avimuttaṃ citta'nti pajānāti. Iti ajjhattaṃ vā citte cittānupassī viharati, bahiddhā vā citte cittānupassī viharati, ajjhattabahiddhā vā citte cittānupassī viharati; samudayadhammānupassī vā cittasmiṃ viharati, vayadhammānupassī vā cittasmiṃ viharati, samudayavayadhammānupassī vā cittasmiṃ viharati. 'Atthi citta'nti vā panassa sati paccupaṭṭhitā hoti. Yāvadeva ñāṇamattāya paṭissatimattāya anissito ca viharati, na ca kiñci loke upādiyati. Evampi kho, bhikkhave, bhikkhu citte cittānupassī viharati.

Cittānupassanā niṭṭhitā.

Dhammānupassanā nīvaraṇapabbaṃ

"Kathañca, bhikkhave, bhikkhu dhammesu dhammānupassī viharati? Idha, bhikkhave, bhikkhu dhammesu dhammānupassī viharati pañcasu nīvaraṇesu. Kathañca pana, bhikkhave, bhikkhu dhammesu dhammānupassī viharati pañcasu nīvaraṇesu?

"Idha, bhikkhave, bhikkhu santaṃ vā ajjhattaṃ kāmacchandaṃ 'atthi me ajjhattaṃ kāmacchando'ti pajānāti, asantaṃ vā ajjhattaṃ kāmacchandaṃ 'natthi me ajjhattaṃ kāmacchando'ti pajānāti; yathā ca anuppannassa kāmacchandassa uppādo hoti tañca pajānāti, yathā ca uppannassa kāmacchandassa pahānaṃ hoti tañca pajānāti, yathā ca pahīnassa kāmacchandassa āyatiṃ anuppādo hoti tañca pajānāti.

"Santaṃ vā ajjhattaṃ byāpādaṃ 'atthi me ajjhattaṃ byāpādo'ti pajānāti, asantaṃ vā ajjhattaṃ byāpādaṃ 'natthi me ajjhattaṃ byāpādo'ti pajānāti; yathā

ca anuppannassa byāpādassa uppādo hoti tañca pajānāti, yathā ca uppannassa byāpādassa pahānaṃ hoti tañca pajānāti, yathā ca pahīnassa byāpādassa āyatiṃ anuppādo hoti tañca pajānāti.

"Santaṃ vā ajjhattaṃ thīnamiddhaṃ 'atthi me ajjhattaṃ thīnamiddha'nti pajānāti, asantaṃ vā ajjhattaṃ thīnamiddhaṃ 'natthi me ajjhattaṃ thīnamiddha'nti pajānāti, yathā ca anuppannassa thīnamiddhassa uppādo hoti tañca pajānāti, yathā ca uppannassa thīnamiddhassa pahānaṃ hoti tañca pajānāti, yathā ca pahīnassa thīnamiddhassa āyatiṃ anuppādo hoti tañca pajānāti.

"Santaṃ vā ajjhattaṃ uddhaccakukkuccaṃ 'atthi me ajjhattaṃ uddhaccakukkucca'nti pajānāti, asantaṃ vā ajjhattaṃ uddhaccakukkuccaṃ 'natthi me ajjhattaṃ uddhaccakukkucca'nti pajānāti; yathā ca anuppannassa uddhaccakukkuccassa uppādo hoti tañca pajānāti, yathā ca uppannassa uddhaccakukkuccassa pahānaṃ hoti tañca pajānāti, yathā ca pahīnassa uddhaccakukkuccassa āyatiṃ anuppādo hoti tañca pajānāti.

"Santaṃ vā ajjhattaṃ vicikicchaṃ 'atthi me ajjhattaṃ vicikicchā'ti pajānāti, asantaṃ vā ajjhattaṃ vicikicchaṃ 'natthi me ajjhattaṃ vicikicchā'ti pajānāti; yathā ca anuppannāya vicikicchāya uppādo hoti tañca pajānāti, yathā ca uppannāya vicikicchāya pahānaṃ hoti tañca pajānāti, yathā ca pahīnāya vicikicchāya āyatiṃ anuppādo hoti tañca pajānāti.

"Iti ajjhattaṃ vā dhammesu dhammānupassī viharati, bahiddhā vā dhammesu dhammānupassī viharati, ajjhattabahiddhā vā dhammesu dhammānupassī viharati; samudayadhammānupassī vā dhammesu viharati, vayadhammānupassī vā dhammesu viharati, samudayavayadhammānupassī vā dhammesu viharati. 'Atthi dhammā'ti vā panassa sati paccupaṭṭhitā hoti. Yāvadeva ñāṇamattāya paṭissatimattāya anissito ca viharati, na ca kiñci loke upādiyati. Evampi kho, bhikkhave, bhikkhu dhammesu dhammānupassī viharati pañcasu nīvaraṇesu.

Nīvaraṇapabbaṃ niṭṭhitaṃ.

Dhammānupassanā khandhapabbaṃ

“Puna caparaṃ, bhikkhave, bhikkhu dhammesu dhammānupassī viharati pañcasu upādānakkhandhesu. Kathañca pana, bhikkhave, bhikkhu dhammesu dhammānupassī viharati pañcasu upādānakkhandhesu? Idha, bhikkhave, bhikkhu – ‘iti rūpaṃ, iti rūpassa samudayo, iti rūpassa atthaṅgamo; iti vedanā, iti vedanāya samudayo, iti vedanāya atthaṅgamo; iti saññā, iti saññāya samudayo, iti saññāya atthaṅgamo; iti saṅkhārā, iti saṅkhārānaṃ samudayo, iti saṅkhārānaṃ atthaṅgamo; iti viññāṇaṃ, iti viññāṇassa samudayo, iti viññāṇassa atthaṅgamo’ti; iti ajjhattaṃ vā dhammesu dhammānupassī viharati, bahiddhā vā dhammesu dhammānupassī viharati, ajjhattabahiddhā vā dhammesu dhammānupassī viharati; samudayadhammānupassī vā dhammesu viharati, vayadhammānupassī vā dhammesu viharati, samudayavayadhammānupassī vā dhammesu viharati. ‘Atthi dhammā’ti vā panassa sati paccupaṭṭhitā hoti. Yāvadeva ñāṇamattāya paṭissatimattāya anissito ca viharati, na ca kiñci loke upādiyati. Evampi kho, bhikkhave, bhikkhu dhammesu dhammānupassī viharati pañcasu upādānakkhandhesu.

Khandhapabbaṃ niṭṭhitaṃ.

Dhammānupassanā āyatanapabbaṃ

“Puna caparaṃ, bhikkhave, bhikkhu dhammesu dhammānupassī viharati chasu ajjhattikabāhiresu āyatanesu. Kathañca pana, bhikkhave, bhikkhu dhammesu dhammānupassī viharati chasu ajjhattikabāhiresu āyatanesu?

“Idha, bhikkhave, bhikkhu cakkhuñca pajānāti, rūpe ca pajānāti, yañca tadubhayaṃ paṭicca uppajjati saṃyojanaṃ tañca pajānāti, yathā ca anuppannassa saṃyojanassa uppādo hoti tañca pajānāti, yathā ca uppannassa saṃyojanassa pahānaṃ hoti tañca pajānāti, yathā ca pahīnassa saṃyojanassa āyatiṃ anuppādo hoti tañca pajānāti.

“Sotañca pajānāti, sadde ca pajānāti, yañca tadubhayaṃ paṭicca uppajjati saṃyojanaṃ tañca pajānāti, yathā ca anuppannassa saṃyojanassa uppādo hoti tañca pajānāti, yathā ca uppannassa saṃyojanassa pahānaṃ hoti tañca pajānāti, yathā ca pahīnassa saṃyojanassa āyatiṃ anuppādo hoti tañca pajānāti.

“Ghānañca pajānāti, gandhe ca pajānāti, yañca tadubhayaṃ paṭicca uppajjati saṃyojanaṃ tañca pajānāti, yathā ca anuppannassa saṃyojanassa uppādo hoti tañca pajānāti, yathā ca uppannassa saṃyojanassa pahānaṃ hoti tañca pajānāti, yathā ca pahīnassa saṃyojanassa āyatiṃ anuppādo hoti tañca pajānāti.

“Jivhañca pajānāti, rase ca pajānāti, yañca tadubhayaṃ paṭicca uppajjati saṃyojanaṃ tañca pajānāti, yathā ca anuppannassa saṃyojanassa uppādo hoti tañca pajānāti, yathā ca uppannassa saṃyojanassa pahānaṃ hoti tañca pajānāti, yathā ca pahīnassa saṃyojanassa āyatiṃ anuppādo hoti tañca pajānāti.

“Kāyañca pajānāti, phoṭṭhabbe ca pajānāti, yañca tadubhayaṃ paṭicca uppajjati saṃyojanaṃ tañca pajānāti, yathā ca anuppannassa saṃyojanassa uppādo hoti tañca pajānāti, yathā ca uppannassa saṃyojanassa pahānaṃ hoti tañca pajānāti, yathā ca pahīnassa saṃyojanassa āyatiṃ anuppādo hoti tañca pajānāti.

“Manañca pajānāti, dhamme ca pajānāti, yañca tadubhayaṃ paṭicca uppajjati saṃyojanaṃ tañca pajānāti, yathā ca anuppannassa saṃyojanassa uppādo hoti tañca pajānāti, yathā ca uppannassa saṃyojanassa pahānaṃ hoti tañca pajānāti, yathā ca pahīnassa saṃyojanassa āyatiṃ anuppādo hoti tañca pajānāti.

“Iti ajjhattaṃ vā dhammesu dhammānupassī viharati, bahiddhā vā dhammesu dhammānupassī viharati, ajjhattabahiddhā vā dhammesu dhammānupassī viharati; samudayadhammānupassī vā dhammesu viharati, vayadhammānupassī vā dhammesu viharati, samudayavayadhammānupassī vā dhammesu viharati. ‘Atthi dhammā’ti vā panassa sati paccupaṭṭhitā hoti. Yāvadeva ñāṇamattāya paṭissatimattāya anissito ca viharati na ca kiñci loke upādiyati.

Evampi kho, bhikkhave, bhikkhu dhammesu dhammānupassī viharati chasu ajjhattikabāhiresu āyatanesu.

Āyatanapabbaṃ niṭṭhitaṃ.

Dhammānupassanā bojjhaṅgapabbaṃ

"Puna caparaṃ, bhikkhave, bhikkhu dhammesu dhammānupassī viharati sattasu bojjhaṅgesu. Kathañca pana, bhikkhave, bhikkhu dhammesu dhammānupassī viharati sattasu bojjhaṅgesu? Idha, bhikkhave, bhikkhu santaṃ vā ajjhattaṃ satisambojjhaṅgaṃ 'atthi me ajjhattaṃ satisambojjhaṅgo'ti pajānāti, asantaṃ vā ajjhattaṃ satisambojjhaṅgaṃ 'natthi me ajjhattaṃ satisambojjhaṅgo'ti pajānāti, yathā ca anuppannassa satisambojjhaṅgassa uppādo hoti tañca pajānāti, yathā ca uppannassa satisambojjhaṅgassa bhāvanāya pāripūrī hoti tañca pajānāti.

"Santaṃ vā ajjhattaṃ dhammavicayasambojjhaṅgaṃ 'atthi me ajjhattaṃ dhammavicayasambojjhaṅgo'ti pajānāti, asantaṃ vā ajjhattaṃ dhammavicaya-sambojjhaṅgaṃ 'natthi me ajjhattaṃ dhammavicayasambojjhaṅgo'ti pajānāti, yathā ca anuppannassa dhammavicayasambojjhaṅgassa uppādo hoti tañca pajānāti, yathā ca uppannassa dhammavicayasambojjhaṅgassa bhāvanāya pāripūrī hoti tañca pajānāti.

"Santaṃ vā ajjhattaṃ vīriyasambojjhaṅgaṃ 'atthi me ajjhattaṃ vīriyasambojjhaṅgo'ti pajānāti, asantaṃ vā ajjhattaṃ vīriyasambojjhaṅgaṃ 'natthi me ajjhattaṃ vīriyasambojjhaṅgo'ti pajānāti, yathā ca anuppannassa vīriyasambojjhaṅgassa uppādo hoti tañca pajānāti, yathā ca uppannassa vīriyasambojjhaṅgassa bhāvanāya pāripūrī hoti tañca pajānāti.

"Santaṃ vā ajjhattaṃ pītisambojjhaṅgaṃ 'atthi me ajjhattaṃ pītisambojjhaṅgo'ti pajānāti, asantaṃ vā ajjhattaṃ pītisambojjhaṅgaṃ 'natthi me ajjhattaṃ pītisambojjhaṅgo'ti pajānāti, yathā ca anuppannassa pītisambojjhaṅgassa uppādo hoti tañca pajānāti, yathā ca uppannassa pītisambojjhaṅgassa bhāvanāya pāripūrī hoti tañca pajānāti.

"Santaṃ vā ajjhattaṃ passaddhisambojjhaṅgaṃ 'atthi me ajjhattaṃ passaddhisambojjhaṅgo'ti pajānāti, asantaṃ vā ajjhattaṃ passaddhisambojjhaṅgaṃ 'natthi me ajjhattaṃ passaddhisambojjhaṅgo'ti pajānāti, yathā ca anuppannassa passaddhisambojjhaṅgassa uppādo hoti tañca pajānāti, yathā ca uppannassa passaddhisambojjhaṅgassa bhāvanāya pāripūrī hoti tañca pajānāti.

"Santaṃ vā ajjhattaṃ samādhisambojjhaṅgaṃ 'atthi me ajjhattaṃ samādhisambojjhaṅgo'ti pajānāti, asantaṃ vā ajjhattaṃ samādhisambojjhaṅgaṃ 'natthi me ajjhattaṃ samādhisambojjhaṅgo'ti pajānāti, yathā ca anuppannassa samādhisambojjhaṅgassa uppādo hoti tañca pajānāti, yathā ca uppannassa samādhisambojjhaṅgassa bhāvanāya pāripūrī hoti tañca pajānāti.

"Santaṃ vā ajjhattaṃ upekkhāsambojjhaṅgaṃ 'atthi me ajjhattaṃ upekkhāsambojjhaṅgo'ti pajānāti, asantaṃ vā ajjhattaṃ upekkhāsambojjhaṅgaṃ 'natthi me ajjhattaṃ upekkhāsambojjhaṅgo'ti pajānāti, yathā ca anuppannassa upekkhāsambojjhaṅgassa uppādo hoti tañca pajānāti, yathā ca uppannassa upekkhāsambojjhaṅgassa bhāvanāya pāripūrī hoti tañca pajānāti.

"Iti ajjhattaṃ vā dhammesu dhammānupassī viharati, bahiddhā vā dhammesu dhammānupassī viharati, ajjhattabahiddhā vā dhammesu dhammānupassī viharati; samudayadhammānupassī vā dhammesu viharati, vayadhammānupassī vā dhammesu viharati, samudayavayadhammānupassī vā dhammesu viharati. 'Atthi dhammā'ti vā panassa sati paccupaṭṭhitā hoti. Yāvadeva ñāṇamattāya paṭissatimattāya anissito ca viharati, na ca kiñci loke upādiyati. Evampi kho, bhikkhave, bhikkhu dhammesu dhammānupassī viharati sattasu bojjhaṅgesu.

Bojjhaṅgapabbaṃ niṭṭhitaṃ.

Dhammānupassanā saccapabbaṃ

"Puna caparaṃ, bhikkhave, bhikkhu dhammesu dhammānupassī viharati catūsu ariyasaccesu. Kathañca pana, bhikkhave, bhikkhu dhammesu dhammānupassī

viharati catūsu ariyasaccesu? Idha, bhikkhave, bhikkhu 'idaṃ dukkha'nti yathābhūtaṃ pajānāti, 'ayaṃ dukkhasamudayo'ti yathābhūtaṃ pajānāti, 'ayaṃ dukkhanirodho'ti yathābhūtaṃ pajānāti, 'ayaṃ dukkhanirodhagāminī paṭipadā'ti yathābhūtaṃ pajānāti. …

[Saccapabbaṃ niṭṭhito.]

"Yo hi koci, bhikkhave, ime cattāro satipaṭṭhāne evaṃ bhāveyya satta vassāni, tassa dvinnaṃ phalānaṃ aññataraṃ phalaṃ pāṭikaṅkhaṃ diṭṭheva dhamme aññā; sati vā upādisese anāgāmitā.

"Tiṭṭhantu, bhikkhave, satta vassāni. Yo hi koci, bhikkhave, ime cattāro satipaṭṭhāne evaṃ bhāveyya cha vassāni…pe… pañca vassāni… cattāri vassāni… tīṇi vassāni… dve vassāni… ekaṃ vassaṃ… tiṭṭhatu, bhikkhave, ekaṃ vassaṃ. Yo hi koci, bhikkhave, ime cattāro satipaṭṭhāne evaṃ bhāveyya satta māsāni, tassa dvinnaṃ phalānaṃ aññataraṃ phalaṃ pāṭikaṅkhaṃ diṭṭheva dhamme aññā; sati vā upādisese anāgāmitā. Tiṭṭhantu, bhikkhave, satta māsāni. Yo hi koci, bhikkhave, ime cattāro satipaṭṭhāne evaṃ bhāveyya cha māsāni…pe… pañca māsāni… cattāri māsāni… tīṇi māsāni… dve māsāni… ekaṃ māsaṃ… aḍḍhamāsaṃ… tiṭṭhatu, bhikkhave, aḍḍhamāso. Yo hi koci, bhikkhave, ime cattāro satipaṭṭhāne evaṃ bhāveyya sattāhaṃ, tassa dvinnaṃ phalānaṃ aññataraṃ phalaṃ pāṭikaṅkhaṃ diṭṭheva dhamme aññā sati vā upādisese anāgāmitā"ti.

"'Ekāyano ayaṃ, bhikkhave, maggo sattānaṃ visuddhiyā sokaparidevānaṃ samatikkamāya dukkhadomanassānaṃ atthaṅgamāya ñāyassa adhigamāya nibbānassa sacchikiriyāya yadidaṃ cattāro satipaṭṭhānā'ti. Iti yaṃ taṃ vuttaṃ, idametaṃ paṭicca vutta"nti.

Idamavoca bhagavā. Attamanā te bhikkhū bhagavato bhāsitaṃ abhinandunti.

Sutta 16 ♦ Glossary

a

aṅga (n.), limb, part, factor, constituent, attribute, quality, determing characteristic.

√*añch*, to stretch, to turn, to drag, to pull.

aññatara (m.n. pr. adj.), a, a certain.

aññā (f.), knowledge, wisdom, insight.

ajjhattaṃ (part.), in, inner, subjective, within oneself.

ajjhattika (adj.), personal, inner, internal, belonging to oneself.

añña (pr. adj.), other, another.

aṭṭhika (n.), bone.

aḍḍha (m.n.), half.

atīta (adj.; ppp. √*i* + *ati*), past, former, beyond, transgressing, become free of; passed away.

atthaṅgama (m.), disappearance, annihilation.

attamana (adj.), mentally uplifted, exalted, pleased, assured, satisfied.

atthi, see √*as.*

adhigama (m.), attainment, acquisition; understanding, realization; experience.

adho (part.), below, beneath.

anāgāmitā (f.), the condition of being an *anāgāmin*, one who does not return.

anuttara (adj.), unsurpassed, unexcelled, excellent, supreme.

anupassana (n.), looking at, viewing, observing, contemplating, realizing.

anupassin (adj.), observing, viewing, considering.

anta (n.), intestines.

antaguṇa (n.), bowels.

antevāsin (m.), pupil, apprentice, student, disciple.

apagata (ppp. √*gam* +*apa*; adj.), gone, gone away from; without stain, without defect.

aparaṃ, see puna.

apāna (n.), exhalation.

api (part.), *adds emphasis to preceding term*; even, even though, also; but.

abhikkanta (ppp. √*kam* + *abhi*), going forward, advancing.

abhijjhā (f.), longing, yearning.

abhi + √*nand*, to rejoice, to take delight, to be glad.

amhi, see √*as.*

ayaṃ (m.f. dem. pron.), this, *etc.*

arañña (n.), forest, wilderness.

ariya (adj.), noble, preeminent, superlative; Buddhist.

√*as*, to be. (Line 37, *atthi* = 3rd pers. sing. indic.; line 43, *amhi* = 1st pers. sing. indic.; line 84, *assa* = 3rd pers. sing. opt.)

asita (ppp. √*as*), eaten, eating.

asucin (adj.), impure, unclean.

assa (m.n. dem. pron.), to him, to that one, *etc.*

assu (n.), tears.

aha (n.), day. (Line 92, initial *a* is elided after *i*, which is lengthened.)

ā

āgāra (n.), house, dwelling, place, spot.

ātāpin (adj.), ardent, strenuous, energetic, applying oneself.

āna (n.), inhalation.

āpo (n.), water.

ā + √*bhuj*, to bend down, to assume a posture.

ā + √*mant*, to address, to advise.

āyatana (n.), resting place, abode; source; region, field, sphere; *tech.* the perceptual sphere, the sensorium: the six sense organs and their respective objects (including mind and thoughts).

āyatiṃ (adv.), in the future.

ālokita (ppp. √*lok* + *ā*), looking forwards.

i

icchā (f.), wish, want, desire, long for.

iti (part.), here, in this/that case; *marks quotation of speech or thought.*

idaṃ (n. dem. pron), this, *etc.*

idha (part.), here, in this connection, now.

imaṃ (m.f.n. dem. pron.), this, *etc.*

imasmiṃ (m.n. dem. pron.), in the, *etc.*

ime (m. dem. pron.), these, *etc.*

iriyāpatha (m.), conduct, way of life, movement, deportment, posture.

u

uccāra (m.), feces.

uju (adj.), straight, upright.

udariya (n.), stomach.

uddesa (m.), instruction, summary exposition, brief statement, recitation.

uddhaṃ (part.), above, vertically.

uddhacca (n.), agitation, over-excitement, distraction.

uddhumātaka (adj.), swollen, bloated.

ud + √*pad*, to come into being, to be produced, to appear, to become available.

upa + √*ṭhā*, to establish, to set up; *caus.* to employ, to attend, to bring near, to bring about.

upa + *saṃ* + √*har*, to draw together, to put together, to focus on, to bring to bear on, to see as similar.

upa + *ā* + √*dā*, to take hold, to grasp, to take up. (Line 38, *upādiyati* = 3. pers. sing. indic.)

upādāna (n.), taking, grasping, appropriating; material support, fuel.

upādi (m.f.), material support, grasping, appropriating.

upāyāsā (m.), anxiety, trouble, disturbance.

upekkhā (f.), equanimity, equipoise, balance.

uppajj° = *ud* + √*pad.*

uppanna (ppp. √*pad* + *ud*), arisen, come into being, aroused.

uppāda (m.), coming into being, appearance, production, manifestation, arising.

ubhatomukha (adj.), with an opening on both sides, facing two directions.

ubhaya (adj.), both.

ū

ūru (m.), thigh.

e

eka (num.; adj.), one; a certain, some.

ekāyana (m.), a narrow path, the only path, a one way path, the direct way.

etaṃ (m.f.n. dem. pron.), this, *etc.* (Line 3, n. *etad* before vowel.)

enaṃ (m.f.n. dem. pron.), him, her, it, that, this, the, *etc.*

eva (part.), *adds emphasis to preceding term*; so, just, even.

evaṃ, (part.), thus, so, such, in this way; yes.

k

kaṅka (m.), heron.

kaṭi (f.), hips.

katama (m.f.n. interg. pron.), which (of several)?, *etc.*

kathaṃ (part), how?

kamma (n.), action, behavior.

kammāsadhamma (m.), *place name.*

karīsa (n.), excrement, feces.

kāka (m.), crow.

kāma (m.n.), desire, sensory pleasure, passion.

kāya (m.), body.

kārin (adj.), doing, making, acting with; one who does, *etc.*

kiñci (n. indef. pron.), certain, some, *etc.*; *with negation*, whatsoever, *etc.*.

kilomaka (n.), lung membrane.

kukkucca (n.), worry, remorse, anxiety.

kulala (m.), raven.

kuru (m.), *peoples' name.*

kesa (m.), hair.

koci (m. indef. pron), any.

kh

khandha (m.), trunk, shoulder; complex, bulk, mass, accumulation; *tech.*, the five existential functions of the human being (namely, materialty, sensation, perception, conceptualization, consciousness).

√*khād*, to eat, to devour. (Line 97, *khajjamāna* = prap.)

khāyita (ppp. √*khā*), chewing.

kheḷa (m.), saliva.

kho (encl. part.), indeed, clearly, surely, certainly.

g

gacchant (prap. √*gam*), going, proceeding, walking.

gata (ppp. √*gam*), going, gone.

√*gam*, to go.

gāmin (adj.), leading to, going toward.

gāvī (f.), cow.

gijjha (m.), vulture.

gīvā (f.), the neck.

goghātaka (m.), butcher.

gopphaka (m.), ankle.

gh

ghāna (n.), nose.

c

cakkhu (n.), eye.

catumahāpatha (m.), town square, crossroads.

catu(r) (num.), four. (Line 7, *cattāro* = four.)

citta (n.), mind, discursive thought, discursive mind.

cīvara (n.), robe.

cuṇṇaka (adj.), powder-like.

cuddasa (num.), fourteen.

ch

cha (num.), six.

chaḍḍita (ppp. √*chaḍḍ*), discarded, thrown away.

chanda (m.), impulse, will, resolution, intention.

j

jaṅghā (f.), lower leg, calf.

jarā (f.), aging.

jāgarita (ppp. √*gar*), awakened.

jāta (ppp. √*jan*), born, grown, become, reduced to.

jāti (f.), birth, generation.

jivhā (f.), tongue.

ñ

ñāṇa (n.), knowledge, recognition, discernment.

ñāya (m.), method, system, proper way.

ṭh

ṭhita (ppp. √*ṭhā*), stood, standing.

t

taṃ (m.f.n. dem. pron.), him, her, it, that, this, the, *etc.* (Line 232, n. *tad* before vowel; also, used adverbially = there.)

taca (n.), skin.

taṇḍula (m.), husked rice.

tatra (part.), there.

tathā (part.), that, thus, in that manner; such, so. (Line 44, *yathā* ... *tathā*, whatever X … that Y.)

tala (n.), flat surface, base; palm, sole.

tassa (m.n. dem. pron.), for him, for that one, *etc.*

ti (part.), marks end of direct speech, a thought, or quoted term. (Note: A short vowel preceding *ti* is lengthened, and *ṃ* is converted to *n.*)

ti (num.), three.

tila (m.), sesame seed.

tuṇhībhāva (m.), silence.

te (2nd pers. per. pron.; m. dem. pron.), by you, yours, to you (sg.); those, them, *etc.*

tejo (n.), fire, heat.

terovassika (adj.), older than a season, dried up, decayed.

th

√*ṭhā*, to stand, to be.

thīna (n.), stagnation, stiffness, unwieldiness, impiability, inflexibility.

d

dakkha (adj.), skilled, able, possessing dexterity.

danta (m.), teeth.

disā, (f.), the four directions, the four principle points of the compass.

dīgha (adj.), long, tall.

dīpin (m.), panther.

dukkha (n.; adj.), unease, distress, trouble, unhappiness, pain; distressful, painful, troublesome.

domanassa (n.), heavy heartedness, depression, abjection.

dosa (m.), hostility, anger.

dvi (num.), two.

dh

dhañña (n.), grain, corn, seed.

dhamma (m.), phenomenon, thing; quality, mental quality, thought; nature; teaching; standard.

dhātu (f.) element, natural condition, property, feature. (Line 81, *dhātuso* = abl., *according to its nature.*)

dhāraṇa (n.), wearing, bearing, holding.

diṭṭha (ppp. √*das*), seen, visible. (Line 322, *diṭṭhe dhamme* = in this world, here and now, in the present.)

n

na (part.), no, not.

naṃ (mfn. dem. pron.), that, *etc.*

nakha (m.), fingernail, toenail.

nava (num.), nine.

nānappakāra (m.), various, manifold.

nānā (part.), various, diverse, different.

nāma (n.), name; *tech.* mental functions, e.g. feeling, perception, conceptualization, intention, attentiveness.

ni, *as noun prefix denoting* being without, lacking, non-, un-, *etc.*

nigama (m.), town.

niṭṭhita (adj.), completed, finished, come to an end.

nibbāna (n.), extinguishing, unbinding, letting go, releasing.

nirāmisa (adj.), immaterial, incorporeal.

nirodha (m.), cessation, ending, stopping.

ni + √*sad*, to sit down.

nisinna (ppp. √*sad* + *ni*), seated, sitting.

nisīd° = *ni* + √*sad.*

nissita (adj.), hanging on, depending on, supported by; by means of, on account of.

nīvaraṇa (m.), hindrance, obstacle, envelopment.

nhāru (m.), sinew.

p

paccupaṭṭhita (ppp. √*ṭhā* + *paṭi* + *upa*), set up, established, brought near, made present.

pa + √*jān*, to know, to realize.

pañca (num.), five.

paṭi + *ava* + √*ikkh*, to see, to regard, to look at, to consider, to realize, to contemplate.

paṭikūla (m.), disgust, repugnance, repulsion, loathing.

paṭikkanta (ppp. √*kam* + *paṭi*), going backwards, returning.

paṭicca (abs. √*i* + *paṭi*), because, on account of, on the basis of.

paṭipadā (f.), path, course, practice, way.

paṭibhāga (adj.), having a likeness, resemblance.

paṭisaṃvedin (adj.), experiencing, feeling, undergoing.

paṭi + √*su*, to respond, to answer; to agree, to assent. (Line 3, *paccassosuṃ* = aor.)

paṭissati (f.), remembrance, awareness, attentiveness.

paṭṭhānā (n.), foundation, establishment; *tech*., setting forth.

paṭhama (ord. num.), first.

pa + *ṇi* + √*dhā*, to put down, to apply, to direct. (Line 18, *paṇidhāya* = abs.)

paṇihita (ppp. √*dhā* + *pa* + *ṇi*), intent on, controlled, applied, directed toward, disposed.

pana (encl. part.), but, however; moreover; now (*continuing particle*).

patta (m.n.), bowl; bowl used by Buddhist mendicants for begging food.

pathavī (f.), earth.

pabba (n.), section, division, part.

parideva (m.), regret, weeping, crying.

parimukhaṃ (part.), in front, immediately before; *lit.*, around the mouth.

pariyanta (m.), limit, end, border, surface, surrounding.

pallaṅka (adj.), crossed-legged.

√*pas*, to see, to look, to regard.

pa + √*sas*, to exhale.

pa + √*sambh*, to calm, to tranquilize. (Line 23, *passambhaya* = prap.)

pasārita (ppp. √*sār* + *pa*), to stretch.

passaddhi (f.), calmness, tranquility, repose, serenity.

passāva (m.), urine.

pahāna (n.), abandonment, rejection, reliquishment.

pahīna (ppp. √*hā*), abandoned, eliminated, put down, left alone.

pāṭikaṅkha (adj.), desired, expected.

pāṇaka (m.), creature, living being.

pāda (m.), base, basis, foundation, footing, foot.

pāripūrī (f.), fulfillment, completion, consummation.

pi (encl. part.), even, also, just so, too; but; *adds emphasis to preceding term.*

piṭṭhi (f.), the back.

pitta (n.), bile.

piya (adj.), dear, agreeable, likable, beloved.

pihaka (n.), spleen

pīta (ppp. √*pī*), having drunk, drinking.

pīti (f.), joy, delight, exuberance, bliss.

puñjakita (adj.), heaped up, heaped together.

pūti (adj.), putrid, rotten, festering.

putoḷi (f.), sack, bag.

puna (part.), again. (Line 42, *puna caparaṃ*, moreover, and something else, furthermore.)

pubbo (m.), pus.

purisa (m.), man, person, people.

pūra (adj.), full.

pe (part.), abridgement of *peyyāla*: repetition, etcetera.

ph

phala (n.), result, fruit.

phāsukā (f.), ribs.

b

bahiddhā (prep.), external, outside.

bāhira (adj.), external, outside, outer.

bilaso (adv.), bit by bit, piece by piece.

bojjha (n.), awakening, wisdom, knowledge.

byaggha (m.), tiger.

byāpāda (m.), hostility, anger, ill-will, antagonism.

bh

bhagavant (adj.), fortunate, illustrious, honorable; fortunate one: *epithet of Gotama.*

bhadante (ind.), *form of respectful address, like E.* sir.

bhamakāra (m.), acrobat.

bhāvanā (f.), developing, producing, cultivating, applying; *tech.* cultivating the mind through meditation.

bhāvin (adj.), being as, having a being, becoming.

bhāsita (ppp. √*bhās*; n.), spoken, speeking; speech, talk.

bhikkhu (m.), mendicant; *tech.*, beggar.

√*bhū*, to be, to become; to cultivate, to nurture, to develop.

m

maṃsa (n.), flesh.

makkhita (ppp. √*makkh*), smeared, pasted, anointed.

magga (m.), path, road, way.

mata (ppp. √*mar*), dead, deceased.

matta (adj.), measured, by measure, as much as; merely, only, not even.

matthaka (m.), head, top.

manas (n.), mind.

manasikāra (n.), attention, attentiveness, consideration, fixed thought.

maraṇa (n.), death.

mahaggata (adj.), extensive, expansive, vast.

mahant (adj.), large, great, extensive.

māsa (m.) kidney beans.

māsa (m.), month.

miñja (n.), marrow, bone.

middha (n.), lethargy, torpor.

mugga (m.), green bean, mung bean.

√*muc*, to release, to free, to liberate; to let out.

mutta (n.), urine.

mūla (n.), root.

me (1st pers. per. pron.), to me, by me, *etc.*

medo (m.), fat.

moha (m.), delusion, confusion, mental dullness.

y

yaṃ (mfn. rel. pron.), that which, *etc.*

yakana (n.), liver.

yathā (part.), as, just as. (Line 44, *yathā ... tathā*, whatever X ... that Y.)

yathāṭhita (adv.), so-being, such and such, as is.

yathābhūtaṃ (part.), as is; in reality.

yadidaṃ (part.), namely, as follows, that is to say; *literally*, which is this.

yāva (part.), as long as, to the extent that, as far as.

yo (m. rel. pron.), he who, that which, *etc.*

r

rassa (adj.), short.

rāga (m.), passion, excitement, infatuation, lust.

rukkha (m.), tree.

rūpa (n.), form, appearance, body, object.

l

√*labh*, to gain, to get, to aquire.

lasikā (f.), joint fluid.

loka (m.), world.

loma (n.), body hair.

lohita (n.), blood.

v

vakka (n.), kidney.

√*vac*, to speak. (Line 3, *avoca* = aor.)

vaṇṇa (m.), color.

√*vadh*, to kill, to slaughter.

vaya (m.), loss, decay, perishing, disappearance.

vasā (f.), skin oil.

vassa (n.), year; *lit.*, rainy season.

vā (encl. part.), or.

vāyo (n.), wind.

vi, *as noun prefix denoting* away from, without, separation, dis-, un-, *etc.*

vikkhitta (ppp. √*khip*), disturbed, scattered, dispersed, deranged, dismembered.

vicaya (m.), search, examination, investigation, inquiry into.

vicikicchā (f.), doubt, perplexity, uncertainty.

viññāṇa, (n.), cognizance, consciousness, cognition.

√*vid*, to know, to feel, to experience.

vidisā, (f.), the four intermediate directions, the four intermeditate points of the compass.

vi + √*nī*, to give up, to put down, to remove. (Line 10, *vineyya* = abs.)

vinīlaka (adj.), bluish-black, discolored.

vipubbaka (adj.), festering.

vi + √*bhaj*, to break apart, to cut up, to divide.

vimutta (ppp. √*muc* + *vi*), liberated, released, freed.

vilokita (ppp. √*lok* + *vi*), looking backwards.

vividha (adj), various, diverse, manifold, different.

visuddhi (f.), excellence, splendor, purity, virtue, clarity, recititude.

vi + √*har*, to live, to stay, to dwell, to abide.

vihita (ppp. √*dhā* + *vi*), arranged, prepared, placed, set.

vīta, (adj.), without, deprived of, free from.

vīriya (n.), vigor, virility, energy, effort.

vīhi (m.), rice.

vutta (ppp. √*vac*), said, spoken.

vedanā (f.), feeling, sensation.

s

sa, *prefix denoting* with, possessed of, having.

sauttara (adj.), inferior; *lit.*, with (*sa*) something greater (*uttara*).

saṃyojana (m.), bond, fetter.

√*sak*, can, to be able to. (Line 22, *sikkh°* = desid., want to be able, *i.e.*, train oneself.)

saṅkha (f.), a shell, conch, mother-of-pearl.

saṅkhalikā (f.), a chain.

saṅkhāra (m.), mental formation, conceptual fabrication; volition, will; anything made, conditioned, fashioned, constructed or put together.

saṅkhitta (ppp. √*khip* + *saṃ*), conventrated, gathered, collected, attentive.

saṅkhittena (part.), in short, in brief, concisely.

saṅghāṭi (f.), the outer robe (of three) of a Buddhist mendicant.

sacca (adj.; n.), real, actual, verifiable; reality, actuality, fact.

sacchikiriyā, (f.), realization, experiencing.

saññā (f.), perception.

sat (prap.), being. (Line 37, *sati* = f. loc. sing.)

sata (ppp. √*sar*), remembered, established in present-momery awareness. (Line 18, *satova* = *sata* + *eva*.)

sati (f.), present-moment awareness, presence of mind, reflective clarity, non-interfering consciousness, lucidity; *lit.* memory; *tech.*, memory-in-the-present.

satimant (adj.), aware, attentive, watchful.

satta (num.), seven.

satta (m.), person, being, sentient being.

santa (prap. √*as*), being.

sabba (adj.), every, all, entire.

samatikkama (m.), going further, passing, passing beyond, overcoming.

samaya (m.), time, occasion.

samādhi (m.), concentration, collectedness, composure, mental intentness.

samāhita (ppp. √*dhā* + *saṃ* + *ā*), collected, composed, gathered together, concentrated, firm.

samiñjita (ppp. √*iñj* + *saṃ*), bending.

sāmisa (adj.), bodily, material, in the flesh, .

samudaya (m.), origin, arising, source.

sampajāna (adj.), attentive, conscientious, thoughtful, fully comprehending.

sampayoga (m.), connection, association, union, relationship.

sambandha (ppp. √*bandh* + *saṃ*), bound, tied, connected.

sambojjha = *bojjha* .

sayāna (prap. √*si*), lying down.

sarīra (n.), body, corpse.

sāli (m..), wheat.

√*si*, to lie down.

siṅgāla (m.), jackel.

siṅghāṇikā (f.), mucus.

sivathika (m.), charnal ground, cremation ground.

sīsakaṭāha (n.), skull.

sukha (n.; adj.), ease, serenity, harmony, happiness, pleasure; gratifying, pleasant, agreeable, harmonious.

suñña (adj.), empty, uninhabited.

suta (ppp. √*su*), heard.

sutta (n.), discourse, dialogue, text; *lit.*, thread, stitching, textile.

sutta (ppp. √*sup*), sleeping.

sunakha (m.), dog.

seta (adj.), white.

seda (m.), sweat.

semha (n.), phlegm.

seyyathā (part.), as if, just as.

sesa (m.), remnant, residue.

so (m. dem. pron.), he, that, that one, the, *etc.*

soka (m), sadness, sorrow, grief.

sota (n.), ear.

h

hattha (m.), the hand.

hanukā (f.), the jaw.

hadaya (m.), the heart.

hi (part.), surely, indeed.

hoti = √*bhū*.

Sutta Translations

NOTE: The texts in the present volume were translated from the *Chaṭṭha Saṅgāyana Pāli Tipiṭaka* (Dhamma Giri, Igatpuri, India: Vipassana Research Institute, 1990). The translations in this section first appeared in Glenn Wallis, *Basic Teachings of the Buddha* (New York: Random House, 2007). Readers may wish to consult the notes to the translations in that volume. Readers, furthermore, are encouraged to consult other translations in addition to those here. To that end, the references given under the text titles are to the following recommended publications:

- *Dīghanikāya* = Walshe, Maurice (trans.), *The Long Discourses of the Buddha: A Translation of the Digha Nikaya* (Boston: Wisdom Publications, 1995).
- *Majjhimanikāya* = Bhikkhu Nanamoli and Bhikkhu Bodhi (trans.), *The Middle Length Discourses of the Buddha: A New Translation of the Majjhima Nikaya* (Boston: Wisdom Publications, 1995).
- *Saṃyuttanikāya* = Bhikkhu Bodhi (trans.), *The Connected Discourses of the Buddha: A Translation of the Samyutta Nikaya* (Boston: Wisdom Publications, 2000).
- *Aṅguttaranikāya* = Nyanaponika Thera and Bhikkhu Bodhi, *Numerical Discourses of the Buddha: an Anthology of Suttas from the Anguttara Nikaya* (Walnut Creek: AltaMira Press, 1999).

Readers should, finally, keep in mind that there may not always be an exact text-translation correspondence. That is, some portions of text may be translated that were elided in the Pali text; and some portions of the Pali text may have been edited out of the translation.

Sutta 1

The Hawk

(*Sakuṇagghi Sutta; Saṃyuttanikāya* 5.47.6)

The Buddha related this story to a group of his followers.

Once, in the distant past, a hawk suddenly swooped down and seized a quail. As the quail was being carried away by the hawk, it lamented, "how unfortunate I am, what little merit I possess to have wandered out of my natural habitat into a foreign domain. If I had wandered within my native domain today, within my own ancestral, natural habitat, this hawk would certainly not have been a match for me in battle."

"What is your native domain, quail, what is your own ancestral, natural habitat?," asked the hawk.

The quail answered, "that clod of earth freshly tilled with a plough."

Then, the hawk, not boasting about its own strength, not mentioning its own strength, released the quail, saying, "go, quail; but having gone there, you can not escape me."

Then, the quail, having gone to the clod of earth freshly tilled with a plough, climbed onto a large clod of earth and, standing there, said to the hawk, "come get me now, hawk, come get me now!"

Now, the hawk, not boasting about its own strength, not mentioning its own strength, folded up its wings and suddenly swooped down on the quail. When the quail fully realized that the hawk was coming, it got inside that clod of earth. And the hawk, striking against it, suffered a blow to its chest.

So it is when someone wanders out of his or her natural habitat into a foreign domain. Therefore, do not wander out of your natural habitat into a foreign domain. Death will gain access to the person who has wandered out of his or her natural habitat into a foreign domain, death will gain a footing.

Now, what is for you a foreign domain, outside of your natural habitat? It is the five-fold realm of sensual pleasure. Which five? Forms perceptible to the eye, which are pleasing, desirable, charming, agreeable, arousing desire, and enticing; sounds perceptible to the ear, which are pleasing, desirable, charming, agreeable, arousing desire, and enticing; scents perceptible to the nose, which are pleasing, desirable, charming, agreeable, arousing desire, and enticing; tastes perceptible to the tongue, which are pleasing, desirable, charming, agreeable, arousing desire, and enticing; tactile objects perceptible to the body, which are pleasing, desirable, charming, agreeable, arousing desire, and enticing. This is for you a foreign domain, outside of your natural habitat. Death will not gain access to the person who lives within his or her native domain, within his or her own ancestral, natural habitat, death will not gain a footing. Now, what is your native domain, your own ancestral, natural habitat? It is the foundation of present-moment awareness in four areas. What are the four areas? Now, being ardent, fully aware, and mindful, and having put down longing and discontentment towards the world, live observing the body *in and as the body*, live observing feelings *in and as feelings*, live observing mind *in and as mind*, and live observing mental qualities and phenomena *in and as mental qualities and phenomena.*

This is your native domain, your own ancestral, natural habitat.

Sutta 2
A Brief Talk to Mālukya

(*Cūḷamālukya Sutta*; *Majjhimanikāya* 63)

This is what I heard. Once, the Fortunate One was staying in Sāvatthī, in Jeta's grove in Anāthapiṇḍika's park.

There, the venerable Mālukya was living in solitary seclusion. Mālukya reflected as follows. "There are certain speculative matters that the Fortunate One has left undetermined, set aside, and rejected. Is the world eternal, or is the world not eternal? Is the world infinite, or is the world finite? Is the life-force identical to the body, or is the life-force different from the body? Does a person who has come to know reality exist after death; not exist after death; both exist and not exist after death; or neither exist nor not exist after death? These are the matters that the Fortunate One has not determined. It does not please me or seem right to me that the Fortunate One has not determined these matters. I will approach the Fortunate One and ask him the reason for this refusal. If he determines these matters for me, then I will continue the training. If he does not determine these matters for me, then I will abandon the training and return to the lowly world."

So, in the evening, Mālukya emerged from his solitude and approached the Fortunate One. After exchanging greetings, he sat down and said, "when I was in solitary seclusion, it occurred to me that you have left undetermined, set aside, and rejected certain speculative matters. Is the world eternal, or is the world not eternal? Is the world infinite, or is the world finite? Is the life-force identical to the body, or is the life-force different from the body? Does a person who has come to know reality exist after death; not exist after death; both exist and not exist after death; or neither exist nor not exist after death? These are the matters that you have not determined:

"It does not please me or seem right to me that you have not determined these matters. So, I thought that I would approach you and ask you the reason for this refusal. If you determine these matters for me, then I will continue the training. If you do not determine these matters for me, then I will abandon the training and return to the lowly world. So, if you know the answers to these questions, then answer me! If you do not know, then it is straightforward for a person who does not know or see to say, 'I do not know, I do not see.'"

The Buddha replies, "Mālukya, did I ever say to you, 'come, Mālukya, train with me, I will determine for you whether the world is eternal or not eternal, infinite or finite,' and so on?"

"No, you did not," responded Mālukya.

"In that case, you fool of a man , who do you think are you, and what is it that you are repudiating?"

The Buddha continues, "Mālukya, if anyone were to say, 'I will not enter the life of training under the Fortunate One until he determines for me whether the world is eternal or not eternal, infinite or finite,' and so on, I would still not determine those matters, and in the meantime that person would die.

"It is, Mālukya, as if a person would be shot by an arrow thickly smeared with poison, and his friends, companions, and relatives would hire a physician to remove the arrow. But that person would say, 'I will not have this arrow removed until I know who shot it; whether he was of the upper, middle or low class; his name and family; whether he was tall, short, or of medium stature; whether he was black, brown, or light skinned; whether he lived in such and such a town, village, or city; and until I know whether the bow that was used to shoot the arrow was a long bow or a cross bow; and until I know whether the bowstring that was used to shoot the arrow was made from the swallowwort plant, from *sanha* hemp, sinew, *maruva* hemp, or from the bark of the *khira* tree; and until I know whether the shaft was made from wild or cultivated wood; and until I know whether the feathers on the shaft were that of a vulture, crow, hawk, peacock, or stork; and until I know whether the sinew used to wrap the shaft was from a cattle, water buffalo, deer, or monkey; and until I know whether the arrow that was used to wound me was razor-tipped, curved, tubular, calf-toothed, or oleander.

"All of this would remain unknown to that person, Mālukya, and in the meantime he or she would die. So, too, Mālukya, someone might say, 'I will not enter the life of training under the Fortunate One until the he determines for me whether the world is eternal or not eternal, infinite or finite,' and so on. Still, these matters would remain undetermined, and in the meantime that person would die."

"Mālukya, because there is the speculative view *the world is eternal*, the training life can not be cultivated. And because there is the speculative view *the world is not eternal*, the training life can not be cultivated. Whether there is the view *the world is eternal* or the view *the world is not eternal*, whether there is the view *the life force is different from the body* or the view *the life force is the same as the body*, and so on, still there is birth, there is ageing, there is death; still there is sadness, regret, unease, depression, and anxiety. It is the destruction of all of *this*, in this very world, that *I* make known.

"It is for this reason, Mālukya, that you should bear in mind that which I have not determined, because it is indeterminate, and that which I have determined, because it is determinate. What have I not determined? I have not determined *the world is eternal*; I have not determined *the world is not eternal*; I have not determined *the world is infinite*; I have not determined *the world is finite*; I have not determined *the life-force is identical to the body*; I have not determined *the life-force is different from the body*; I have not determined *a person who has come to know reality exists after death, a person who has come to know reality does not exist after death, a person who has come to know reality both exists and does not exist after death, or a person who has come to know reality neither exists nor does not exist after death.*

"And why, Mālukya, have I not determined these matters? To do so does not lead to what is beneficial, to the beginning of training, to disenchantment, to dispassion, to cessation, to peace, to direct knowing, to awakening, to unbinding. That is the reason that I have not determined these matters.

"And what, Mālukya, *have* I determined? I have determined *this is unease.* I have determined *this is the arising of unease.* I have determined *this is the cessation of unease.* I have determined *this is the path leading to the cessation of unease.*

"And why, Mālukya, have I determined these matters? To do so leads to what is beneficial, to the beginning of training, to disenchantment, to dispassion, to cessation, to peace, to direct knowing, to awakening, to unbinding. That is the reason that I have determined these matters.

"It is for this reason, Mālukya, that you should bear in mind that which I have not determined, because it is indeterminate, and that which I have determined, because it is determinate."

This is what the Fortunate One said. Exalted, the venerable Mālukya rejoiced at the words of the Fortunate One.

Sutta 3

Three-fold Knowledge

(*Tevijja Sutta*; *Dīghanikāya* 13)

This is what I heard. Traveling in Kosala with a large group of five hundred mendicants, the Fortunate One approached the Brahmin village Manasākaṭa. The Fortunate One stayed there, just north of the village, in the mango grove on the banks of the river Aciravatiyā. Many renowned and wealthy religious authorities lived in Manasakāṭa at that time.

Now, Vāseṭṭha and Bhāradvāja were wandering, strolling along the road, when a dispute arose between them concerning the right and wrong paths. The young Brahmin Vāseṭṭha said, "*this* is the direct path, this is the straight path that leads to salvation, and leads one who follows it to communion with God. This is what is proclaimed by the Brahmin Pokkharasāti."

And the young Brahmin Bhāradvāja said: "*This* is the direct path, this is the straight path that leads to salvation, and leads one who follows it to communion with God. This is what is proclaimed by the Brahmin Tārukkha." But neither could Vāseṭṭha convince Bhāradvāja, nor Bharadvaja convince Vaseṭṭha.

Then Vaseṭṭha said to Bhāradvāja, "Bhāradvāja, the ascetic Gotama Sakyaputta, who went forth from the Sakya clan, is staying north of Manasākaṭa, in the mango grove on the banks of the river Aciravatiyā. A favorable reputation has preceded the honorable Gotama. It is said that the Fortunate One is worthy, completely awakened, perfected in knowledge and conduct, happy, knowledgeable in the ways of the world, unsurpassed as a trainer of people needing to be tamed, a teacher of humans and resplendent beings, awakened, fortunate. Let's go Bhāradvāja, to where the ascetic Gotama is. Let's approach him, and ask about this matter. Whatever the ascetic Gotama answers, we will take to heart."

"Very well, friend," consented Bhāradvāja.

So, Vāseṭṭha and Bhāradvāja approached the Fortunate One, exchanged friendly greetings and polite conversation with him, then sat down on one side. Having done so, Vāseṭṭha spoke to the Fortunate One. "We were wandering, friend Gotama, strolling along the road here, when a dispute arose concerning the right and wrong paths. I said, '*this* is the direct path, this is the straight path that leads to salvation, and leads one who follows it to communion with God. This is what is proclaimed by the Brahmin Pokkharasāti.'"

Then the young Brahmin Bhāradvāja said, "And I said, '*this* is the direct path, this is the straight path that leads to salvation, and leads one who follows it to communion with God. This is what is proclaimed by the Brahmin Tārukkha."

"It is in this matter, friend Gotama, that there is an argument, a disagreement, a difference of opinion."

The Buddha replied, "so, Vāseṭṭha, you say this: '*this* is the direct path, this is the straight path that leads to salvation, and leads one who follows it to communion with God. This is what is proclaimed by the Brahmin Pokkharasāti.' Bhāradvāja says this: '*this* is the direct path, this is the straight path that leads to salvation, and leads one who follows it to communion with God. This is what is proclaimed by the Brahmin Tārukkha.' So what, then, Vāseṭṭha, does the dispute, the argument, the difference of opinion between you, concern?"

Vāseṭṭha said, "the right and wrong paths, friend Gotama. Various religious authorities declare various paths. Do they all lead the one who follows them to communion with God? For example, there might be many different paths near a village or a town. Do they all necessarily merge in the village? Similarly, various religious authorities declare various paths. Do they all lead the one who follows them to communion with God?"

"Are you asking whether, 'they lead,' Vāseṭṭha?" asked the Buddha.

"I'm asking whether, 'they lead,' friend Gotama," Vāseṭṭha replied.

"Are you asking whether, 'they lead,' Vāseṭṭha?" repeated the Buddha.

"I'm asking whether, 'they lead,' Gotama," Vāseṭṭha replied.

"Are you asking whether, 'they lead,' Vāseṭṭha?" repeated the Buddha.

"I'm asking whether, 'they lead,' friend Gotama," Vāseṭṭha replied.

The Buddha said, "Vāseṭṭha, is there even a single religious authority among those versed in their tradition who has seen God face to face?"

"Certainly not, friend Gotama," responded Vāseṭṭha.

"Vāseṭṭha, is there even a single teacher among those religious authorities versed in their tradition, who has seen God face to face?"

"Certainly not, friend Gotama."

"Vāseṭṭha, is there even a single teacher of teachers among those religious authorities versed in their tradition who has seen God face to face?"

"Certainly not, friend Gotama."

"Vāseṭṭha, is there anyone among those religious authorities versed in their tradition, going back as far as seven generations of teachers, who has seen God face to face?"

"Certainly not, friend Gotama."

"Vāseṭṭha, those ancient visionaries among the religious authorities versed in their tradition, those creators and expounders of the sacred verses that are preserved, sung, and declared, and which the religious authorities of today continually recite and endlessly repeat – did those ancient visionaries say, 'we know, we see where, how, and when God appears'?"

"Certainly not, friend Gotama."

"So, Vāseṭṭha, there is not a single religious authority, teacher of religious authorities, teacher of those teachers going back seven generations who has seen God face to face. Nor did the ancient visionaries declare, 'we know, we see where, how, and when God appears.' So, those religious authorities versed in tradition are saying, 'that path, which we neither know nor have seen, we declare to be the path to union; this is the direct path, this is the straight path that leads to salvation, and leads one who follows it to communion with God.' What do you think, Vāseṭṭha, this being the case, doesn't the talk of those religious authorities turn out to be ridiculous?"

"Certainly, friend Gotama."

"Good, Vāseṭṭha. That which those religious authorities neither know nor see, they nonetheless declare to be the path to union: 'this is the direct path, this is the straight path that leads to salvation, and leads one who follows it to communion with God.' This just is not possible."

"Vāseṭṭha, it is just as if there were a single file of blind men clinging to one another: the first one sees nothing, the middle one sees nothing, and the last one sees nothing. The talk of the religious authorities is similarly nothing but blind talk: the first one sees nothing, the middle one sees nothing, and the last one sees nothing. The talk of these religious authorities turns out to be ridiculous, mere words, vacuous, and desolate.

"What do you think, Vāseṭṭha, do those religious authorities see the sun and moon, just as other people do? And when the sun and moon rise and set, do they entreat, extol, honor, and worship them with folded hands?"

Vāseṭṭha responds, "yes, Gotama."

"So, what do you think, Vāseṭṭha, are those religious authorities able to point out the path to union with the sun and moon, which they see, saying, 'this is the direct path, this is the straight path that leads one who follows it to communion with the sun and moon'?"

"Of course not, friend Gotama."

"So, Vāseṭṭha, those religious authorities are not able to point out the path to union with the sun and moon, which they see. And none of them, nor their teachers going back seven generations, nor the ancient visionaries, can say, 'we know, we see where, how, and when God appears.' So, those religious authorities versed in tradition are saying, 'that path, which we neither know nor have seen, we declare to be the path to union; this is the direct path, this is the straight path that leads to salvation, and leads one who follows it to communion with God.' "What do you think, Vāseṭṭha, this being the case, doesn't the talk of those religious authorities turn out to be ridiculous?"

"Certainly, friend Gotama."

"Good, Vāseṭṭha. That which those religious authorities neither know nor see, they nonetheless declare to be the path to union: 'this is the direct path, this is the straight path that leads to salvation, and leads one who follows it to communion with God.' This just is not possible.

"Vāseṭṭha, it is as if a man were to say, 'I am going to seek out and love the most beautiful woman in the land.' And the people would ask him, 'this "most beautiful woman in the land," do you know which class she belongs to?' Asked this, he would have to answer, 'no.' And then the people would ask him, 'this "most beautiful woman in the land" whom you will seek out and love, do you know her name, or her family name, whether she is tall, short, or of medium height, dark, brown, or golden in complexion, or in what village or town or city she lives?' Asked this, he would have to answer, 'no.' And then people might say to him, "so then, you neither know nor see the one whom you seek and desire?" Asked this, he would have to answer, 'yes, that is correct.'

"Now what do you think, Vāsettha? This being the case, does not the talk of that man turn out to be ridiculous?"

"Yes, friend Gotama, it does," said Vāseṭṭha.

"In the same way, the claim of the religious authorities to know the path to union with God is just not viable."

"Vāseṭṭha, it is just as if a man were to make a staircase at a crossroads, leading up to a palace. And people would say to him, 'this staircase leading to the palace, do you know whether it is for a palace that will face east, south, west or north, or whether it will be of high, low or medium size?' Asked this, he would have to answer, 'no.' And people would say to him, 'you are making a staircase leading to a palace that you neither know nor see?' And when asked, he would have to answer, "yes, that is correct.'"

"Now, what do you think, Vāseṭṭha? This being the case, does not the talk of that man turn out to be mind-numbing?"

"Yes, friend Gotama, it does," said Vāseṭṭha.

"In the same way, the claim of the religious authorities to know the path to union with God is just not viable."

"Vāseṭṭha, it is just as if there were a river that was so full with water that cows and crows could drink out of it; and a man would come to it, desiring to cross over to the other bank. Standing on the near bank, he calls out to the farther bank, "come, farther bank, come!'"

"What do you think, Vāseṭṭha, would the far bank of the river come to the near bank as a result of his calling, pleading, requesting, and cajoling?"

"Certainly not, Gotama," said Vāseṭṭha.

"Vāseṭṭha, in just the same way, do the religious authorities, who persistently neglect the duties of a religious authority and persistently undertake what such an authority should not do, declare, 'we summon the supernatural beings!' That such religious authorities, as a result of their cajoling, should, after death, when the body is dissolved, realize communion with God, is simply not reasonable."

"Vāseṭṭha, it is just as if there were a river that was so full with water that cows and crows could drink out of it; and a man would come to it, desiring to cross over to the other bank. This man's arms are bound tightly behind his back with a strong cord.

"What do you think, Vāseṭṭha, could this man go from the near bank of the river to the far bank?"

"Certainly not, friend Gotama," said Vāseṭṭha.

The Buddha continued, "there are five cords of sensory desire, called 'fetters and binds' in the Buddhist discipline. What are the five cords? Forms perceptible to the eye, which are pleasing, desirable, charming, agreeable, arousing desire, and enticing; sounds perceptible to the ear, which are pleasing, desirable, charming, agreeable, arousing desire, and enticing; scents perceptible to the nose, which are pleasing, desirable, charming, agreeable, arousing desire, and enticing; tastes perceptible to the tongue, which are pleasing, desirable, charming, agreeable, arousing desire, and enticing; tactile objects perceptible to the body, which are pleasing, desirable, charming, agreeable, arousing desire, and enticing.

"These five cords of sensory desire are called 'fetters and binds' in the Buddhist discipline. Vāseṭṭha, those religious authorities are enslaved and infatuated by these five cords of sensory desire, enjoying them guiltily, not realizing the danger, and knowing no way out.

"These religious authorities, who persistently neglect the duties of a religious authority and persistently undertake what such an authority should not do, are enslaved and infatuated by these five cords of sensory desire, enjoying them guiltily, not realizing the danger, and knowing no way out. Bound by the binds of sensory desire, the possibility that they would realize communion with God after death, when the body is dissolved, is simply not viable.

"Vāseṭṭha, it is just as if there were a river that was so full with water that cows and crows could drink out of it; and a man would come to it, desiring to cross over to the other bank. But this man would lie down on the near bank, his head covered with a cloth. What do you think, Vāseṭṭha, could this man go from the near bank of the river to the far bank?"

"Certainly not, friend Gotama," said Vāseṭṭha.

The Buddha continued, "there are five hindrances called 'obstructions, obstacles, coverings, envelopings' in the Buddhist discipline. What are the five hindrances? The impulse toward desire, hostility, heavy lethargy, agitated worry, and debilitating doubt. These are called the 'five hindrances.'"

"These religious authorities are obstructed, enveloped, covered, and ensnared by these five hindrances. They persistently neglect the duties of a religious authority and persistently undertake what such an authority should not do. Hindered as they are, the possibility that they would realize communion with God after death, when the body is dissolved, is simply not viable.

The Buddha asked, "what do you think, Vāseṭṭha, have you heard the venerable, accomplished teachers of the religious authorities saying whether or not God is wrapped up in possessions?"

"Not wrapped up in possessions, friend Gotama," said Vāseṭṭha.

"Ill-tempered or composed?" continued the Buddha.

"Composed, friend Gotama."

"Antagonistic or gracious?

"Gracious, friend Gotama."

"Corrupt or honest?"

"Honest, friend Gotama."

"Domineering or compliant?"

"Compliant, friend Gotama."

"Now, what do you think, Vāseṭṭha, are the religious authorities wrapped up in possessions or not?"

"Wrapped up in possessions, friend Gotama," said Vāseṭṭha.

"Ill-tempered or composed?" continued the Buddha.

"Ill-tempered, friend Gotama."

"Antagonistic or gracious?

"Antagonistic, friend Gotama."

"Corrupt or honest?"

"Corrupt, friend Gotama."

"Domineering or compliant?"

"Domineering, friend Gotama."

"So,' the Buddha continued, "is there then any communion or commonality between the religious authorities – who are wrapped up in possessions, ill-tempered, antagonistic, corrupt, and domineering – and God – who is not wrapped up in possessions, composed, gracious, honest, and compliant?"

"Certainly, not, Gotama," answered Vāseṭṭha.

"Very good, Vāseṭṭha. So, the idea that these authorities will realize communion with God after death, when the body is dissolved, is simply not viable.

"These authorities, having come to the near shore thinking that they will cross over to the dry bank, sink down and fall into despair. Therefore, this knowledge of the religious authorities is called a desert-like knowledge, a wilderness of knowledge, the ruin of knowledge."

This having been said, Vāseṭṭha spoke to the Fortunate One. "I have heard that you – the ascetic Gotama – know the path to communion with God."

The Buddha replied, "what do you think, Vāseṭṭha; is the town of Manasākaṭa near here, and not distant?"

"Yes, friend Gotama, it is near and not distant."

"Now," the Buddha continued, "imagine this. There is a person born and raised in the town of Manasākaṭa. Someone who was just leaving the town asks him about the town road. Would there be any perplexity or hesitation on the part of that person when so asked?"

"Certainly not, Gotama," said Vāseṭṭha.

"And why not?"

"Because that person, born and raised in the town, would know all of the town's paths," said Vāseṭṭha.

"It may be that a person is perplexed and hesitant when asked about the path to the town, but the Tathāgata, when asked about the province of God/exceptional integrity or the way leading to the province of God/exceptional integrity, is neither perplexed nor hesitant. So, Vāseṭṭha, I know God/ exceptional integrity and the province of God/exceptional integrity and the way leading to the province of God/ exceptional integrity. I have entered and realized the province of God/exceptional integrity, so, yes, I do know that."

This having been said, Vāseṭṭha spoke to the Fortunate One. "I have heard that you – the ascetic Gotama – teach the path to communion with God. Please teach the path to communion with God! Please help God's progeny!"

"Now, listen, and concentrate completely on what I will now say," said the Buddha.

"Yes, I will," replied Vāseṭṭha to the Fortunate One.

The Fortunate One spoke. "Here, a Tathāgata – a person who has come to know reality – arises in the world, an accomplished person, a perfectly awakened person, adept in conduct and knowledge, going well through life, understanding the world, an unsurpassed guide of people in need of training, a teacher of resplendent beings and humans, an awakened, fortunate one. Having realized directly, come to know thoroughly for himself, he makes this known to the world, to this world with its resplendent beings, with its death and God, with its ascetics and upper class, with its royalty and common people. He elucidates a teaching that is good in the beginning, good in the middle, good at the end, complete and entire in both letter and spirit, a teaching that clearly illuminates the training life."

The Buddha continues. "A person, having heard the teaching, develops confidence in the Tathāgata. That person reflects as follows. 'The householder's life is filled with pressure and much dust; a mendicant's life is open and spacious. It is not easy for the person living a householder's life to live the life of training to its utmost fulfillment, purity, and splendor. Let me shave my hair and beard, put on the yellow robes of the mendicant, and go from home into homelessness. After a short period, he gives away his amassed possessions, great and small; he lets go of his circle of relationships, significant and insignificant; and he shaves his hair and beard, puts on the yellow robes of the mendicant, and goes from home into homelessness.

"Now a mendicant seeker, he lives guarded by the restraints of the rules, grazing in the field of good conduct. Seeing danger even in the slightest faults, he undertakes the training precepts. Skilled in beneficial bodily and verbal conduct, he sustains his life through pure means, perfected in integrity. Watchful at the gateways to the senses, he is skilled in present-moment awareness and attention, and is contented.

"And how, Vāseṭṭha, is the practitioner a mendicant who is perfected in integrity? Having renounced the destruction of life, he is a person who abstains from the destruction of life. He has put down all weapons. He lives as a conscientious and kind person, anxious for the welfare of all sentient beings. In this way he becomes accomplished in integrity.

"Having renounced the taking of what is not given, he is a person who abstains from taking what is not given, who takes only what is given and desires only what is given. So, he spontaneously lives purely and genuinely. In this way he becomes accomplished in integrity.

"Having renounced sexual activity, he is a person who lives distanced from it, as a person who abstains from the sexual practices of the world. In this way he becomes accomplished in integrity.

"Having renounced useless speech, he is a person who abandons useless speech, who speaks according to the case, who is truthful, reliable, trustworthy, and not deceitful towards others. In this way he becomes accomplished in integrity.

"Having renounced malicious speech, he is a person who abstains from malicious speech. Hearing something here, he does not repeat it there in order to create division among others. He is thus a reconciler of those who are divided and an inspirer of those who are together. He is someone who speaks delighting in harmony, taking pleasure in harmony, and creating harmony. In this way he becomes accomplished in integrity.

"Having renounced harsh speech, he is a person who abstains from harsh speech. The words that he speaks are pleasant to the ear and affectionate; they go straight to the heart, and are humane, pleasing many people, agreeable to many people. He is a person whose speech has such qualities. In this way he becomes accomplished in integrity.

"Having renounced chatter, he is a person who abstains from chatter. He is a person whose speech is timely, in accordance with the case, beneficial, just, and edifying. He is a person whose speech is a real treasure. In this way he becomes accomplished in integrity.

"And how, Vāseṭṭha, is the practitioner someone who is watchful at the gateways to the senses? Here, a practitioner, on seeing an object with his eyes, does not grasp at its general appearance or its accompanying characteristics. Because desire and dejection, as well as detrimental and unskillful qualities, would overcome him if he lived unrestrained in the eye faculty, he follows the method of restraining this faculty, he protects the eye faculty, he manifests restraint in the eye faculty. And the practitioner does so similarly for the ear and sounds, nose and scents, tongue and tastes, body and tactile objects, mind and thoughts. Maintaining this noble restraint of the senses, he experiences an unimpaired sense of ease within himself. In this way, Vāseṭṭha, he is watchful at the gateways to the senses.

"And how, Vāseṭṭha, is the practitioner someone who is endowed with clear attention and present-moment awareness? Here, he is a person who acts with clear attentiveness when going back or forth, when looking ahead or behind, when bending or stretching, when getting dressed. He acts with clear attentiveness when eating, drinking, chewing, and tasting. He is a person who acts with clear attentiveness when defecating and urinating. When walking, standing, sitting, sleeping, waking, speaking, and remaining silent he is a person who acts with clear attentiveness. In this way, Vāseṭṭha, the practitioner is someone who is endowed with clear attention and present-moment awareness.

"And how, Vāseṭṭha, is the practitioner someone who is contented? He is content with a robe for the care of his body, and with alms for the care of his stomach. Taking up these items only, he wanders widely. Just as a winged bird flies here and there burdened only by its wings. In this way, Vāseṭṭha, the practitioner is someone who is contented.

"Possessing these noble traits of integrity, restraint in the senses, clear attentiveness and present-moment awareness, and contentment, the practitioner resorts to an isolated place. He sits down in a cross-legged position, holds his body erect, and establishes present-moment awareness in front of him.

"Abandoning his longing for the world, he abides with his mind freed from longing. This causes his mind to be thoroughly purified of longing.

"Abandoning hostility and anger, he abides with a friendly mind, as a person who pulses with compassion for all sentient beings. This causes his mind to be thoroughly purified of hostility and anger.

"Abandoning sluggishness and drowsiness, he abides free of sluggishness and drowsiness, as one who perceives with luminous clarity. Being attentive and mindful causes his mind to be thoroughly purified of sluggishness and drowsiness.

"Abandoning agitation and anxiety, he abides well balanced, as one whose mind is quieted from within. This causes his mind to be thoroughly purified of agitation and anxiety.

"Abandoning indecisiveness, he is a person who abides having overcome indecisiveness. By virtue of being a person who no longer wonders 'why' or 'how' concerning the development of skillful qualities, his mind is purified of indecisiveness.

"Recognizing that theses five hindrances have been eliminated, delight arises in the practitioner. Out of this delight emerges joy. Because his mind is filled with joy, his body becomes calm, and a body that is calmed experiences ease. Now, as a result of this ease, his mind becomes concentrated. Disengaged from sensual desire and unskillful qualities, he enters into and abides in the first meditative absorption, which entails applied and sustained cognizance, is born of detachment and filled with joy and ease. He suffuses his body, pervades, fills, and permeates it with joy and ease born of detachment. There is no part whatsoever of his entire body that is not saturated by this joy and ease born of detachment.

"The practitioner persists in gradually suffusing the entire world and all of space with a heart and mind filled with friendliness towards others, vast, expansive, boundless, and peaceful. Just as a powerful trumpeter could with ease make a proclamation known throughout space, the practitioner leaves nothing in the sensuous sphere untouched or unaffected by this heart released through the cultivation of friendliness.

"Then, the practitioner persists in gradually suffusing the entire world and all of space with a heart and mind filled with compassion, vast, expansive, boundless, and peaceful. And further, the practitioner persists in gradually suffusing the entire world and all of space with a mind filled with joy, vast, expansive, boundless, and peaceful. And yet further, the practitioner persists in gradually suffusing the entire world and all of space with a heart and mind filled with equanimity, vast, expansive, boundless, and peaceful.

"Just as a powerful trumpeter could with ease make a proclamation known throughout space, the practitioner leaves nothing in the sensuous sphere untouched or unaffected by this heart released through the cultivation of friendliness, compassion, sympathetic joy, and equanimity.

"Vāseṭṭha, *this* is the path to communion with God/exceptional goodness."

The Buddha continued. "What do you think, Vāseṭṭha, is a Buddhist practitioner who lives in this manner wrapped up in possessions or not?"

"Not wrapped up in possessions, friend Gotama," said Vāseṭṭha.

"Ill-tempered or composed?" "Composed, friend Gotama."

"Antagonistic or gracious?

"Gracious, friend Gotama."

"Corrupt or honest?"

"Honest, friend Gotama."

"Domineering or compliant?"

"Compliant, friend Gotama."

"So, Vāseṭṭha," the Buddha continued, "the practitioner is not wrapped up in possessions, and God is not wrapped up in possessions. Is there then any likeness or unity shared by the practitioner and God?"

"Yes, there is, friend Gotama," said Vāseṭṭha.

"Good, Vāseṭṭha. That a practitioner who is not wrapped up in possessions could, after death, when the body is dissolved, realize communion with God, who is also not wrapped up in possessions – that is a reasonable notion. And it is the same for a practitioner who, like God, is composed, gracious, honest, and possessing self-mastery. That a practitioner possessing such qualities could, after death, when the body is dissolved, realize communion with God, who is also possesses such qualities – that is a reasonable notion."

Vāseṭṭha and Bhāradvāja then spoke to the Fortunate One. "Wonderful, wonderful, friend Gotama! It is just as if someone were to set up what had been upset, uncover what had been concealed, divulge the path to someone who had gotten lost, hold up a lamp in the darkness so that those with eyes could finally see visible forms. Friend Gotama has illuminated the teaching in various ways. We go for refuge to the fortunate Gotama, and to the teaching and the community of practitioners. May the fortunate Gotama accept us as lay followers who have gone for refuge from this day for the rest of our lives!

Sutta 4

Discourse in Kesamutta

(*Kesamutti Sutta*; *Aṅguttaranikāya* 3.65)

This is what I heard. Once, the Fortunate One was wandering in Kosala with a large group of mendicants when he came to a village of the Kālāmas named Kesamutta.

Now, the Kālāmas of Kesamutta heard that the seeker Gotama Sakyaputta, who had left the Sakya clan to enter into a life of mendicancy, had settled in Kesamutta. They said, "a favorable reputation has preceded this honorable Gotama. It is said that he is an accomplished person, a perfectly awakened person, adept in conduct and wisdom. It is certainly good to see an accomplished person like him."

So the Kālāmas of Kesamutta went to the Fortunate One. Some greeted him respectfully and then sat down next to him, some exchanged friendly greetings with him and then sat down, some bowed with their hands together in a gesture of reverence and then sat down, some told him their clan name and then sat down, some remained silent and then sat down. When they were all seated, the Kālāmas of Kesamutta spoke to the Fortunate One.

"Certain mendicants and religious authorities come to Kesamutta. They explain and illuminate their own doctrines while cursing, reviling, despising, and emasculating the doctrines of others. Then come other mendicants and religious authorities to Kesamutta. And they explain and illuminate *their* own doctrines while cursing, reviling, despising, and emasculating the doctrines of others. We have doubts and perplexity concerning which of these illustrious teachers are speaking truthfully and which are speaking falsely."

The Buddha replied, "Kālāmas, it is understandable that you are uncertain; and it is understandable that you are perplexed. Being uncertain in this matter, you have become perplexed. You should not go by unconfirmed reports, by tradition, by hearsay, by scriptures, by logical reasoning, by inferential reasoning, by reflection on superficial appearances, by delighting in opinions and speculation, by the appearance of plausibility, or because you think 'this person is our teacher.'

"Kālāmas, when you know for yourselves, 'these teachings are detrimental, these teachings are faulty, these teachings would be censured by the wise, these teachings, when fully taken up, lead to harm, to trouble' – then, Kālāmas, you should reject those teachings.

"What do you think, Kālāmas," the Buddha continued, "when infatuation, hostility, and delusion arise in a person, is it harmful or beneficial?"

"It is harmful," replied the Kālāmas.

"A desirous, offensive, or confused person is overpowered by infatuation, hostility, and delusion. His mind overcome by these qualities, such a person also destroys life, takes what is not freely given, engages in damaging sexual relations, speaks falsely, and incites others to do the just the same. Such a person is subject to harm and trouble for a long time."

And the Kālāmas reply, "that is true, sir."

The Buddha continued, "now, what do you think, Kālāmas, are these qualities beneficial or detrimental?"

The Kālāmas respond, "detrimental."

"Are they with or without fault?"

"With fault."

"Would they be censured or approved of by the wise."

"They would be censured by the wise," answered the Kālāmas.

The Buddha continued. "When fully carried out, do they or do they not lead to harm and trouble? Now, how is it in such a case?"

"Fully carried out, they lead to harm and trouble. That is how it seems to us to be in such a case."

"Yes, Kālāmas! And it is for this reason that I have advised you as I have not [to] go by unconfirmed reports, by tradition, by hearsay, by scriptures, by logical reasoning, by inferential reasoning, by reflection on superficial appearances, by delighting in opinions and speculation, by the appearance of plausibility, or because you think 'this person is our teacher.' It is for this reason that I said that when you know for yourselves, 'these teachings are detrimental, these teachings are faulty, these teachings would be censured by the wise, these teachings, when fully taken up, lead to harm, to trouble,' that you should reject those teachings."

The Buddha continued, "you should not go by unconfirmed reports, by tradition, by hearsay, by scriptures, by logical reasoning, by inferential reasoning, by reflection on superficial appearances, by delighting in opinions and speculation, by the appearance of plausibility, or because you think 'this person is our teacher.'

"Kālāmas, when you know for yourselves, 'these teachings are beneficial, these teachings are without fault, these teachings would be approved of by the wise, these teachings, when fully taken up, lead to welfare, to ease' – then, Kālāmas, you should live embracing those teachings.

"What do you think, Kālāmas: when infatuation, hostility, and delusion do not arise in a person, is it harmful or beneficial?"

"It is beneficial."

"A non-desirous, non-offensive, or non-confused person is not overpowered by infatuation, hostility, and delusion. His mind not overcome by these qualities, such a person does not destroy life, does not take what is not freely given, does not engage in damaging sexual relations, does not speak falsely, and does not incite others to behave in such ways. Such a person is subject to well being and ease for a long time."

And the Kālāmas reply, "that is true, sir."

The Buddha continues, "now, what do you think, Kālāmas, are these qualities beneficial or detrimental?"

The Kālāmas respond, "beneficial."

"Are they with or without fault?"

"Without fault."

"Would they be censured or approved of by the wise."

"They would be approved of by the wise," said the Kālāmas.

The Buddha continued. "When fully carried out, do they or do they not lead to well being and ease? Now, how is it in such a case?"

"Fully carried out, they lead to well being and ease. That is how it seems to us to be in such a case."

"Yes, Kālāmas! And it is for this reason that I have advised you as I have not [to] go by unconfirmed reports, by tradition, by hearsay, by scriptures, by logical reasoning, by inferential reasoning, by reflection on superficial appearances, by delighting in opinions and speculation, by the appearance of plausibility, or because you think 'this person is our teacher.' It is for this reason that I said that when you know for yourselves, 'these teachings are beneficial, these teachings are without fault, these teachings would be accepted by the wise, these teachings, when fully taken up, lead to well being, to ease,' that you should live embracing those teachings."

The Buddha continues, "Kālāmas, the superlative practitioner, who, thus embracing beneficial teachings, becomes free from desire, free from hostility, without confusion, attentive, and mindful, dwells gradually pervading the world with a heart suffused with friendliness. He dwells, pervading the entire cosmos with a vast, expansive, boundless heart suffused with friendliness, free from hostility, free from ill-will.

"The practitioner dwells gradually pervading the world with a heart suffused with compassion. He dwells, pervading the entire cosmos with a vast, expansive, boundless heart suffused with compassion , free from hostility, free from ill-will.

"The practitioner dwells gradually pervading the world with a heart suffused with joy. He dwells, pervading the entire cosmos with a vast, expansive, boundless heart suffused with joy, free from hostility, free from ill-will.

"The practitioner dwells gradually pervading the world with a heart suffused with equanimity. He dwells, pervading the entire cosmos with a vast, expansive, boundless heart suffused with equanimity, free from hostility, free from ill-will.

"The practitioner, thus manifesting the four boundless qualities, becomes a person whose heart is kind and gentle, open and clear. For such a person, the four comforts are realized here and now:

If there is an afterlife, and if there is such a possibility as the ripening of positive and negative actions, then, after the dissolution of my body following death, I will be reborn in positive circumstances in the resplendent world beyond the starry vault. This is the first comfort realized by the practitioner.

If there is not an afterlife, and if there is no such a thing as the ripening of positive and negative actions, then I will take care of myself here and now, well at ease, undisturbed, without hostility or ill-will. This is the second comfort realized by the practitioner.

If something harmful is done to someone who has himself done harm, then I do not wish harm on that person or on anyone else. How, then, can trouble touch me, since I did not perform the harmful action? This is the third comfort realized by the practitioner.

If no harm is done to someone who has himself done harm, then in both cases I view myself as untainted. This is the fourth comfort realized by the practitioner."

The Kālāmas replied, "wonderful, wonderful, sir! . . . It is just as if someone were to set up what had been upset, uncover what had been concealed, divulge the path to someone who had gotten lost, hold up a lamp in the darkness so that those with eyes could finally see visible forms. The Fortunate One has illuminated the teaching in various ways. We go for refuge to the Fortunate One, and to the teaching and the community of practitioners. May the Fortunate One accept us as lay followers who have gone for refuge from this day for the rest of our lives!"

Sutta 5

The All

(*Sabba Sutta*; *Saṃyuttanikāya* 4.25.23)

This was spoken by the Buddha at Sāvatthi.

I will teach you the all. Listen to what I say.

What is the all? The eye and forms, the ear and sounds, the nose and scents, the tongue and tastes, the body and tactile objects, the mind and thoughts. This is called the all.

Someone might say, "I reject this all, I will declare another all." But because that is simply a groundless assertion, such a person, when asked about it, would not be able to explain, and would, moreover, meet with distress. What is the reason for that distress? Because *that* all is not within his or her sensorium.

Sutta 6

Like a Ball of Foam

(*Pheṇapiṇḍūpama Sutta*; *Saṃyuttanikāya* 3.22.95)

Once, the Fortunate One was staying at Ayodhya, on the banks of the Ganges River. There, he addressed some mendicants.

Imagine that a large ball of foam were to float out of the *Ganges River*, and that a person with good vision would look at it, reflect on it, and carefully examine it. Looking in such a manner, it would appear as empty, hollow, and insubstantial. For, what substance could there be in a ball of foam? In the same way, whatever appearance there may be, whether in the past, present, or future, internal or external, subtle or massive, inconsequential or exalted, close at hand or in the distance, you should look at it, reflect on it, and carefully examine it. Looking in such a manner, it will appear as empty, hollow, and insubstantial. For, what substance could there be in an appearance?

Imagine that in autumn, when massive rain is falling, a water bubble appears on the surface of a puddle, and then dissolves. A person with good vision would look at it, reflect on it, and carefully examine it. Looking in that manner, it would appear as empty, hollow, and insubstantial. For, what substance could there be in a water bubble? In the same way, whatever feeling there may be, whether in the past, present, or future, internal or external, subtle or massive, inconsequential or exalted, close at hand or in the distance, you should look at it, reflect on it, and carefully examine it. Looking in that manner, it will appear as empty, hollow, and insubstantial. For, what substance could there be in a feeling?

Imagine that at noon, late in the summer months, a shimmering mirage appears. A person with good vision would look at it, reflect on it, and carefully examine it. Looking in that manner, it would appear as empty, hollow, and insubstantial. For, what substance could there be in a mirage? In the same way, whatever perception there may be, whether in the past, present, or future, internal or external, subtle or massive, inconsequential or exalted, close at hand or in the distance, you should look at it, reflect on it, and carefully examine it. Looking in that manner, it will appear as empty, hollow, and insubstantial. For, what substance could there be in a perception?

Imagine that a person, needing heartwood, searching for wood, wandering around looking for heartwood, takes a sharp ax and goes into a forest. There, the person would see the trunk of a plantain tree, straight, fresh, of enormous height. He would cut the root, then cut the top, then cut off the outer bark. Cutting off the outer bark of the tree, the person would not even find soft wood, much less heartwood. A person with good vision would look at the tree's woodless core, reflect on it, and carefully examine it. Looking in that manner, it would appear as empty, hollow, and insubstantial. For what substance could there be in the trunk of a plantain tree? In the same way, whatever conceptual fabrications there may be, whether in the past, present, or future, internal or external, subtle or massive, inconsequential or exalted, close at hand or in the distance, you should look at them, reflect on them, and carefully examine them. Looking in that manner, they will appear as empty, hollow, and insubstantial. For, what substance could there be in conceptual fabrications?

Imagine that a magician or a magician's apprentice were to conjure up a magical illusion in the city square. A person with good vision would look at it, reflect on it, and carefully examine it. Looking in that manner, it would appear as empty, hollow, and insubstantial. For what substance could there be in a magical illusion? In the same way, whatever cognizance there may be, whether in the past, present, or future, internal or external, subtle or massive, inconsequential or exalted, close at hand or in the distance, you should look at it, reflect on it, and carefully examine it. Looking in that manner, it will appear as empty, hollow, and insubstantial. For what substance could there be in cognizance?

Seeing in this manner, as a learned superlative practitioner, you become disenchanted with appearances, disenchanted with feeling, disenchanted with perception, disenchanted with conceptual fabrication, disenchanted with cognizance. Being disenchanted, you are free from infatuation. Because of this dispassion, you are liberated. Being liberated, the knowledge is present: *I am liberated.* And you clearly know: *Generation is exhausted. The exalted life has been lived. What had to be done was done. There is no further becoming in this state.*

This is what the Fortunate One said. Having done so, the well-farer, the teacher further said the following:

As was pointed out by the kinsman of the sun,
appearance is like a ball of foam, feeling, like a water bubble;
perception is like a mirage, conceptual fabrications like a plantain tree;
and cognizance is like a magical display.

However you reflect on or it carefully examine the matter,
to whoever looks at it with care, each is empty and hollow.

As for the body, the one with extensive insight has taught
three matters concerning its abandonment.

Seeing these, you will cast away your physical form.
The body, when devoid of vitality, heat, and cognizance
lies there, discarded, food for some other being, without volition.

Such is the continuum, this illusory charmer of the childlike,
Said to be a slayer, no substance is found here.

That is how you should regard the aggregates of being,
day and night, energetically, ardently, mindfully.

You should dissolve all bonds, make a refuge for yourself,
and live as if your head were ablaze,
yearning for the way that is never-vanishing.

Sutta 7

Evidence of Selflessness

(*Anattalakkhaṇa Sutta*; *Saṃyuttanikāya* 3.22.59)

The Fortunate One was once staying at Varanasi in the deer park at Isipatana. There, he addressed the group of five mendicants.

The body does not constitute a self. If the body constituted a self, then it would not give us trouble, and it would be possible to manipulate the body by making determinations such as *let my body be this way, let my body not be that way.* So, because the body does not constitute a self, it *does* give us trouble, and it *is not* possible to manipulate the body by making determinations such as, *let my body be this way, let my body not be that way.*

Feeling does not constitute a self. If feeling constituted a self, then it would not give us trouble, and it would be possible to manipulate feeling by making determinations such as, *let my feeling be this way, let my feeling not be that way.* So, because feeling does not constitute a self, it does give us trouble, and it is not possible to manipulate feeling by making determinations such as, *let my feeling be this way, let my feeling not be that way.*

Perception does not constitute a self. If perception constituted a self, then it would not give us trouble, and it would be possible to manipulate perception by making determinations such as, *let my perception be this way, let my perception not be that way.* So, because perception does not constitute a self, it does give us trouble, and it is not possible to manipulate perception by making determinations such as, *let my perception be this way, let my perception not be that way.*

Conceptual fabrications do not constitute a self. If conceptual fabrications constituted a self, then they would not give us trouble, and it would be possible to manipulate conceptual fabrications by making determinations such as, *let my conceptual fabrications be this way, let my conceptual fabrications not be that way.* So, because conceptual fabrications do not constitute a self, they do give us trouble, and it is not possible to manipulate conceptual fabrications by making determinations such as, *let my conceptual fabrications be this way, let my conceptual fabrications not be that way.*

Cognizance does not constitute a self. If cognizance constituted a self, then it would not give us trouble, and it would be possible to manipulate cognizance by making determinations such as, *let my cognizance be this way, let my cognizance not be that way.* So, because cognizance does not constitute a self, it does give us trouble, and it is not possible to manipulate cognizance by making determinations such as, *let my cognizance be this way, let my cognizance not be that way.*

The Buddha then questioned the five mendicants.

"What do you think, are the body, feeling, perception, conceptual fabrications, and cognizance permanent or impermanent?"

The five mendicants replied, "impermanent."

"And is that which is impermanent distressing or gratifying?"

"Distressful."

"And is it correct to see that which is impermanent, distressful, and subject to change in terms of *this is mine, I am this, this is my self*?

"Certainly not," said the five mendicants.

"Therefore," the Buddha continues, "whatever body there is, whether past, present or future, internal or external, subtle or massive, inconsequential or exalted, close at hand or in the distance, every body should be seen with thorough understanding for what it is: *this is not mine, I am not this, this is not my self.*

"Similarly, whatever feeling, perception, conceptual fabrications, and cognizance there are, whether past, present or future, internal or external, subtle or massive, inconsequential or exalted, distant or near, each of these should be seen with thorough understanding for what it is: *this is not mine, I am not this, this is not my self.*

"Seeing in this way, as a trained practitioner you become disenchanted with the body, feeling, perception, conceptual fabrications, and cognizance. Being disenchanted, you are free from infatuation. Because of this dispassion, you are liberated. Being liberated, the knowledge is present: *I am liberated.* And you clearly know: *Generation is exhausted. The exalted life has been lived. What had to be done was done. There is no further becoming in this state.*

This is what the Fortunate One said. Exalted, the five mendicants rejoiced at the words of the Fortunate One. As this exposition was being spoken, the five mendicants' minds were freed from the habituated impulses through letting go.

Sutta 8

The Burden

(*Bharā Sutta*; *Saṃyuttanikāya* 3.22.22)

This is what I heard. The Fortunate One was once staying in Sāvatthi, in Jeta's grove in Anāthapiṇḍika's park. There, he spoke to a group of mendicants.

I will teach you about the burden. I will teach you about the bearer of the burden, the taking up of the burden, and the putting down of the burden. Listen to what I say.

What, then, is the burden? To this, it should be said, *the five existential functions subject to grasping.* Which five? The materiality function subject to grasping; the feeling function subject to grasping; the perception function subject to grasping; the conceptual fabrication function subject to grasping; and the cognizance function subject to grasping. This is what is called the burden.

And what is the bearer of the burden? To this, it should be said, *the person.* This person named so and so, from such and such a family. This is what is called the bearer of the burden.

And what is the taking up of the burden? It is this craving that leads to further being, accompanied by passion and delight, seeking pleasure here and there. It is, namely, craving for sensual pleasures, craving for becoming, and craving for non-becoming. This is what is called the taking up of the burden.

And what is the putting down of the burden? It is the complete dissolution and cessation of precisely that craving, the relinquishment and rejection of it, freedom from it, non-attachment to it. This is what is called putting down the burden.

This is what the Fortunate One said. And when he had finished, he spoke further, as follows.

Such burdens are the five existential functions subject to grasping.
And the bearer of the burden is the person.
Taking up the burden in this world is painful.
Putting down the burden is happiness.

Having put down the heavy burden,
another burden should not be taken up.
Craving eradicated, together with its root,
you are sated and quenched.

Sutta 9
Turning the Wheel of the Teaching

(*Dhammacakkappavattana Sutta*; *Saṃyuttanikāya* 5.56.11)

This is what I heard. The Fortunate One was once staying at Varanasi, in the deer park at Isipatana. There he addressed the group of five mendicants as follows.

"There are two extremes that are not to be embraced by a person who has set out on the path. Which two? The practice of clinging to sensory pleasure in sensory objects. This practice is lowly, common, ordinary, dishonorable, and unprofitable. And the practice of exhausting oneself with austerities. This practice is distressful, dishonorable, and unprofitable.

"Not tending towards either of these extremes, a Tathāgata – person who has come to know reality – has completely awakened to the middle way. The middle way engenders insight and understanding, and leads to calmness, to direct knowledge, to full awakening, to unbinding. So what is that middle way completely awakened to by a Tathāgata? It is precisely this preeminent eight-component course; namely, sound view, sound inclination, sound speech, sound action, sound livelihood, sound effort, sound awareness, and sound concentration. This is the middle way, realized by a Tathāgata, which gives rise to vision and knowledge, and leads to calmness, to direct knowledge, to full awakening, to unbinding.

"Now, this is unease. It is a preeminent reality. Birth is unsettling, aging is unsettling, illness is unsettling, death is unsettling, association with what is displeasing is unsettling, separation from what is pleasing is unsettling, not getting what is wanted is unsettling. In short, the five existential functions subject to grasping are unsettling.

"This is the origination of unease. It is a preeminent reality. It is this craving that leads to further being, accompanied by passion and delight, seeking pleasure here and there. It is, namely, craving for sensual pleasures, craving for being, and craving for non-being.

"This is the cessation of unease. It is a preeminent reality. It is the complete dissolution and cessation of precisely that thirst, the relinquishment and rejection of it, freedom from it, non-attachment to it.

"This is the way leading to the cessation of unease. It is a preeminent reality. It is this preeminent eight-component course; namely, sound view, sound inclination, sound speech, sound action, sound livelihood, sound effort, sound awareness, and sound concentration.

"Realizing, *this is unease*, there arose in me vision, insight, discernment, knowledge, and clarity concerning things that have not been previously heard. Realizing, *this unease is to be fully recognized*, there arose in me vision, insight, discernment, knowledge, and clarity concerning things that have not been previously heard. Realizing, *this unease has been fully recognized*, there arose in me vision, insight, discernment, knowledge, and clarity concerning things that have not been previously heard.

"Realizing, *this is the origin of unease*, there arose in me vision, insight, discernment, knowledge, and clarity concerning things that have not been previously heard. Realizing, *the arising of unease is to be abandoned*, there arose in me vision, insight, discernment, knowledge, and clarity concerning things that have not been previously heard. Realizing, *the arising of unease has been abandoned*, there arose in me vision, insight, discernment, knowledge, and clarity concerning things that have not been previously heard.

"Realizing, *this is the cessation of unease*, there arose in me vision, insight, discernment, knowledge, and clarity concerning things that have not been previously heard. Realizing, *the cessation of unease is to be realized*, there arose in me vision, insight, discernment, knowledge, and clarity concerning things that have not been previously heard. Realizing, *the cessation of unease has been realized*, there arose in me vision, insight, discernment, knowledge, and clarity concerning things that have not been previously heard.

"Realizing, *this is the path leading to the cessation of unease*, there arose in me vision, insight, discernment, knowledge, and clarity concerning things that have not been previously heard. Realizing, *the path leading to the cessation of unease is to be cultivated*, there arose in me vision, insight, discernment, knowledge, and clarity concerning things that have not been previously heard. Realizing, *the path leading to the cessation of unease has been cultivated*, there arose in me vision, insight, discernment, knowledge, and clarity concerning things that have not been previously heard.

"As long as my insight and vision concerning these four preeminent realities just as they are, in their three sequences and twelve aspects, was not completely purified, I did not claim to have fully realized unsurpassed, complete awakening in this world with its resplendent beings, God, and death, with its seekers and priests, its supernatural beings and humans. But as soon as my insight and vision concerning these four preeminent realities just as they are was completely purified, then did I claim to have fully realized unsurpassed, complete awakening. The insight and vision arose in me: *unwavering is my release*; *this is the final birth, there is now no further becoming.*"

That is what the Fortunate One said. Exalted, the group of five mendicants delighted at the words of the Fortunate One. And while this discourse was being spoken, there arose for the venerable Koṇḍañña this dustless, stainless insight: *all that is subject to origination is subject to cessation.*

And when the Fortunate One had set in motion the wheel of teaching, the resplendent earth-dwelling beings cried out, "at Varanasi, in the deer park at Isipatana, the Fortunate One has set in motion the unexcelled wheel of the teaching, which cannot be stopped by any seeker or priest, any resplendent being, by God or death, or by anyone in the world!" Hearing the resplendent earth-dwelling beings' cry, resplendent beings throughout the cosmos cried out in the exact fashion.

Thus, at that moment, at that instant, at that second, the cry extended as far as the *brahmā* realm, and this ten thousand-fold cosmos trembled, shook, and violently quaked, and an immeasurable, great radiance appeared in the cosmos, exceeding the brilliant majesty of the resplendent beings themselves.

Then the Fortunate One exclaimed this inspired utterance: "So you really know, Koṇḍañña! So you really know!" And that is how the venerable Koṇḍañña acquired the name Añña-Koṇḍañña – Koṇḍañña-Who-Knows.

Sutta 10
Gotama's Discourse

(*Gotama Suttaṃ*; *Saṃyuttanikāya* 2.1.10)

"Before my awakening, being still an aspirant to awakening and not yet a fully awakened person, it occurred to me: *How troubled is this world! It is born, it decays, and it dies. It falls away and then appears yet again. And people understand but little about the escape from unease, from aging-and-death. When will an escape from this unease, this aging-and-death, be understood?*

"From this consideration, it occurred to me: *There being what, does aging-and-death come to be? By means of what condition is there aging-and-death?* Because of my complete attentiveness to this matter, I came, through penetrative insight, to full comprehension: *There being birth, aging-and-death comes to be. Aging-and-death is founded on birth.*

"From this consideration, it occurred to me: *There being what, does birth come to be? By means of what condition is there birth?* Because of my complete attentiveness to this matter, I came, through penetrative insight, to full comprehension: *There being existence, birth comes to be. Birth is founded on existence.*

"From this consideration, it occurred to me: *There being what, does existence come to be? By means of what condition is there existence?* Because of my complete attentiveness to this matter, I came, through penetrative insight, to full comprehension: *There being grasping, existence comes to be. Existence is founded on grasping.*

"From this consideration, it occurred to me: *There being what, does grasping come to be? By means of what condition is there grasping?* Because of my complete attentiveness to this matter, I came, through penetrative insight, to full comprehension: *There being craving, grasping comes to be. Grasping is founded on craving.*

"From this consideration, it occurred to me: *There being what, does craving come to be? By means of what condition is there craving?* Because of my complete attentiveness to this matter, I came, through penetrative insight, to full comprehension: *There being feeling, craving comes to be. Craving is founded on feeling.*

"From this consideration, it occurred to me: *There being what, does feeling come to be? By means of what condition is there feeling?* Because of my complete attentiveness to this matter, I came, through penetrative insight, to full comprehension: *There being contact, feeling comes to be. Feeling is founded on contact.*

"From this consideration, it occurred to me: *There being what, does contact come to be? By means of what condition is there contact?* Because of my complete attentiveness to this matter, I came, through penetrative insight, to full comprehension: *There being the six sense fields, contact comes to be. Contact is founded on the six sense fields.*

"From this consideration, it occurred to me: *There being what, do the six sense fields come to be? By means of what condition are there the six sense fields?* Because of my complete attentiveness to this matter, I came, through penetrative insight, to full comprehension: *There being the mind-body entity, the six sense fields come to be. The six sense fields are founded on the mind-body entity.*

"From this consideration, it occurred to me: *There being what, does the mind-body entity come to be? By means of what condition is there the mind-body entity?* Because of my complete attentiveness to this matter, I came, through penetrative insight, to full comprehension: *There being cognizance, the mind-body entity comes to be. The mind-body entity is founded on cognizance.*

"From this consideration, it occurred to me: *There being what, does cognizance come to be? By means of what condition is there cognizance?* Because of my complete attentiveness to this matter, I came, through penetrative insight, to full comprehension: *There being fabrications cognizance comes to be. Cognizance is founded on fabrications.*

"From this consideration, it occurred to me: *There being what, do fabrications come to be? By means of what condition are there fabrications?* Because of my complete attentiveness to this matter, I came, through penetrative insight, to full comprehension: *There being ignorance, fabrications come to be. Fabrications are founded on ignorance.*

"So, with ignorance as the condition, there are fabrications.

With fabrications as the condition, there is cognizance.

With cognizance as the condition, there is the mind-body entity.

With the mind-body entity as the condition, there are the six sense fields.

With the six sense fields as the condition, there is contact.

With contact as the condition, there is feeling.

With feeling as the condition, there is craving.

With craving as the condition, there is grasping.

With grasping as the condition, there is existence.

With existence as the condition, there is birth.

With birth as the condition, there is aging-and-death.

"Thus is the emergence of this entire mass of unease. It occurred to me *this is the emergence, this is the emergence.* And there arose in me an eye for previously unheard of matters, there arose in me direct knowledge, penetrative insight, wisdom, and clear seeing.

"From this consideration, it occurred to me: *There not being what, does aging-and-death not come to be? From the cessation of what does aging-and-death come to cessation?* Because of my complete attentiveness to this matter, I came, through penetrative insight, to full comprehension: *When there is not birth, aging-and-death does not come to be. The cessation of aging-and-death comes from the cessation of birth.*

"From this consideration, it occurred to me: *There not being what, does birth not come to be? From the cessation of what does birth come to cessation?* Because of my complete attentiveness to this matter, I came, through penetrative insight, to full comprehension: *When there is not existence, birth does not come to be. The cessation of birth comes from the cessation of existence.*

"From this consideration, it occurred to me: *There not being what, does existence not come to be? From the cessation of what does existence come to cessation?* Because of my complete attentiveness to this matter, I came, through penetrative insight, to full comprehension: *When there is not grasping, existence does not come to be. The cessation of existence comes from the cessation of grasping.*

"From this consideration, it occurred to me: *There not being what, does grasping not come to be? From the cessation of what does grasping come to cessation?* Because of my complete attentiveness to this matter, I came, through penetrative insight, to full comprehension: *When there is not craving, grasping does not come to be. The cessation of grasping comes from the cessation of craving.*

"From this consideration, it occurred to me: *There not being what, does craving not come to be? From the cessation of what does craving come to cessation?* Because of my complete attentiveness to this matter, I came, through penetrative insight, to full comprehension: *When there is not feeling, craving does not come to be. The cessation of craving comes from the cessation of feeling.*

"From this consideration, it occurred to me: *There not being what, does feeling not come to be? From the cessation of what does feeling come to cessation?* Because of my complete attentiveness to this matter, I came, through penetrative insight, to full comprehension: *When there is not contact, feeling does not come to be. The cessation of feeling comes from the cessation of contact.*

"From this consideration, it occurred to me: *There not being what, does contact not come to be? From the cessation of what does contact come to cessation?* Because of my complete attentiveness to this matter, I came, through penetrative insight, to full comprehension: *When there are not the six sense fields, contact does not come to be. The cessation of contact comes from the cessation of the six sense fields.*

"From this consideration, it occurred to me: *There not being what, do the six sense fields not come to be? From the cessation of what do the six sense fields come to cessation?* Because of my complete attentiveness to this matter, I came, through penetrative insight, to full comprehension: *When there is not the mind-body entity, the six sense fields do not come to be. The cessation of the six sense fields comes from the cessation of the mind-body entity.*

"From this consideration, it occurred to me: *There not being what, does the mind-body entity not come to be? From the cessation of what does the mind-body entity come to cessation?* Because of my complete attentiveness to this matter, I came, through penetrative insight, to full comprehension: *When there is not cognizance, the mind-body does not come to be. The cessation of the mind-body entity comes from the cessation of cognizance.*

"From this consideration, it occurred to me: *There not being what, does cognizance not come to be? From the cessation of what does cognizance come to cessation?* Because of my complete attentiveness to this matter, I came, through penetrative insight, to full comprehension: *When there are no fabrications, cognizance s does not come to be. The cessation of cognizance comes from the cessation of fabrications.*

"From this consideration, it occurred to me: *There not being what, do fabrications not come to be? From the cessation of what do fabrications come to cessation?* Because of my complete attentiveness to this matter, I came, through penetrative insight, to full comprehension: *When there is not ignorance, fabrica-*

tions do not come to be. The cessation of fabrications comes from the cessation of ignorance.

"So, with the cessation of ignorance, the cessation of fabrications.

With the cessation of fabrications, the cessation of cognizance.

With the cessation of cognizance, the cessation of the mind-body entity.

With the cessation of the mind-body entity, the cessation of the six sense fields.

With the cessation of the six sense fields, the cessation of contact.

With the cessation of contact, the cessation of feeling.

With the cessation of feeling, the cessation of craving.

With the cessation of craving, the cessation of grasping.

With the cessation of grasping, the cessation of existence.

With the cessation of existence, the cessation of birth.

With the cessation of birth, the cessation of aging-and-death.

"Thus is the cessation of this entire mass of unease. It occurred to me *this is cessation, this is cessation.* And there arose in me an eye for previously unheard of matters, there arose in me direct knowledge, penetrative insight, wisdom, and clear seeing."

Sutta 11

Destination

(*Parāyana Sutta*; *Saṃyuttanikāya* 4.43.44)

The Buddha spoke as follows.

"I will teach the destination and the path leading to the destination. Listen to what I say. What is the destination? The eradication of infatuation, the eradication of hostility, and the eradication of delusion is what is called the destination. And what is the path leading to the destination? Present-moment awareness directed towards the body. This awareness is what is called the path leading to the destination.

In this way, I have taught to you the destination and the path leading to the destination. That which should be done out of compassion by a caring teacher who desires the welfare of his students, I have done for you.

There are secluded places. Meditate, do not be negligent! Don't have regrets later! This is my instruction to you.

Sutta 12

Quenched

(*Nibbuta Sutta*; *Aṅguttaranikāya* 3.55)

Once, a man called Jāṇussoṇi approached the Fortunate One. Exchanging greetings, he sat down next to the Fortunate One, and spoke.

"It is said, 'unbinding is conspicuous, unbinding is conspicuous.' In what regard, friend Gotama, is unbinding conspicuous? In what regard is it palpable, leading the practitioner to *come and see*, and to be personally realized by the wise?"

The Buddha replied, "Jāṇussoni, an infatuated, hostile, and deluded person comes to the realization that, through the overwhelming power of infatuation, hostility, and delusion he has become mentally exhausted, and that he is hurting himself and others. And that person becomes depressed and distressed. He realizes that if infatuation, hostility, and delusion were eradicated he would no longer hurt himself, he would no longer hurt others, and he would no longer experience depression and distress. It is in this way, Jāṇussoṇi, that unbinding is conspicuous. Because a person realizes the absolute eradication of infatuation, the absolute eradication of hostility, and the absolute eradication of delusion, unbinding is conspicuous, palpable, leading the practitioner to *come and see*, and to be personally realized by the wise."

Sutta 13

Signs of the Fabricated

(*Saṅkhatalakkhaṇa Sutta; Aṅguttaranikāya* 3.47)

The Buddha spoke as follows.

"There are three signs that something is fabricated. What are the three? Its arising is evident. Its vanishing is evident. And its alteration while persisting is evident. These are the three signs that something is fabricated."

Sutta 14

Signs of the Unfabricated

(*Asaṅkhatalakkhaṇa Sutta; Aṅguttaranikāya* 3.48)

The Buddha spoke as follows.

"There are three signs that something is unfabricated. What are the three? No arising is evident. No vanishing is evident. And no alteration while persisting is evident. These are the three signs that something is unfabricated."

Sutta 15

Present-moment Awareness with Breathing

(*Ānāpānasati Sutta, Majjhimanikāya* 118)

This is what I heard. The Fortunate One was once staying in Sāvatthi, in the eastern park of Migāra's mother's palace, together with many highly distinguished senior disciples. The venerable Sāriputta, the venerable Mahāmoggallāna, the venerable Mahākassapa, the venerable Mahākaccaya, the venerable Ānanda, and many others were there.

At that time, the senior practitioners were teaching and instructing the novice practitioners. Some were teaching ten, others twenty, thirty, or forty novices. So, these novices gradually realized increasingly excellent progress.

Now, at this time, the Fortunate One was surrounded by the community of practitioners, sitting in the open air. This was on the day of assembly, during the Pavāraṇā ceremony, on the fifteenth night of the month, when the moon is full. The Fortunate One, surveying the utterly silent community, said, "I am pleased with this progress. In my heart I am pleased with this progress. So, you should energetically exert yourselves still more, mastering what you have not yet mastered, experiencing what you have not yet experienced, realizing what you have not yet realized. I will return here to Sāvatthi on the full moon day of the 'white water lily' month, the fourth month."

When the practitioners living in the countryside heard this, they left in due course to go see the Fortunate One. There, the senior practitioners still more intensely taught and instructed the novice practitioners.

Then, on the day of assembly, on the night of the full moon of the fourth month, the Buddha was surrounded by the community of practitioners, sitting in the open air. Surveying the utterly silent community, the Fortunate One gave the following discourse.

"This assembly is free from mindless chatter, this assembly is free from trivial prattle. It is established purely in the heart of the matter. Such is the nature of this community, such is the nature of this assembly, that it is deserving and worthy of the world's offerings and respect as an incomparable field of merit. Such is the nature of this community that a small offering to it becomes great, and a great offering becomes even greater. Such is the nature of this community that the world rarely ever sees something of its kind. Such is the nature of this community that it would be worth traveling many miles just to see an assembly of its kind.

"There are practitioners in this community who are accomplished, *arahants.* They have destroyed their habituated impulses, fulfilled the training, done what had to be done, put down the burden, reached the ideal state beyond rebirth, completely destroyed the bonds of existence. These accomplished ones have been completely liberated through sound knowledge. There are indeed practitioners of such a kind in this community.

There are practitioners in this community who, by means of destroying the five lower bonds spontaneously reappear elsewhere, becoming unbound there, not to return from that world. There are indeed practitioners of such a kind in this community.

There are practitioners in this community who, by means of the destruction of the three bonds and the gradual elimination of attraction, aversion, and delusion, return to this world only once, as once-returners, bringing distress to an end. There are indeed practitioners of such a kind in this community.

There are practitioners in this community who are stream-enterers, no longer subject to frustration, steady, bound for awakening. There are indeed practitioners of such a kind in this community.

There are practitioners in this community who live applying themselves to the practices of cultivating the application of present-moment awareness in the four areas, the four sound efforts, the four bases of success, the five natural strengths, the five developed powers, the seven factors of awakening, and the preeminent eight-component course. There are indeed practitioners of such a kind in this community.

There are practitioners in this community who live applying themselves to the practices of cultivating friendliness, compassion, joy, and equanimity, and of cultivating the perception of impermanence and impurity. There are indeed practitioners of such a kind in this community.

There are practitioners in this community who live applying themselves to the practice of cultivating present-moment awareness with breathing. When present-moment awareness with breathing is persistently practiced and cultivated it is rich in results and of great benefit. This practice perfects present-moment awareness in the four areas. When present-moment awareness in the four areas is persistently practiced and cultivated, the seven factors of awakening are perfected. When these seven factors of awakening are persistently practiced and cultivated, this perfects higher knowledge and release.

1. PLACE AND POSTURE

And how is present-moment awareness with breathing persistently practiced and cultivated so that it is rich in results and of great benefit? Now, go to the woods, to the root of a tree, or to an empty hut, sit down in a crossed-leg position and straighten your body. Establishing present-moment awareness right where you are, breathe in, simply aware, then breathe out, simply aware.

2. SIXTEEN-POINT PRACTICE

BODY

(1) Breathing in long, know directly *I am breathing in long.* Breathing out long, know directly *I am breathing out long.*

(2) Breathing in short, know directly *I am breathing in short.* Breathing out short, know directly *I am breathing out short.* You should train as follows:

(3) I breathe in, sensitive to the entire body. I breathe out, sensitive to the entire body.

(4) I breathe in, quieting the bodily formation. I breathe out, quieting everything that constitutes the body.

FEELING

You should train as follows:

(5) I breathe in, sensitive to delight. I breathe out, sensitive to delight.

(6) I breathe in, sensitive to ease. I breathe out, sensitive to ease.

(7) I breathe in, sensitive to mental reactions. I breathe out, sensitive to mental reactions.

(8) I breathe in, calming mental reactions. I breathe out, calming mental reactions.

MIND

You should train as follows:

(9) I breathe in, sensitive to the mind. I breathe out, sensitive to the mind.

(10) I breathe in, gladdening the mind. I breathe out, gladdening the mind.

(11) I breathe in, composing the mind. I breathe out, composing the mind.

(12) I breathe in, releasing the mind. I breathe out, releasing the mind.

MENTAL QUALITIES AND PHENOMENA

You should train as follows:

(13) I breathe in, observing impermanence. I breathe out, observing impermanence.

(14) I breathe in, observing dissolution. I breathe out, observing dissolution.

(15) I breathe in, observing cessation. I breathe out, observing cessation.

(16) I breathe in, observing relinquishment. I breathe out, observing relinquishment.

"It is in this manner that present-moment awareness with breathing, when persistently practiced and cultivated, is rich in results and of great benefit."

3. THE FOUR AREAS OF PRESENT-MOMENT AWARENESS

"And how does present-moment awareness with breathing, when cultivated and persistently practiced, constitute mastery of present-moment awareness in the four areas?

BODY

(1) When attending to the bodily phenomena as described above, you should dwell observing the body *in and as the body*, ardent, fully aware, and attentive, having given up longing and discontentment towards the world. I am speaking here of a certain kind of body among bodies; namely, this inhalation and exhalation of the breath. This is why the practitioner abides at that time observing the body *in and as the body*, ardent, fully aware, and attentive, having given up longing and discontentment towards the world.

FEELING

(2) "When attending to the sensations of feeling and perception as described above, the practitioner dwells observing feelings *in and as feelings*, ardent, fully aware, and attentive, having given up longing and discontentment towards the world. I am speaking here of a certain kind of feeling among feelings, namely, thorough attentiveness to the inhalation and exhalation of the breath. This is why the practitioner abides at that time observing feelings in and as feelings, ardent, fully aware, and attentive, having given up longing and discontentment towards the world.

MIND

(3) "When attending to the mind as described above, the practitioner abides observing mind *in and as mind*, ardent, fully aware, and attentive, having given up longing and discontentment towards the world. I am *not* saying that there is awareness of breathing for a person who is not fully aware and forgetful. This is why the practitioner abides at that time observing mind in and as mind, ardent, fully aware, and attentive, having given up longing and discontentment towards the world.

MENTAL QUALITIES AND PHENOMENA

(4) "When attending to thoughts as described above, the practitioner abides observing mental qualities and phenomena *in and as mental qualities and phenomena*, ardent, fully aware, and attentive, having given up longing and discontentment towards the world. Having seen, having realized the abandonment of longing and discontentment, the practitioner becomes a person who observes with care and equanimity. This is why the practitioner abides at that time observing mental qualities and phenomena in and as mental qualities and phenomena, ardent, fully aware, and attentive, having given up longing and discontentment towards the world.

"It is in this manner that present-moment awareness with breathing, when cultivated and persistently practiced, constitutes mastery of present-moment awareness in the four areas.

4. THE SEVEN FACTORS OF AWAKENING

"And how does mastery of present-moment awareness in the four areas, when cultivated and persistently practiced, constitute mastery of the seven factors of awakening?

PRESENT-MOMENT AWARENESS

(1) "When practicing in the manner described above, present-moment awareness becomes established and continuous. And when it does, the awakening factor of present-moment awareness is aroused. At that moment when it is aroused, the practitioner cultivates the awakening factor of present-moment awareness. Cultivating it, the awakening factor of present-moment awareness is brought to fulfillment.

INVESTIGATION OF QUALITIES

(2) "Abiding aware in this way, the practitioner examines and investigates each mental quality with insight, and undertakes a thorough inquiry into it. Doing so, the awakening factor of investigation into qualities is aroused. So aroused, the practitioner cultivates the awakening factor of investigation into qualities.

Cultivating it, the awakening factor of investigation into qualities is brought to fulfillment.

ENERGY

(3) "In the practitioner who examines and investigates each phenomenon with insight and undertakes a thorough inquiry into it, invigorating energy is aroused. At this moment, the awakening factor of energy is manifested. So manifested, the practitioner cultivates the awakening factor of energy. Cultivating it, the awakening factor of energy is brought to fulfillment.

DELIGHT

(4) "In the practitioner who has aroused invigorating energy, there is born unfleshly delight. At this moment, the awakening factor of delight is manifested. So manifested, the practitioner cultivates the awakening factor of delight. Cultivating it, the awakening factor of delight is brought to fulfillment.

TRANQUILITY

(5) "For the practitioner who has aroused delight, the body is quiet, and the mind is quiet. At this moment, the awakening factor of tranquility is aroused. So aroused, the practitioner cultivates the awakening factor of tranquility. Cultivating it, the awakening factor of tranquility is brought to fulfillment.

CONCENTRATION

(6) "For the practitioner whose body is calm and who is at ease, the mind becomes concentrated. At this moment, the awakening factor of concentration is aroused. So aroused, the practitioner cultivates the awakening factor of concentration. Cultivating it, the awakening factor of concentration is brought to fulfillment.

EQUANIMITY

(7) "With his mind concentrated in this way, the practitioner becomes a person who observes with thoroughgoing care and equanimity. At this moment, the awakening factor of equanimity is aroused. So aroused, the practitioner cultivates the awakening factor of equanimity. Cultivating it, the awakening factor of equanimity is brought to fulfillment. "Cultivated and persistently practiced in this way, present-moment awareness in the four areas fulfills the seven factors of awakening."

Penetrative insight and release

"How do the seven factors of awakening, when cultivated and persistently practiced, fulfill penetrative insight and release? Each of the factors of awakening, rooted in detachment, dispassion, and dissolution, ripens in relinquishment. It is in this way that the seven factors of awakening, when cultivated and persistently practiced, fulfill penetrative insight and release."

This is what the Fortunate One said. Exalted, those practitioners delighted in the words of the Fortunate One.

Sutta 16

The Application of Present-moment Awareness

(*Satipaṭṭhāna Sutta*; *Majjhimanikāya* 10)

This is what I heard. On one occasion, the Fortunate One was staying in the region of the Kurus, where there was a village called Kammāsadhamma. There, the Fortunate One spoke to the mendicants.

The Fortunate One said, "the direct path for the purification of beings, for the overcoming of sadness and distress, for the cessation of unease and depression, for finding the way, and for the direct realization of unbinding is this: the application of present-moment awareness in four areas. What are the four areas? Now, being ardent, fully aware, and mindful, and having put down longing and discontentment towards the world, you should live observing the body *in and as the body*, live observing feelings *in and as feelings*, live observing mind *in and as mind*, and live observing mental qualities and phenomena *in and as mental qualities and phenomena.*

I. The Body

First Practice: Present-Moment Awareness with Breathing

How should you live observing the body in and as the body? Now, go to the woods, to the root of a tree, or to an empty hut, sit down in a crossed-leg position and straighten your body. Establishing present-moment awareness right where you are, breathe in, simply aware, then breathe out, simply aware. Breathing in long, know directly *I am breathing in long.* Breathing out long, know directly *I am breathing out long.* Breathing in short, know directly *I am breathing in short.* Breathing out short, know directly *I am breathing out short.* Train as follows: *I breathe in experiencing the whole body. I breathe out experiencing the whole body. I breathe in quieting everything that constitutes the body. I breathe out quieting everything that constitutes the body.*

Just as a skilled acrobat or his apprentice, when making a long turn, knows directly, *I am making a long turn*, or, making a short turn knows directly, *I am making a short turn*, so do you, breathing in a long breath, know directly, *I am breathing in a long breath*, or, breathing out a short breath know directly, *I am breathing out a short breath*. Train in this manner: *experiencing the whole body, I breathe in and out*; *quieting everything that constitutes the body, I breathe in and out*.

In just this manner should you live observing the body, either your own or others', in and as the body. Live observing the nature of arising within the body, or the nature of cessation within the body, or both simultaneously. Even just realizing that *this is a body*, awareness is made present. To just the extent that you directly know and are simply mindful are you one who lives unattached, not grasping at anything whatsoever in the world. This is how a practitioner lives observing the body in and as the body."

Second Practice: The Four Postures

Furthermore, when walking, know directly *I am walking*; when standing, know directly *I am standing*; when sitting, know directly *I am sitting*; or, when lying down, know directly *I am lying down*. However your body is disposed, know that directly.

In just this manner should you live observing the body, either your own or others', in and as the body, and so on, as above. This is how a practitioner lives observing the body in and as the body.

Third Practice: Full Attention

Furthermore, when going here or there, do so with full attention; when looking here or there do so with full attention; when bending over or stretching out do so with full attention; when getting dressed do so with full attention; when eating, drinking, chewing, and tasting do so with full attention; when defecating or urinating do so with full attention; when walking, standing, sitting, sleeping, being awake, speaking, remaining silent do so with full attention.

In just this manner should you live observing the body, either your own or others', in and as the body, and so on, as above. This is how a practitioner lives observing the body in and as the body.

Fourth Practice: Careful Consideration of Repulsive Bodily Features

Furthermore, investigate your body from the soles of the feet upwards, and from the hair on the head downwards – this body wrapped in skin, full of various kinds of repulsive features. Investigate as follows: *in or on this body of mine there is head hair, skin hair, nails, teeth, flesh, tendons, bones, marrow, kidneys, heart, liver, diaphragm, spleen, lungs, intestines, bowels, stomach, excrement, bile, phlegm, pus, blood, sweat, fat, tears, oils, saliva, mucus, joint fluid, and urine.*

Just as if there were a sack filled at both ends with various kinds of grains, such as rice and seeds, and someone with eyes to see, opening that sack, would investigate them as follows – *this one is a piece of rice, this one is a seed* – just so should you investigate your body from the soles of the feet upwards, and from the hair on the head downwards.

In just this manner should you live observing the body, either your own or others', in and as the body, and so on, as above. This is how a practitioner lives observing the body in and as the body.

FIFTH PRACTICE: CAREFUL CONSIDERATION OF THE ELEMENTS

Furthermore, you should investigate your body just as it is, however it is disposed, as consisting of elements, as follows: *in this very body of mine there is the earth element, solidity; the water element, liquidity; the fire element, combustion; and the air element, currency.*

Just as if a skilled butcher or butcher's apprentice who, having slaughtered a cow and divided it into pieces, were to sit down at a crossroads – just so should you investigate your body just as it is, however it is disposed, as consisting of the four elements.

In just this manner should you live observing the body, either your own or others', in and as the body, and so on, as above. This is how a practitioner lives observing the body in and as the body.

THE NINE CREMATION GROUND CONTEMPLATIONS

SIXTH PRACTICE: Now, imagine that you were to see, in a cremation ground, a corpse that had been discarded for several days and become swollen, discolored, and festering. Making your body the focal point, reflect: *this body of mine is of the same nature as that one; it will become just like that one; it, too, is not free from death.*

SEVENTH PRACTICE: Next, imagine that you were to see a discarded corpse that had been devoured by various wild animals. Making your body the focal point, reflect: *this body of mine is of the same nature as that one; it will become just like that one; it, too, is not free from death.*

EIGHTH PRACTICE: Next, imagine that you were to see a discarded corpse, a skeleton retaining some flesh, still bound by tendons. Making your body the focal point, reflect: *this body of mine is of the same nature as that one*; *it will become just like that one*; *it, too, is not free from death.*

NINTH PRACTICE: Next, imagine that you were to see a discarded corpse, a fleshless skeleton smeared with blood, still bound by tendons. Making your body the focal point, reflect: *this body of mine is of the same nature as that one*; *it will become just like that one*; *it, too, is not free from death.*

TENTH PRACTICE: Next, imagine that you were to see a discarded corpse, a skeleton completely devoid of flesh, still bound by tendons. Making your body the focal point, reflect: *this body of mine is of the same nature as that one*; *it will become just like that one*; *it, too, is not free from death.*

ELEVENTH PRACTICE: Next, imagine that you were to see completely disconnected bones, strewn here and there – hand bone, foot bone, ankle bone, calf bone, thigh bone, hip bone, ribs, backbone, shoulder bone, neck bone, jaw bone, teeth, skull. Making your body the focal point, reflect: *this body of mine is of the same nature as that one*; *it will become just like that one*; *it, too, is not free from death.*

TWELFTH PRACTICE: Next, imagine that you were to see a discarded corpse, bones as white as pearl. Making your body the focal point, reflect: *this body of mine is of the same nature as that one*; *it will become just like that one*; *it, too, is not free from death.*

THIRTEENTH PRACTICE: Next, imagine that you were to see a discarded corpse, bones piled up and decayed. Making your body the focal point, reflect: *this body of mine is of the same nature as that one*; *it will become just like that one*; *it, too, is not free from death.*

FOURTEENTH PRACTICE: Next, imagine that you were to see a discarded corpse, bones reduced to powder. Making your body the focal point, reflect: *this body of mine is of the same nature as that one*; *it will become just like that one*; *it, too, is not free from death.*

In just this manner should you live observing the body, either your own or others', in and as the body. Live observing the nature of arising within the body, or the nature of cessation within the body, or both simultaneously. Even just realizing that *this is a body*, awareness is made present. To just the extent that you directly know and are simply mindful are you one who lives unattached, not grasping at anything whatsoever in the world. This is how a practitioner lives observing the body in and as the body.

II. FEELINGS

FIFTEENTH PRACTICE: Now, how should you live observing feelings in and as feelings? Experiencing an agreeable feeling, know directly *I am experiencing an agreeable feeling.* Experiencing a disagreeable feeling, know directly *I am experiencing a disagreeable feeling.* Or, experiencing a feeling that is neither agreeable nor disagreeable, know directly *I am experiencing a feeling that is neither agreeable nor disagreeable.* Experiencing a material feeling, whether agreeable, disagreeable, or neither, know that directly. Or, experiencing an immaterial feeling, whether agreeable, disagreeable, or neither, know that directly.

In just this manner should you live observing feelings, either your own or others', in and as feelings. Live observing the nature of arising within feelings, or the nature of cessation within feelings, or both simultaneously. Even just realizing that *this is a feeling,* awareness is made present. To just the extent that he directly knows and is simply mindful are you one who lives unattached, not grasping at anything whatsoever in the world. This is how a practitioner lives observing feelings in and as feelings.

III. MIND

SIXTEETH PRACTICE: Now, how should you live observing mind in and as mind? Know a mind possessed of infatuation directly as a mind possessed of infatuation. Know a mind free from infatuation directly as a mind free from infatuation. Know a mind possessed of anger directly as a mind possessed of anger. Know a mind free from anger directly as a mind free from anger. Know a mind possessed of delusion directly as a mind possessed of delusion. Know a mind free from delusion directly as a mind free from delusion. A practitioner knows an attentive mind directly as an attentive mind. Know an inattentive mind directly as an inattentive mind. Know an expansive mind directly as an expansive mind. Know a contracted mind directly as a contracted mind. Know an undignified mind directly as an undignified mind. Know a dignified mind directly as a dignified mind. Know a concentrated mind directly as a concentrated mind. Know a scattered mind directly as a scattered mind. Know a relaxed mind directly as a relaxed mind. Know a tense mind directly as a tense mind.

In just this manner should you live observing mind, either your own or others', in and as mind. Live observing the nature of arising within the mind, or the nature of cessation within the mind, or both simultaneously. Even just realizing that *this is mind,* awareness is made present. To just the extent that you directly know and are simply mindful are you one who lives unattached, not grasping at anything whatsoever in the world. This is how a practitioner lives observing mind in and as mind.

IV. MENTAL QUALITIES AND PHENOMENA

SEVENTEENTH PRACTICE: OBSERVING MENTAL QUALITIES AND PHENOMENA IN RELATION TO THE FIVE HINDRANCES

Now, how should you live observing mental qualities and phenomena in an as mental qualities and phenomena? You do so by observing mental qualities and phenomena in an as mental qualities and phenomena in relation to the five hindrances. How do you do this?

When there is an impulse within toward sensual desire, know directly *there is an impulse toward sensual desire within me.* When there is no impulse within toward sensual desire, know directly *there is no impulse toward sensual desire within me.* As for the arising of a previously unarisen impulse toward sensual desire, know that directly. As for the cessation of a previously arisen impulse toward sensual desire, know that directly. As for the non-arising in the future of a ceased impulse toward sensual desire, know that directly.

When there is hostility within, know directly *there is hostility within me.* When there is no hostility within, know directly *there is no hostility within me.* As for the arising of previously unarisen hostility, know that directly. As for the cessation of previously arisen hostility, know that directly. As for the non-arising in the future of ceased ill-will towards others, know that directly.

When there is heavy lethargy within, know directly *there is heavy lethargy within me.* When there is no heavy lethargy within, know directly *there is no heavy lethargy within me.* As for the arising of previously unarisen heavy lethargy, know that directly. As for the cessation of previously arisen heavy lethargy, know that directly. As for the non-arising in the future of ceased heavy lethargy, know that directly.

When there is agitated worry within, know directly *there is agitated worry within me.* When there is no agitated worry within, know directly *there is no agitated worry within me.* As for the arising of previously unarisen agitated worry, know that directly. As for the cessation of previously arisen agitated worry, know that directly. As for the non-arising in the future of ceased agitated worry, know that directly.

When there is debilitating doubt within, know directly *there is debilitating doubt within me.* When there is no debilitating doubt within, know directly *there is no debilitating doubt within me.* As for the arising of previously unarisen debilitating doubt, know that directly. As for the cessation of previously arisen debilitating doubt, know that directly. As for the non-arising in the future of ceased debilitating doubt, know that directly.

In just this manner should you live observing mental qualities and phenomena, either your own or others', in an as mental qualities and phenomena.

EIGHTEENTH PRACTICE: OBSERVING MENTAL QUALITIES AND PHENOMENA IN RELATION TO THE FIVE EXISTENTIAL FUNCTIONS SUBJECT TO GRASPING

Furthermore, you should live observing mental qualities and phenomena in an as mental qualities and phenomena in relation to the five existential functions subject to grasping. How do you do this? Reflect as follows: (1) *This is an appearance. This is the arising of the appearance. This is the disappearance of the appearance.* (2) *This is a feeling. This is the arising of the feeling. This is the disappearance of the feeling.*(3) *This is a perception. This is the arising of the perception. This is the disappearance of the perception.* (4) *These are conceptual fabrications. This is the arising of conceptual fabrications. This is the disappearance of conceptual fabrications.* (5) *This is cognizance. This is the arising of cognizance. This is the disappearance of cognizance.*

In just this manner should you live observing mental qualities and phenomena, either your own or others', in an as mental qualities and phenomena.

NINETEENTH PRACTICE: MENTAL QUALITIES AND PHENOMENA IN RELATION TO THE SPHERES OF PERCEPTION

Furthermore, you should live observing mental qualities and phenomena in an as mental qualities and phenomena in relation to the six internal and external spheres of perception. How do you do this?

Know the eye directly; and directly know visible forms. Know the ear directly; and directly know sounds. Know the nose directly; and directly know scents. Know the tongue directly; and directly know tastes. Know the body directly; and directly know tactile objects. Know the mind directly; and directly know thoughts. And in each case, when, on the basis of the two – eye, visible form; ear, sounds, and so on – a bind is produced, know that directly. As for the production of a previously unproduced bind, know that directly. As for the cessation of a previously produced bind, know that directly. As for the non-production in the future of ceased bind, know that directly.

In just this manner should you live observing mental qualities and phenomena, either your own or others', in and as mental qualities and phenomena.

Twentieth Practice: Observing Mental Qualities and Phenomena in Relation to the Factors of Awakening

Furthermore, you should live observing mental qualities and phenomena in and as mental qualities and phenomena in relation to the seven factors of awakening. How do you do this?

When the awakening factor of present-moment awareness is present within you, know directly *the awakening factor of present-moment awareness is present within me.*

When the awakening factor of investigation of qualities is present within you, know directly *the awakening factor of investigation of qualities is present within me.*

When the awakening factor of energy is present within you, know directly *the awakening factor of energy of is present within me.*

When the awakening factor of delight is present within you, know directly *the awakening factor of delight is present within me.*

When the awakening factor of tranquility is present within you, know directly *the awakening factor of tranquility is present within me.*

When the awakening factor of concentration is present within, know directly *the awakening factor of concentration is present within me.*

When the awakening factor of equanimity is present within, know directly *the awakening factor of equanimity of is present within me.*

In just this manner should you live observing mental qualities and phenomena, either your own or others', in and as mental qualities and phenomena.

Twenty-first Practice: Mental Qualities and Phenomena in Relation to the Preeminent Realities

Furthermore, you should live observing mental qualities and phenomena in and as mental qualities and phenomena in relation to the four preeminent realities. How do you do this?

This is unease: know this directly, just as it is. *This is the arising of unease*: know this directly, just as it is. *This is the cessation of unease*: know this directly, just as it is. *This is the path leading to the cessation of unease*: know this directly, just as it is.

In just this manner should you live observing mental qualities and phenomena, either your own or others', in and as mental qualities and phenomena.

Live observing the nature of arising within mental qualities and phenomena, or the nature of cessation within mental qualities and phenomena, or both simultaneously. Even just realizing that these are mental qualities or phenomena, awareness is made present. To just the extent that you directly know and are simply mindful are you one who lives unattached, not grasping at anything whatsoever in the world. This is how a practitioner lives observing mental qualities and phenomena in and as mental qualities and phenomena.

FRUITS OF THE PRACTICE

Whoever cultivates these four applications of present-moment awareness for seven years can expect one of two results: penetrative insight right here and now; or, if there is a remnant of the grasping tendency, the state of a non-returner.

Let alone seven years, whoever cultivates these four applications of present-moment awareness for six, five, four, three, two years, or even one year, can expect one of those two results.

Let alone one year, whoever cultivates these four applications of present-moment awareness for seven, six, five, four, three, two months, one month, or even half a month, can expect one of those two results.

Let alone half a month, whoever cultivates these four applications of present-moment awareness for seven days, can expect one of two results: penetrative insight right here and now; or, if there is a remnant of the grasping tendency, the state of a non-returner. The basis for my assertion that the direct path for the purification of beings, for the overcoming of sadness and distress, for the cessation of unease and depression, for finding the way, and for the direct realization of unbinding is this: the application of present-moment awareness in four areas.

This is what the Fortunate One said. Exalted, the practitioners rejoiced at the words of the Fortunate One.

ABOUT PARIYATTI

Pariyatti is dedicated to providing affordable access to authentic teachings of the Buddha about the Dhamma theory (*pariyatti*) and practice (*paṭipatti*) of Vipassana meditation. A 501(c)(3) non-profit charitable organization since 2002, Pariyatti is sustained by contributions from individuals who appreciate and want to share the incalculable value of the Dhamma teachings. We invite you to visit www.pariyatti.org to learn about our programs, services, and ways to support publishing and other undertakings.

Pariyatti Publishing Imprints

Vipassana Research Publications (focus on Vipassana as taught by S.N. Goenka in the tradition of Sayagyi U Ba Khin)

BPS Pariyatti Editions (selected titles from the Buddhist Publication Society, co-published by Pariyatti in the Americas)

Pariyatti Digital Editions (audio and video titles, including discourses)

Pariyatti Press (classic titles returned to print and inspirational writing by contemporary authors)

Pariyatti enriches the world by

- disseminating the words of the Buddha,
- providing sustenance for the seeker's journey,
- illuminating the meditator's path.

www.ingramcontent.com/pod-product-compliance
Lightning Source LLC
Chambersburg PA
CBHW081913170426
43200CB00014B/2722
* 9 7 8 1 6 8 1 7 2 3 2 9 7 *